T0362429

ROUTLEDGE LIBRARY EDITIONS:
BRITISH IN INDIA

Volume 8

ESSAYS ON THE TRANSFORMATION OF INDIA'S AGRARIAN ECONOMY

ESSAYS ON THE TRANSFORMATION OF INDIA'S AGRARIAN ECONOMY

CHIRANJIB SEN

LONDON AND NEW YORK

First published in 1984 by Garland Publishing, Inc.

This edition first published in 2017
by Routledge
2 Park Square, Milton Park, Abingdon, Oxon OX14 4RN

and by Routledge
711 Third Avenue, New York, NY 10017

Routledge is an imprint of the Taylor & Francis Group, an informa business

© 1984 Chiranjib Sen

British Library Cataloguing in Publication Data
A catalogue record for this book is available from the British Library

ISBN: 978-1-138-22929-7 (Set)
ISBN: 978-1-315-20179-5 (Set) (ebk)
ISBN: 978-1-138-63346-9 (Volume 8) (hbk)
ISBN: 978-1-315-20729-2 (Volume 8) (ebk)

Publisher's Note
The publisher has gone to great lengths to ensure the quality of this reprint but points out that some imperfections in the original copies may be apparent.

Disclaimer
The publisher has made every effort to trace copyright holders and would welcome correspondence from those they have been unable to trace.

Essays on
the Transformation of
India's Agrarian Economy

Chiranjib Sen

Garland Publishing, Inc.
New York & London, 1984

Library of Congress Cataloging in Publication Data

Sen, Chiranjib, 1946–
    Essays on the transformation of India's agrarian
economy.

    (Outstanding dissertations in economics)
    Thesis (Ph.D.)—Stanford University, 1978.
    Bibliography: p.
    1. Agriculture—Economic aspects—India—History.
I. Title. II. Series.
HD2072.S425 1984   338.1'0954   79-52692
ISBN 0-8240-4155-0

All volumes in this series are printed on acid-free,
250-year-life paper.

Printed in the United States of America

ESSAYS ON THE TRANSFORMATION OF INDIA'S AGRARIAN ECONOMY

A DISSERTATION

SUBMITTED TO THE DEPARTMENT OF ECONOMICS

AND THE COMMITTEE ON GRADUATE STUDIES

OF STANFORD UNIVERSITY

IN PARTIAL FULFILLMENT OF THE REQUIREMENTS

FOR THE DEGREE OF

DOCTOR OF PHILOSOPHY

By

Chiranjib Sen

February 1978

I certify that I have read this thesis and that in my opinion
it is fully adequate, in scope and quality, as a dissertation
for the degree of Doctor of Philosophy.

Duncan K. Foley
(Principal Adviser)

I certify that I have read this thesis and that in my opinion
it is fully adequate, in scope and quality, as a dissertation
for the degree of Doctor of Philosophy.

I certify that I have read this thesis and that in my opinion
it is fully adequate, in scope and quality, as a dissertation
for the degree of Doctor of Philosophy.

Approved for the University Committee
on Graduate Studies:

Dean of Graduate Studies

iii

ACKNOWLEDGEMENTS

I would like to thank my dissertation committee--Professors Duncan Foley, Donald Harris and Tibor Scitovsky. Their criticisms, comments and suggestions have clarified my understanding and enabled me to make substantial improvements on earlier drafts. Professor Foley, my principal adviser, has been particularly generous with his time.

I have also benefited greatly from very detailed comments on specific chapters from my friends, Professors Jon S. Cohen (University of Toronto) and Bridget O'Laughlin (Department of Anthropology). Professor J. G. Gurley's comments during several of my verbal presentations were also beneficial.

Many of my ideas and interests evolved in the course of participation at the Political Economy Seminar and summer workshops at Stanford.

My greatest debt, however, is to my wife, Gita. She has helped me in every stage of preparation of this study. I have discussed practically every substantive issue in this thesis with her. But more than anything else, her love and support made it easy to meet the challenges that have come my way.

There are several other people I would like to thank. Stimulating conversations with Susan Carter, Ian Parker, Robert Williams and Naved Hamid, among others, helped to keep my level of enthusiasm high. Mr. Charles Milford of the Food Research Institute library was exceptionally cooperative and always made studying there a pleasure. Betty K. Smith, Rina Benmayor and Ashok Khanna provided much appreciated, timely help.

Lillian Salzman efficiently typed the final draft under pressure of time.

All of the above-named persons have earned my sincere gratitude. I, alone, am responsible for any remaining errors and omissions.

iv

TABLE OF CONTENTS

Page

ACKNOWLEDGEMENTS   iv

CHAPTER

I   INTRODUCTION: AGRARIAN STRUCTURE AND TRANSFORMATION--
         CONCEPTS, THEORY AND METHOD   1

         I.1.   Theoretical Objectives and Preconceptions   7
         I.2.   Agriculture and the Development Process--
                  A Review of Major Theoretical Approaches   17
         I.2(a)   'Dualistic Development' Theories   18
         I.2(b)   The 'Agricultural Development Approaches'   22
         I.2(c)   The Neoclassical Theory of Peasant Behavior   28
         I.2(d)   Historical Approaches to Agrarian Trans-
                  formation   32
         I.3.   The Approach of This Study   44
         I.4.   Conclusion   52

II   AGRARIAN CHANGE IN THE COLONIAL PERIOD: THE EMERGENCE
         OF SURPLUS AGRICULTURAL POPULATION IN GREATER BENGAL
         (1793-1947)   55

         II.1.   Introduction   55
         II.2.   Conventional Discussions of Surplus Labor   58
         II.3.   Amartya Sen on Surplus Labor   61
         II.4.   An Alternative Formulation   70
         II.5.   Relative Overpopulation in Agrarian Bengal   74
         II.5(a) The Pre-existent Agrarian System   77
         II.5(b) Transition to a Colonial System of Agriculture   80
         II.5(c) Transformation of Social Structure and
                  Economic Relations   84
         II.5(d) Evolution of Forces of Production in the
                  Colonial System   94
         II.5(e) Population Size and Relative Overpopulation   103
         II.5(f) The Non-Availability of Alternative
                  Employment Opportunities   106
         II.6.   Conclusion   109

CHAPTER

III   AGRARIAN STRUCTURE, CONDITIONS OF PRODUCTION,
PEASANT ECONOMIC ACTIVITY AND MARKET PARTICI-
PATION IN INDIA, 1950-1970   118

     III.1.   Introduction   118
     III.2.   Land Ownership, Operational Holdings and
           Consumption Levels   123
     III.3.   Cross-sectional Variation in Productivity
           and Resource Utilization   128
     III.4.   Agrarian Hierarchy and Land Relations
           during 1950-1961   132
     III.5.   Conditions of Production and the Character
           of Market Participation   139
     III.6.   Economic Reproduction and Exchange in
           Agriculture--Further Theoretical Issues
           and Implications   163
     III.7.   Short-run Price Responsiveness of
           Agricultural Marketed Output   168
     III.8.   Conclusion   189

IV   AGRARIAN TRANSFORMATION IN INDIA, 1948-EARLY 1970's:
A PROCESS OF DIFFERENTIAL DEVELOPMENT OF THE PEASANTRY

     IV.1.   Introduction   196
     IV.2.   A Theoretical Conceptualization of Agrarian   199
           Change in India since Independence
     IV.3.   The Evolution of State Policies Towards
           Agriculture   217
     IV.3(a)   Policies during the Pre-'Green Revolution'
           Phase (1948-1965)   217
     IV.3(b)   Structural Reasons for the Shift Towards
           the 'Green Revolution' Phase   226
     IV.3(c)   New Agricultural Strategy and the 'Green
           Revolution' Phase   231
     IV.4.   Structural Transformation of Agricultural
           Production--Evidence and Analysis   234
     IV.4(a)   Tendency toward 'Capitalist' Cultivation   240
     IV.4(b)   Trend Towards the Emergence of Capitalist
           Production Relations and a Wage-Labor Force   247
     IV.4(c)   Evidence on Changes in Extent and Structure
           of Tenancy   268
     IV.5.   Conclusion   272

REFERENCES   278

CHAPTER I

INTRODUCTION: AGRARIAN STRUCTURE AND TRANSFORMATION--
CONCEPTS, THEORY AND METHOD

The central problem to which this study is addressed is the transformation of agrarian structure as it historically evolved in India. The
term 'structure', however, has multiple meanings. The sense in which we
use the term refers to the system of production, including the pattern
of its composition in terms of micro-units of production, and the social
and economic relations by which they are integrated. Our concrete analysis
and examination of the evidence of Indian agriculture is undertaken from
this perspective. What follows is therefore intended as a contribution
both to the theory of agrarian change as well as an interpretation of the
development of Indian agriculture.

Our treatment of the Indian historical experience divides into
two parts. The first part deals with the colonial period, where we focus
specifically on the period between the Land Revenue Settlement and independence from British rule (1793-1947). In this part we deal not with
India as a whole, but only with the northeastern region, Greater Bengal,
which consists of the area now divided into West Bengal, Bangladesh, Bihar
and Orissa. Availability of information, the great diversity of agrarian
systems, and more important, the historical differences in contact with
colonialism between regions influenced the decision to treat a limited
geographical region. It would not be correct to generalize the process of
Indian agriculture during the colonial period. Nevertheless, it is very

likely that many other regions have undergone processes of change similar in their essentials to that of Greater Bengal. The second part covers the modern period from independence till the early 1970's, and attempts to deal with Indian agriculture in its geographical entirety. The two parts of this study are unified by a common theme--the process of agrarian change in the Indian economy and together, they provide a sequential analysis of this process in terms of phases of transformation which are linked by historical continuity. They are unified also by a common methodology of analysis of the agrarian structure and its transformation. Moreover, in both parts the evolution of agrarian structure is viewed as emerging in response to, and fundamentally conditioned by, the development of capitalism. However, the two parts of the concrete analysis are distinct in that they analyze two distinct phases in the process of agrarian transformation. This means, in other words, that the process itself becomes distinct in many essential features--the starting point, i.e., the pre-existent structure is distinct and the mechanisms bringing about change are distinct. Therefore, the logic and content of the process of change, and consequently the end product are all different in the two phases of history.

What distinguishes these two phases historically? In 1947, political power shifted from a colonial regime to a national government. This was associated with a sharp change in the economic role of the state with regard to the accumulation of capital. In the latter period the government has been involved directly and indirectly to a much greater extent in investment activity. The pace of capital accumulation and the growth rate particularly in industry increased dramatically relative to the pre-independence period, in the latter period. This was true both of the public and the private sectors of the economy. Thus, a basic difference between the two phases lies in the magnitude and character of the accumulation process itself.

In the analysis of the process of transformation, these differences in the accumulation process have certain consequences. The range of economic opportunities, the ways of deriving incomes in the agrarian system and outside it are different. The relationship between the state and the agrarian system is different, both with regard to the mechanisms of appropriation of agricultural product (taxation) and investment in agriculture. The legal and political intervention in redefining property relations and in terms of social groups favored by legislation in the two periods are different. The extent and pace of monetization and market participation are also different. In short, the external mechanisms operating on the agrarian system differ between the two phases.

Internally, i.e., in terms of the social structure and economic relations of production, the two phases undergo different kinds of change. In the colonial phase the village community system is broken down and in its place emerges a system based on landlord--intermediaries--petty tenants' relations. In the modern period, there are tendencies towards the development of wage labor, the relative decline of the old pure rent-earning landlords with very large landholdings, yet completely divorced from actual agricultural production and the emergence of a stratum (owners, owner-tenants, large tenants) who are economically and politically dominant and economically more involved with agricultural production, credit and marketing operations. Thus, the nature and logic of the transformation of economic relations are very different in the two phases.

A brief summary of the historical experience in these two phases may be useful. The salient features of the broad sequence of events as

evidenced in Greater Bengal during the colonial period were as follows:
prior to the transition to British dominion, the agrarian system under the
Moghals was organized into self-sufficient village communities which related
to the state at a communal level in regard to the payment of taxes. Private property in land did not exist, but peasant families possessed usufructuary rights in land. The nature of the internal division of labor pre-
cluded the possibility of the extended or expansionary development of exchange and commodity production. The system of production was based on
subsistence agriculture and a balance between industry and agriculture,
internal to the village community. This seemingly stable system was, however, radically transformed in consequence of its contact with colonialism,
which initially was a direct outgrowth of British merchant capitalism.
Initially, the growth of local operations of the East India Company affected
mainly the urban-based artisanry, indigenous merchant-houses. The products
of the former were purchased and exported, while the latter were subordinated
and converted to middlemen in the drive for monopoly so characteristic of
the merchant capitalist era. But after 1765, upon the collapse of the Moghal
Empire through internal dissension, the East India Company gained control
over the state in Bengal. The policies of the colonial state, especially
after the land revenue settlement of 1793, created the conditions for the
drastic transformation of the agrarian system which followed. The village
community system was shattered and in its place grew a system based on the
domination of landlord-tax collectors and petty tenants, with intermediate
layers of individuals with rights to the appropriation of parts of the surplus due to subinfeudation and private property in land. It is this process
of transformation with its consequences for the decay of productive forces
and its manifestation as relative overpopulation of agriculture, which is

The nature of intervention into the agrarian system during the colonial period itself followed a succession of phases (connected with the evolution of British capitalism itself) which left its imprint on the agriculture of Bengal. Initially, during the merchant capitalist phase, the predominant element in the relationship was the extraction of taxes. But with the ascendancy of industrial capitalism in Britain, the power of the East India Company declined and finally was lost altogether. The next phase, so far as agriculture was concerned, was the growth of exports of certain agricultural products--cash crops such as jute, indigo for use as industrial intermediate goods in Britain, and also of foodgrains. This latter development accelerated monetization and, in the specific context of the colonial system, served to speed up the process of expropriation of the peasantry. While the entire process, as we have already stated, was made possible and conditioned by contact with capitalism, yet during the colonial period, agricultural production was not carried out on the basis of wage labor. This was true not only for Bengal, but also for all of India. Not only was wage labor not established, capital was not invested in agricultural production. With regard to the relations of production, the broad trend was the transformation on the one hand of the large mass of the peasantry from independent, subsistence producers to immiserized, landless (or tiny plot-owning) petty tenants. On the other hand, a rapid process of subinfeudation created numerous layers of intermediary tenures and a complex system of distribution of rent.

By contrast, the period after independence saw the far more rapid pace of capitalist accumulation in the urban areas. This was accompanied by growth in money incomes and to growing demand for the products of the agricultural sector. The nature of state policies towards agriculture altered--the zamindari system was abolished and land reforms were legislated and implemented. Flows of credit and access to technological innovations were increased. Capital developed within the agrarian structure in new ways and has been gradually increasing its direct involvement with the production process itself--levels of monetization of production, as measured by the proportion of purchased inputs in total and the proportion of output marketed have been increasing. Simultaneously, there has been an increase in the incidence of wage labor, and changes in the modes of tenancy. But the process of transformation is not uniform across the body of the peasantry. Our conceptualization of the process of change during this period is one of differential development of the peasantry in response to the penetration of capital. We analyze the logic, nature and implications of this rather complex socio-economic process in the second part of the study, relating it to the development of industrial capitalism in India during the period. We do this in sequence, first by analyzing from a theoretical and empirical standpoint the agrarian structure during the 1950's. We establish thereby the essential features of the differentiation between the peasantry in terms of a fundamental qualitative distinction in the content of their economic reproduction process. Fundamentally, this distinction arises from the degree of control over the means of agricultural production, chiefly land, in relation to the subsistence requirement of the cultivating household. We term these "viable" and "nonviable" cultivators, the former category consisting of those cultivators whose landholdings are adequate to yield subsistence output, and the latter consisting of those whose resource position is the opposite. We argue that the nature of the economic decisions and the economic relations in which they engage are different.

This argument is supported and illustrated by differential patterns in the
quantitative aspects of production activity and short-run responsiveness
to price changes. Finally, we explain the agrarian development of India
from independence to the early 1970's in terms of the differential evolution of production units constituting the agrarian economy, by showing how
this emerges from an interaction between the process of penetration of
capital and the basic distinction in the conditions of reproduction of
different groups of agriculturists. The specific historical events which
serve as mechanisms activating the process of agrarian development are:
land reforms, secular improvements in agriculture's terms of trade with
industry and technological change associated with the green revolution.
It is the response of different economic groups in the agrarian economy to
economic influences associated with these events which constitutes the
core of the development process.

I.1.   Theoretical Objectives and Preconceptions

The theoretical conceptualization and objectives of analysis
which underlie our approach to the empirical material differs in some basic
ways from that of neoclassical and other 'modern' approaches to economic
development. It might, therefore, be useful to outline them explicitly
in order to locate this study in relation to the existing literature.

Our approach to the problem of economic development is historical.
That is to say, economic development cannot be adequately represented
analytically as a mechanical process independent of historical time. Not
only is it a dynamic phenomenon in the traditional economic sense of the
term, meaning that it involves "time in an essential way", but rather, it
is a process of change.

But what precisely does 'change' mean? It refers to that phenomenon by which the economic system becomes something other than what it
was. There are many aspects of change. Some of these are simple and
easily quantifiable, such as are typically analyzed in economics through
measures of economic activity, income, consumption and resource utilization. In these cases, change involves simply increase or decrease of
magnitudes. However, this is not all that changes in an economy in the
course of historical development. The system itself often alters pro-
foundly in manner that is fundamentally qualitative. Very often, these
quantitative changes reflect underlying structural and qualitative changes
in the economy. The simultaneous occurrence of quantitative and qualitative transformation during the course of economic development is, of
course, commonly recognized, but typically the two aspects are not integrated and remain disjointed in the analysis. In the neoclassical literature, it is usually the quantitative aspect which receives emphasis. A
very significant presupposition of this study is that from the long run
or historical perspective, these two aspects are analytically inseparable
parts of the same event, an explicit recognition of which fact is necessary
for our theoretical understanding of the process of economic development.
The basic analytical preconception which underlies the study, therefore,
is that economic development must be viewed as an evolutionary process--
an historical process of structural transformation of the qualitative
basis and the quantitative intensity of economic activity.

But what precisely do we mean by qualitative transformation of
structure in this context? Here we are not referring to the vast multitude
of describable but nonquantifiable attributes of society and economy which
may be used to characterize an economic system in a loose and general way.

Our concern is somewhat more specific and based on the notion of an economic system in general (and an agrarian system in particular). An economic system is a collection of component economic units. But it is not a collection in the same sense that--to borrow a metaphor used by Marx-- potatoes in a sack make up a sack of potatoes. In other words, there exist connections in the form of economic (and other) relations between these individual economic units. In fact, the organic unity of an economic system derives precisely from the economic relations which bind these units together. Further, these component units of the economic system themselves are not ultimate in any fundamental sense. In any given historical situation, they can be identified concretely. But all these units--the farm, the family, the industrial firm--change over time, i.e., are reconstituted in new forms. The same is true of the relations between them. Qualitative change refers to the transformation of the economic basis of the constituent units of the economic system (i.e., the logic of economic operation) and the economic relations between them. It is clear that because of the existence of economic relations, the economic behavior of any individual economic unit is conditioned by that of others. The same is true for economic change, i.e., the process of change in any individual economic unit needs to be studied not in isolation, but as an interconnected process in which the transformation of one set of units affects that of another. This pattern of interconnected transformation of constituent units we call systemic change and it may be systematically analyzed.

For a complete analysis of economic transformation of the agrarian economy it is necessary to take account of:
1) the nature of economic relations of production and distribution;
2) the logic of economic activity underlying agricultural producers;

3) the mechanisms which create the conditions for systemic change.
In this study, we have given closer attention to the logic of economic
activity and have attempted to identify the mechanisms of change which
have been operating on the agrarian economy. This lays the groundwork
for a detailed concrete analysis of the variety of relations of production, but this latter task is not attempted in any depth in this study
and is left for future work.

By "logic of economic activity" in the preceding paragraph, we
refer to the basic motivation governing production and the labor process.
There are distinctions between different categories of producers at a point
in time, as well as changes over a period. Production may be carried out
primarily for subsistence consumption by independent cultivators or for
the extraction of rents by leasing land or for making money profits.
Clearly, the logic of economic activity is not independent of the relations of production but rather is closely connected with it. But the distinction is useful because the logic of economic activity is directly
associated with the process of economic reproduction and thus helps us to
analyze the different ways in which different groups of cultivators evolve
over time and also to explain the rate and distribution of agricultural investments.

By "mechanisms" of change, here we are referring to the set of
historically specific events which create the economic and the legal-
political environment for systemic change. In this study, we have identified them for the colonial phase as: (a) the transformation of property
rules and the reorganization of the land revenue system affected the nature
of the process of appropriation of agricultural product by rents and taxation, and (b) the insignificant pace of capital accumulation under the

colonial economic relationship between India and Britain. For the modern phase, we have identified them as: (a) land reforms and their biased implementation, (b) the growth of state investments in agriculture, (c) the improving terms of trade for agricultural products as a result of higher accumulation in industry and higher demands for agricultural products, and (d) technological change associated with the green revolution.

Our categorization of mechanisms of change in this way might convey a misleading impression that structural change occurs purely as a result of external influences. In fact, the underlying assumption of this study is that both internal and external developments occur simultaneously and their interaction governs the actual process of agrarian development. The internal developments are essentially connected with evolution of different social and economic groups, (the difference being rooted in different conditions of economic strength and economic existence) and mutual economic relations amongst them. There are evolving relations of dominance and dependence, and competition and collaboration. The external mechanisms create the conditions for differential development amongst the agriculturists precisely because of the existence of fundamental, latent "internal" differences. Different groups are able to respond differently to these changes in the economic and political environment. Some are favored; others are hurt. Indeed, some groups are actively engaged in the political processes which influence and help bring about the mechanisms of change.

Thus far we have clarified what we mean by economic system or structure and what we mean by systemic change or structural transformation. Two aspects need further elaboration--the nature of economic relations which exist between the different constituent units of an economic system, and second, the relationship between the qualitative and quantitative aspects

of economic change. Let us consider each in turn. Neoclassical economic
theory has, of course, an elaborate and sophisticated formulation of
economic relations in its theory of exchange. It has also a corresponding
formulation of an economic system (more precisely, a market system) in
the theory of general equilibrium. However, our formulation is different.
This difference arises in a fundamental way from our use of the concept of
the process of reproduction as a central theoretical tool of analysis.

This notion, given the structure of neoclassical theory and its
foundations in subjective utility, has no counterpart in that theoretical
system. There it is not possible to distinguish clearly the qualitative
basis of exchange (and economic relations in general) because utility has
merely a quantitative dimension--all exchange is homogeneous in the sense
of being utility maximizing (or 'rational') activity, but there is no room
for recognizing the differential basis of economic motivation. Moreover,
there is no explicit foundation within the theory of utility in the material
conditions of economic existence, except rather obliquely through the principle of diminishing marginal utility--the less there is of a commodity in
the consumption bundle of an individual, the more its desirability. In
contrast, the notion of the reproduction process emphasizes the differences
in the basis of economic motivation and attempts to locate the essential
non-homogeneity of economic relations in the differential material conditions of economic existence. Economic change is synonymous with changes
in the nature of the reproduction process. And the interconnectedness of
the conditions of reproduction of individual economic units is the reason
why change in conditions of reproduction of one group affects that of
another. The idea of reproduction underlies the thinking of Marx and it
is one of the most significant contributions to economic method.

For this study, the consequences of thinking in terms of reproduction are several. The most important consequence is the ability to analyze the differential basis of economic activity among producing units in agriculture, e.g., between 'viable' and 'nonviable' cultivators engaged in the superficially similar activity of producing a given crop. And furthermore, it provides the ability to establish its connection with the historical events affecting the distribution of means of production (land, livestock, machinery and finance) and the level and distribution of productive technology. From this perspective, we are led to think of economic structure as a collection of units of production and to concentrate on its conditions of operation (economic logic, relations of production, technology).

There are two broad dimensions to the process of reproduction. The first, which is generally given the most, almost exclusive, attention in the literature within the Marxian tradition, takes a 'macro' view of reproduction. This refers to the aggregative or social conditions which guarantee the continued existence of a given economic system. For example, under the capitalist mode, social reproduction is predicated upon the continued availability of wage labor and upon the continuing accumulation of capital. The second aspect, which is more crucial in this study, is the 'micro' aspect of reproduction. Here, attention is focussed on the individual production unit. However, it should be emphasized that the 'macro' and 'micro' aspects are distinct only in the sense of being different perspectives on the same general economic process.

In agriculture, the traditional basis of production is subsistence production, i.e., production for the exclusive purpose of immediate and direct consumption by the producers themselves. Even when the sale of agricultural products takes place, a substantial, if not major, portion of agricultural output is directly consumed. This is true for agriculture perhaps more than for any other branch of production simply because the means of subsistence are mainly agricultural products. Yet in the course of capitalist development as it spreads to agriculture, the dominant logic of production shifts from subsistence production to production for exchange, and then for profit, as in other capitalist industries. This transformation is not sudden however and involves a long period of time in which subsistence production continues. In dealing with peasant agriculture, it is natural to take as our starting point subsistence production and to examine the processes and mechanisms by which this basis of production is altered.

A key idea in our subsequent analysis, on the basis of which we draw a qualitative distinction in the conditions of reproduction of peasant producers, is that of 'viability'. While it forms the basis for a qualitative differentiation in economic activity, at the same time viability is rooted in a quantitative condition--namely, the degree of control over the means of agricultural production. When the peasant household has the capacity to produce (and retain) sufficient quantities of its means of subsistence for its continued existence as self-producing farmers, we say from the point of view of its conditions of reproduction that it is viable. When this is not the case, it is nonviable. And there is a further quantitative distinction possible in terms of the degree of viability or nonviability, (i.e., a spectrum within the basic bipolarity).

A major advantage in drawing this fundamental distinction between viable and nonviable cultivators is the facility it provides for grasping essential features of differentiation in Chapter III where we analyze the empirical information pertaining to Indian agriculture of the mid-1950's. The actual economic relations (forms of exchange of labor power and mode of

tenancy) vary greatly between regions and across the peasantry in a region.
Thus, one cannot meaningfully classify the agricultural population in terms
of categories such as landlord, tenant, worker, etc., because within any
such category there are agriculturists of very different types in terms
of their reproduction conditions. Besides, there are numerous intermediate
groups which are part-landlord and part-tenant or part-worker, or part-
self-cultivator. In other words, 'pure' categories in terms of which side
of the market for land, labor, or credit, households cannot be established.
Our distinction, insofar as the broad tendencies towards economic change
are concerned, cuts through the maze of these complications and goes
directly to the heart of the economic distinction among agriculturists.

Thus, the main significance of this qualitative difference lies
in this--they are differently placed with regard to the possibility of
economic change, i.e., they are likely to evolve in different ways. Conditions of reproduction moreover affect the character of economic relations
entered into by the household. Here, a comparison with capitalism may help
to elucidate the point. Capitalism represents an extreme situation where
the separation between the producer (wage-worker) and the ownership and
control over the means of production is complete. The difference in the
conditions of reproduction between the worker and the owner of capital and
also in the economic rationale underlying participation in exchange is
very clear and sharp. But in peasant agriculture, where the worker still
controls directly the means of production, where markets exist and yet the
specialization of economic activities is incomplete, qualitative distinctions in the nature of economic relations are not as obvious. For example,
the whole cross-section of peasant households may be selling a portion of
their output in the market. It is a mistake, however, to assume that ex-

change in the product market is a homogeneous activity. An examination
of their conditions of reproduction reveals the qualitative difference
in exchange participation--some may be attempting to obtain means of subsistence while others may be converting the form of their surplus.

The recognition of qualitative distinction in what is superficially a uniform economic exchange (selling of agricultural product,
renting of land, for example), which is made possible by thinking in terms
of reproduction process, has this significance. It enables us to infer
the direction in which the form of production and relations of production
will change. For instance, the nonviable peasant household has a higher
probability of becoming wage laborers. Furthermore, in the case of mutual
economic relations between peasant households, we are led to notice the
unequal basis of these relations by virtue of the control over the conditions of reproduction exercised by one group over another.

What is the connection between the qualitative and quantitative
dimensions of agrarian economic activity and change? The qualitative--
contained in the conditions of reproduction--supplies the logic of economic
activity. The quantitative constitutes the measurable effects of the
activity. Different conditions of reproduction between different agriculturists at any point in time find expression in numerous aspects of pro-
duction--labor intensity, degree of market participation, the pattern of
crops planted.[1] But the implications become more sharply apparent when
mechanisms of historical change become effective. On the other hand,
qualitative differences in conditions of reproduction themselves emerge
from quantitative differences with regard to the degree of control over
the means of production (size of landholding, the level of accumulations
of financial and physical assets). In other words, qualitative and quan-

titative features are inseparably intertwined. We make the distinction, however, in order to differentiate the conditions of reproduction which control the responsiveness to mechanisms of change and the character of economic relations (e.g., dominance, dependence, independence).

The basic theoretical preconceptions of this study have been elaborated. It still remains for us to explain more fully the theory of agrarian transformation underlying our empirical procedure. We shall turn to this after critically reviewing some of the major approaches in the literature of agrarian development. This should serve to place our discussion in better perspective.

I.2. Agriculture and the Development Process--A Review of Major Theoretical Approaches

In this section, let us consider very briefly the chief features of some of the major theoretical approaches which have appeared in the literature dealing with agriculture in relation to the development process. We shall be concerned with the work of a few key authors who have been influential in shaping the literature. Consequently, various mini-traditions of writing have emerged, each of which embodies a common set of basic assumptions and focus. Accordingly, we shall structure our discussion as follows, dealing in turn with (1) dualistic development theories (Lewis, Ranis-Fei, Jorgenson), (2) 'agricultural development' approaches (Mellor), (3) the (neoclassical) theory of peasant agriculture (Chayanov, Sen, Mellor), (4) historical analyses of agrarian transformation (Lenin, Kautsky). The first, second and fourth groups share a common focus in that they are concerned with the long-run process of development. The third set deals with the theoretical formulation of traditional or peasant agriculture from a static viewpoint, but which nevertheless underlies the thinking of many writers in the first and second groups.

I.2.(a) 'Dualistic Development' Theories

Theories of dualistic development are associated with the work of W. A. Lewis, G. Ranis, J. C. H. Fei and D. W. Jorgenson, among others.[2] Beginning in the mid-1950's, these theories have dominated the modern literature on economic development until recently. They have been concerned for the most part with the development experience of the less developed countries of modern times. From our perspective, it should first be noted that these theories have not been directly focussed on the transformation of agriculture, but have dealt with it as a part of the general process of economic development in Third World economies. The dualism refers typically to that between (capitalist, advanced) industry and (backward, traditional) agriculture. The theories essentially present the process of development in abstract terms as one in which the advanced industrial sector of the dual economy expands more rapidly in the early phase because of its greater productivity and accumulation potential. The rapid growth of the industrial sector is, however, facilitated by the presence of the backward agricultural sector through the existence of certain mechanisms of transfer of resources (products and labor-power) from agriculture to industry. Eventually the agricultural sector itself is affected by this growth process and the 'dualism' disappears. A virtue of these theories is that they help to identify some of the major avenues of interaction between the agricultural and non-agricultural sectors. However, they are more concerned with the ways in which agriculture assists the industrial development process than on the transformation of agriculture itself. The major points of interaction, or rather, avenues through which industrial development taps agriculture are: (i) labor supplies--the process of development visualizes a major shift in labor (and population) from the agricultural to the non-agricultural sector because of wage differentials (made possible by the gap in productivity), (ii) the supply of agricultural products which are used as industrial raw materials or for food by the urban (industrial) population, (iii) the acquisition of 'investible surplus' directly through taxation or by the re-export of agricultural products and retaining the foreign exchange proceeds for industrial investment, (iv) agriculture as a market for industrial products.

There are two major strands in dualistic models. In the Lewis-Ranis-Fei type models, the agricultural sector is assumed to initially contain surplus labor in the form of open or disguised unemployment. In the Jorgenson model this is not assumed. For both types of development processes, however, the most important link between industry and agriculture is through the transfer of labor from the latter. From our perspective, it is useful to note some salient features of this type of formulation for the sake of contrast. First, the growth process is visualized in exclusively quantitative terms. The method cannot deal adequately with the transformation of one economic system to another except somewhat crudely. The process of development is envisioned simply as one in which the quantitative significance of agriculture relative to industry declines through a progressively efficient resource allocation in the economy: labor resources move from low productivity to high productivity uses. However, in fact important qualitative changes in the conditions of reproduction may be occurring as this quantitative shift of population takes place. These theories, in effect, ignore the process of qualitative change

and conceptualize structural change as a simple break between the labor
surplus phase and the phase in which surplus labor is exhausted. This
quantitative bias is evident also in the identifying criteria used for
defining the 'backward' and 'advanced' sectors. The agricultural sector
(in the initial 'traditional' phase) is characterized by the payment of
labor according to its average product and the 'advanced' sector by the payment of labor according to its marginal product. According to the Lewis-
Ranis-Fei version, the first phase consists of the transfer of surplus
labor. When the surplus labor pool is exhausted, the 'traditional' sector
is assumed to transform itself, through an inadequately specified process,
into a marginal product regime. Thus, the quantitative bias in thinking
is easily associated with a mechanical treatment of the process of change.
By contrast, in this study we have attempted to analyze the qualitative
transformation in economic relations and modes of economic existence which
are associated with economic development.

Second, the methodology is ahistorical. The formulation is in
terms of an abstract formula of growth which is not grounded on the concrete
historical experience of an economy. Consequently, while the starting
point (e.g., low productivity, high population, high unemployment agriculture, etc.) is a realistic abstraction for many countries, the predicted
pattern of development is not. For example, it is not possible to identify
the various stages of transformation of agriculture in a sharp manner in
any actual case. Historical change simply does not occur in sequence from
one static system to another. It is a process of continuous adjustment
over time, where one form often blurs and blends into the next. The quantitative and ahistorical biases together have led to (seemingly unnecessary)
controversy over whether or not the marginal productivity of labor in

plus labor.[3]

Third, these models do not deal explicitly with the precise mechanisms by which the transfer of food from agriculture takes place. In the Lewis-Ranis-Fei version, the basic idea is that workers who are employed but are unproductive in the surplus labor phase, can be moved to the industrial sector and be employed there. But, of course, this presupposes that the consumption bundle they were entitled to while in agriculture is now available to them as wage goods. It is assumed in the models that this is accomplished. However, the exact mechanism is historically important, i.e., whether or not the remaining peasants step up the marketing of agricultural products, or whether they are simply taxed, makes a difference in the nature of agrarian transformation. Fourth, the peasant households working in agriculture are assumed to be all homogeneous. The entire agricultural population is assumed to be living at a subsistence level. While possibly true for the bulk of the peasants, nevertheless this is unrealistic in the sense of ignoring the existing differentiation among agriculturists, especially the large farmers who may control quite significant proportions of land resources.

Our approach differs in each of the above salient characteristics from the dualistic development school. On the other hand, the underlying idea within this tradition, that it is the growth process in the advanced (capitalist) industrial sector which provides the dynamic towards agrarian transformation, is extremely pertinent. The same is true of the notion in the Jorgenson version that technological change in agriculture comes to play a crucial role. But the central notion of the transfer of labor as the key mechanism of interaction transforming agriculture is certainly belied by the experience of India, often regarded as a typical 'dual' economy.

Here there is little historical evidence of a dramatic shift in the proportions of urban to rural population in favor of the former in the entire period under consideration. Nor is it true that the occupational structure has shifted markedly in favor of industry relative to agriculture in terms of proportions of population employed. Evidently, the rate of expansion of industrial employment has not far exceeded that of population size.

I.2.(b) The 'Agricultural Development Approaches'

These approaches take as their guiding principle an activity or social engineering perspective on the problem of agrarian development. In this they differ from the dualistic development school which was more concerned with the theoretical conceptualization of the process, although in mechanical terms. And on the same count, they differ from the perspective taken in this study. Agricultural development approaches lack the coherence and logical completeness of a full-blown theory of agricultural development. But they are richer in attention to empirical detail and practical policy considerations. J. W. Mellor is a leading exponent of this group and we present here a sifting of some of his ideas.[4]

First, Mellor very explicitly takes up the process of agrarian transformation. This is termed the 'process of modernization of agriculture' and it is very clearly identified with the increase in the role of 'capital' in agriculture. In 'traditional' agriculture and during the early period of development, the 'stock of capital' is low because of (i) attitudes towards saving, investment and consumption, and (ii) the marginal returns to capital investment are low. The latter is the case because of the very low level of productivity and technology which itself reduces the productivity of non-labor inputs, e.g., fertilizer.[5] But the process of modernization raises returns.

Second, while Mellor and others of this school are also concerned about the overall process of capitalist development in the poor countries, they differ from dualistic approaches in taking the policy position that the most effective way of insuring rapid accumulation is to increase the productivity of agriculture and thus integrate accumulation in industry and agriculture to the benefit of both sectors. They stress this, as opposed to a strategy of drawing resources out of a technologically backward agriculture for fostering industrial accumulation. The concern of these writers is therefore focussed on the use of the state machinery to stimulate the modernization process in agriculture, and to devise appropriate strategies of intervention to achieve this end.

Third, the process of modernization is essentially the process of increasing agricultural productivity through technological innovation which becomes the key mechanism. The modernization process is, however, viewed in a somewhat broader way, namely as the process of introduction of new 'inputs'--and it is emphasized that this includes not only what is understood normally as inputs, i.e., physical factors of production, but also 'institutional' inputs. This refers to the provision through the policy of appropriate institutions, such as incentive-preserving land systems, marketing systems, credit facilities, with the simultaneous introduction of a 'package' of measures to stimulate modernization: (i) institutions to provide incentives, (ii) research in the development of technology suited to specific local conditions, (iii) availability of new and improved physical inputs--high-yielding varieties of seed, inorganic fertilizer, pesticides, herbicides, irrigation, better breeds of livestock, etc.,

(iv) the servicing of the new technology through marketing, distribution (including "aggressive" promotion policy)[6] and credit provisions, (v) the improvement of farmer communications--ways to educate and inform peasant farmers about alternative possibilities. This insistence on policy measures and instruments over the standard orthodox preference for laissez-faire is commonly justified by the argument that social aid is necessary because farmers independently cannot evolve the institutional support system necessary for the <u>coordination</u> of input supplies essential for the success of the new technology. Inevitably, the relative emphasis on exact measures to be adopted varies. Mellor emphasizes marketing, research and education, and coordination of the supplies of modern inputs. Others, such as McKinnon and Shaw, have insisted upon the removal of 'fragmentation' of rural financial markets and then rely upon the market mechanism. Mellor also outlines a brief sketch of <u>phases</u> of modernization. This is very explicitly ahistorical in that they neither attempt to explain the past evolution of present agriculture nor its current evolution. Rather, they represent the phases which are "generally optimal for a low income country to follow in the present day".[7] There are three phases. Phase I is a 'technologically stagnant' phase. Expansion of production is held back because of the absence or scarcity of complementary 'modern inputs' which can make possible the increased productivity of abundant 'traditional' inputs such as labor, fixed capital and land. These modern inputs, as noted earlier, are not necessarily physical factors of production; they contribute to the economic environment of production. But they are called inputs because they can be introduced through policy decision. Measures designed to stimulate increasing productivity, if introduced singly, do not have much of an impact in isolation, e.g., land reform. Phase II is the phase of "technologically dynamic agriculture with a low capital technology" and a crucial part of the modernization process. At the beginning of this phase, the following general characteristics are typical. Agriculture remains quantitatively important in the economy relative to industry. Industrial accumulation, however, is proceeding apace and capital is scarce. Demand for agricultural products is rising rapidly due to demographic and income effects. The pressure of population upon the land makes it impossible to increase the average acreage per farm. Incidentally, it is noteworthy how similar the above-mentioned features are to the concrete conditions of Indian agriculture in the early part of the modern period.[8] In Phase II, technological innovation occurs on a number of fronts. The efficiency of agricultural processes is increased and productivity rises at a continuous rate. These technological improvements diffuse through agriculture by degress. Initially, large production increases are made possible by limited adoption of technological improvements in limited geographical areas. This may take place "even in the face of a number of remaining imperfections in the land tenure system, marketing situation, credit facilities, and so on", i.e., without institutional reforms. With the progress of agriculture into Phase II, continuing innovations may be slowly introduced, and it is a dynamic "phase for which a stream of innovation is generated by the process itself". A constant development and adoption of technology in agriculture takes place. However, labor-displacing machinery is not introduced and this is the sense in which it is a "low capital technology" variant of dynamic agriculture. Phase III is that of "technologically dynamic high capital agriculture" involving the steady introduction of machinery which raises labor productivity at a rapid rate. This phase approximates the agricultural systems of the advanced capitalist countries (U.S., West

Europe). It is not relevant to our present study and we may ignore its detailed features in this discussion.

It should be obvious from the above account that the agricultural development school can be accurately characterized as having a social engineering approach. It is not interested so much in providing a theoretical explanation of the process of development or of the condition of under-development, as it is with presenting a blueprint of action or a set of prescriptions. The connection between this set of arguments and the 'green revolution' strategies adopted in India and elsewhere in the Third World is so clear that they might be regarded as their conscious rationalization. Though the perspective taken in the study is diametrically opposite, this literature has been very useful in pinpointing the concrete mechanisms of agrarian transformation in the modern period. They identify very clearly the outlines and logic of the government policies associated with the 'green revolution'. Of particular importance is the emphasis on technological change of a special type--a seed-fertilizer revolution, backed up by a state machinery which aids the distribution of new inputs, provides the finances necessary, disseminates technological information, and makes other complementary investments.

By way of a critical appraisal, several further remarks may be made. It shares with 'dualistic' models the property of being ahistorical. Not only are the 'phases' of modernization of this type, but the whole conception of agricultural backwardness and the process of development is excessively technological. It refuses to recognize any essential distinction between institutional and other elements of modernization, such as new seeds and fertilizer--they are all 'decision variables'. Backwardness is the absence of these 'modern inputs' and modernization is the process of their acquisition. It ignores the fact that the mechanisms of institutional change are vastly different, subject to political constraints. This fundamental incapacity to view technological change properly within its social framework and their interaction is the basic reason why these approaches are unprepared for the actual consequences of 'green revolution' strategies--its "ironies" and "paradoxes". We are referring to the growing concern with the growth in rural unemployment and continued poverty of the large bulk of the population in 'green revolution' areas.[9] In other words, while technological change constitutes a major mechanism of transformation, the form of the transformation does not follow the presumed scenarios--a serious weakness even within this mode of analysis.

Moreover, this approach is ahistorical also in that it appears to assume that each national economy is developing separately and autonomously, whereas in actuality, the development of other nations may play a conditioning role in the development of any nation. For example, the development of capitalism in Britain played a key role in the evolution of India's economy in the colonial period and the 'green revolution' in India and elsewhere is associated with U.S. agro-industries and foreign aid policies.

Finally, it does not address itself to the qualitative aspects of the process of structural transformation, specifically the change in the economic relations between agriculturists which occurs in its course.

The notion of phases of transformation which we have employed in this study is very different from Mellor's. Our conception of phases, as we have explained above, is grounded in the concrete historical experience of the Indian economy and has no connection with supposedly 'optimal' phases. We share the view that government policies with regard to institutional reforms, investments and credit policies and, more im-

portant, technological change play a critical role in agrarian transformation. However, in contrast to Mellor's approach, we attempt to locate
this in the context of the Indian agrarian structure and the implications
for change within it. Specifically, we are concerned with the differential development of the peasantry, which is closely associated with institutional and technological changes. Indeed, contrary to Mellor, we show
that these processes are interconnected, namely that the existing social
and economic structure places bounds on the character and pace of technological and institutional change, and at the same time is moulded by it.
This is evident in our analysis of both phases of agrarian transformation.

I.2.(c) The Neoclassical Theory of Peasant Behavior

Both the above sets of literature on agricultural development
take as their starting point an implicit conception of the economy of
traditional agriculture. This view appears in a theoretically refined
form in the neoclassical models of peasant behavior.[10] In Chapter II,
we treat in some detail the neoclassical formulation. Here we shall be
brief and confine ourselves to some salient features of methodology and
assumptions.

Traditional agriculture, i.e., the agricultural system prior to
the process of modernization, is typically assumed to be a peasant economy.
This is taken to mean a system of privately owned and family operated
farms. The level of technology and productivity of land is low. Production is geared to self consumption by the family. The basic 'economic
decision' made on the farm is with respect to the allocation of family
labor. The 'surplus labor' version of 'dualism' models supposed that the
marginal productivity of labor (under disguised unemployment) is driven to

zero. This generated a controversy about the 'rationality' of peasant agriculture and led to empirical investigation of the proposition. Out of this emerged a sharper theoretical formulation of peasant behavior in a neoclassical framework. A leading contribution was that of A. K. Sen, which resolved the controversy by dissociating surplus labor from zero marginal productivity.[11]

The neoclassical formulation consists primarily of using a subjective choice theoretic framework and adapting the utility apparatus of consumer behavior to a more general problem.[12] Peasant farming is viewed as the maximization of household welfare by achieving an equilibrium between the disutility of work and the utility from consumption of the products of labor under the usual fairly general assumptions about utility functions and production functions. The equilibrium condition is that level of labor utilization which equates the marginal product of labor to the 'real cost' of labor (determined by the marginal rate of indifferent substitution between work and consumption). Explanations for many observed features of peasant economy--such as the existence of disguised unemployment, wage differentials (i.e., returns to labor) between industry and agriculture and within agriculture itself, negative responses to price increases in the labor and product markets--have been advanced in terms of this framework. We have argued in Chapter II that these are explanations in the peculiar sense of proving the consistency of these phenomena with the assumed mode of rational economic behavior. They do not illuminate our understanding of the historical existence of observed conditions. But we shall not belabor this point as it is elaborated upon in later discussion.

There are several other features of this approach. In general, the peasantry is theoretically treated as though it were a homogeneous body, differing only with respect to farm size or technology. More specifically, it fails to recognize the distinction between independent and dependent conditions of peasant cultivation. Even though some peasants may be small landowners, with cultivation largely by family labor and thus on the surface appearing to correspond to the conventional notion of the family farm, there is, in fact, a substantial difference in the motivational structure between farmers with holdings below and above subsistence size. As we have tried to establish in Chapters III and IV, this not only has implications at any point in time for the pattern of resource utilization, but also for long-run change. A related point concerns the neglect within this conception of the significance of actual economic relations, and thus to grasp the essential nature of non-market and market relations and linkages between agriculturalists.

In trying to emphasize the distinction between peasant systems and the competitive capitalist production conditions of the industrial firm, this approach overstresses the internal non-market logic of family farming to the point of overlooking the concrete economic relations between production units. This leads to an unrealistic characterization of the economic structure of agrarian economies such as India and elsewhere. For understanding the processes of historical transformation, the recognition of manifest and latent differences between agriculturists and of the unequal basis of their production conditions and economic relations are of crucial importance.

The notion of reproduction has provided us with an alternative mode of thought to the subjective formulation. It differs from the latter in confronting directly the qualitative distinctions in economic motivations--profit, simple commodity production, subsistence. It attempts to ground these in the objective conditions under which production is carried out, rather than through properties of an unobservable utility surface. It draws attention to the dominant/dependent character of many economic relations in the agrarian system. In this way it provides a more general framework for conceptualizing economic structures, of which the system of self-working, self-sufficient, independent family farming is just one form, while that of capitalist farming with wage labor is another, and that of landlord-tenant farming still another. It is therefore more adequate for the study of agrarian development.

The theoretical approaches discussed thus far share a feature in common--ahistoricity. Fundamentally, they conceptualize the agrarian economy and its development in terms which either explicitly abstract from actual historical experience of an economy (Mellor), or in terms which provide an unrealistic characterization of phases of transformation (dualism theories), ignoring the concrete process of structural change. This derives partly from a mechanical conception of change and partly from the inability to deal adequately with the social and economic structure of the agrarian system and economic relations within it. The conceptualization of 'traditional agriculture' as consisting of homogeneous subsistence producing family farms implicit in these formulations and made explicit in the neoclassical theory of peasant behavior, provides an unrealistic characterization of the actual structure of India's agrarian economy, ignoring as it does differences among peasants with regard to conditions of economic existence and mutual economic relations. We consider next some leading historical approaches.

I.2.(d) Historical Approaches to Agrarian Transformation

In this section, we shall examine two of the best-known studies on the transformation of agriculture from a Marxist perspective--those of Lenin and Kautsky.[13] We shall discuss them from a methodological standpoint, attempting specifically to elicit the theory of agrarian change underlying these studies. This is necessary because the form of these studies--empirical, concretely historical, illustrated with numerous examples--tends to conceal the clear outlines of the theoretical conceptualization. This would be useful in providing points of comparison with the procedure we have adopted in this study. Both these studies are set in Europe and deal with the transformation of agriculture under the influence of capitalism. We shall treat each author in turn.

Lenin on Agriculture in The Development of Capitalism in Russia

Lenin's study does _not_ attempt to offer a general theory of agrarian transformation. It is more directly an attempt to analyze the development of capitalism in Russia during the post-Reform and pre-Revolution period.[14] As such, it does not even deal exclusively with agriculture, though the latter constitutes a substantial portion. Nevertheless, it remains a classic work on Marxian analysis of agrarian transformation. For this reason it is useful to study its underlying method as an example of historical analysis. We shall focus only on the part dealing with agriculture.

The task undertaken by Lenin is primarily to study a _concrete_ phenomenon. Consequently, the approach is historically _specific_ and _empirically_ founded. Lenin conceptualizes an ongoing process of development in terms of which he links and explains the variety of empirical evidence. This central unifying process is, according to him, the formation of a home market for capitalism. This is essentially synonymous with the spread of capitalism and the associated increase in the social division of labor with the growth of the commodity economy. The development of industry is itself a part of this increasing specialization--activities which exchange commodities with each other and with agriculture. Eventually agriculture proper itself becomes an industry and the same process of specialization takes place within it. However, the exchange economy, and especially the capitalist form of production, grows more rapidly in industry, diverting an ever-growing part of the population from agriculture to manufacturing industry. The formation of the home market is accompanied by, and in fact created, by the separation of the direct producer (worker) from control over the means of production, as expropriation occurs. The means of production themselves become commodities and are converted to capital (in the Marxian sense of implying production for profit). Therefore, the products also become commodities. Even the means of subsistence become increasingly obtained through the market as wage labor grows in importance, supplementing household production as the principal source. The development of capitalism in a nation can occur, Lenin asserts in opposition to some contemporary opinions, without the necessity of a foreign market to absorb its production. The expansion of the home market depends on the spread of exchange in the domestic economy, but particularly on the growth of the market for labor power.

The historical process sketched in the last paragraph forms for Lenin an hypothesis, or more accurately, a theoretical vision of historical development. He analyzes the empirical material with a view to proving its validity and at the same time to concretize the abstract process.

What emerges from the analysis is an interpretation of economic transformation of Russia during this period. Within this broad and general
process of development, there are numerous aspects of change--subprocesses
of change which are interconnected and which Lenin selects for closer
examination, always seeking to locate their origins and assess their significance with respect to the larger process of formation of the home
market for capitalism. In regard to agriculture, Lenin locates three such
aspects: (i) the process of disintegration of the peasantry, (ii) the
transformation of a landlord economy from the corvée system to capitalist
production, and (iii) the evolution of commercial agriculture. All three
are clearly seen by Lenin as interrelated aspects of the same larger process.

Lenin's analysis of the peasant economy of post-Reform Russia
is directed at showing that a profound transformation was taking place,
which he terms the process of the disintegration of the peasantry. He
argues that the notion of the peasant economy as one which is based on
independent self-cultivation or self-consumption by the farming family,
with a minimal participation in the market place, and socially organized
around the peasant community, was no longer a valid and realistic characterization. That system simply no longer existed and could not be re-
created, according to Lenin, in sharp opposition to the views of the Narod-
nik economists. The Russian peasantry was at the time completely subordinated to the market and dependent upon it for personal consumption and
husbandry and to pay poll taxes. The dominance of the market place in
the peasant's economic framework is Lenin's first observation.

Second, he argues that the system of socio-economic relations
and the form of economic behavior existing among the peasantry are common
to capitalism, e.g., competition, struggle for economic independence, ten-

dencies towards concentration--'snatching up' of land by purchase or lease, and also concentration in the volume of production. Under these conditions, the 'utter dissolution' of the 'old patriarchal peasantry' occurs. Lenin stresses that this is not simply a process of differentiation in the mere quantitative sense of inequality in property ownership. It is transformation--dissolution of the existing and replacement by new types of rural inhabitants. The disintegration of the peasantry is accompanied by a polarization and the creation of two new types of peasants--(a) the well-to-do peasantry or rural bourgeoisie who are independent, commercial farmers or owners of rural commercial or industrial establishments. From this group a class of capitalist farmers is created who make cash profits and invest in money lending, trade and land purchase or improvements. This group is numerically a minority, but economically and politically are the 'masters of the contemporary countryside'. (b) The rural proletariat who consist of landless, propertyless cultivators, but also of small landholders who own tiny plots. The latter group is quite numerous and comprises half of the total number of rural proletarians. Group (b) takes part in paid work on farms and in rural handicrafts, but increasingly agriculture becomes a subsidiary occupation.[15]

      Lenin regards as too stereotyped the proposition that a capitalist system of production requires for its existence a free, landless wage worker. He argues that reality is more complex and allows for greater variation, and notes further that in agriculture, the small plot owning worker appears in all capitalist countries. This last statement brings up the familiar methodological problem which continues to reappear in all theoretical discussions of economic change; namely, the distinction of 'essence' from the superficial appearance. The small plot owning peasant is in this case 'essentially' a wage worker, despite the fact that he owns and operates land. Fundamentally, this essence refers to the dominant aspect of the conditions of economic reproduction of the small peasant and it infers the propensity towards the direction of change.

An intermediate category to the polar opposites (a) and (b) is the middle peasantry. It is distinguished by the least development of commodity production. However, it is in a marginal, precarious position. There is some sale of labor power, some borrowing. But its position fluctuates in accordance with the good or bad crop year. Crop failures push these peasants into the ranks of the proletarians. The process of development, in sum, is one of polarization which splits the agrarian structure into two extreme types. Lenin establishes this from a detailed analysis of empirical material contained in the Zemstvo statistics, which gives data on different categories of farms. These fundamental emergent differences make it misleading to aggregate and analyze the 'average' peasant.[16]

This process of disintegration expands the home market for capitalism--both groups increase purchases from the market. The rural bourgeoisie purchases means of production and items of luxury consumption. The rural proletarians buy articles of subsistence consumption, stimulating the growth of industries such as cotton textiles. Lenin is unsure about the exact pace of disintegration, but concludes on the basis of general and fragmentary evidence that there is "uninterrupted and rapidly increasing disintegration: on the one hand the 'peasants' are abandoning and leasing land, the number of horseless peasants growing, the peasants fleeing to the towns, etc.; on the other hand the 'progressive trends in peasant farming' are taking their course".[17] Lenin notes certain catalyzing and retarding factors in the process. In the former category is migration (by the middle peasantry), the operation of usurer's and merchant's capital

which brings the town and country closer. In the latter category is the
persistence of some forms of labor exchange--the payment of labor in kind.

The second aspect of agrarian transformation concerns that
occurring on the landlord farms. Prior to the reforms, the system worked
by allotting the peasants' land, who in turn supply labor to the landlord.
Its preconditions include: (i) the predominance of natural economy,
(ii) the attachment of the worker to the land, and (iii) the personal
dependence of the peasant to the landlord. These conditions are under-
mined by the abolition of serfdom and a transformation occurs from the pre-
existent system of labor--"otrabotki"--to a "diametrically opposite"
basis--wage labor.[18] The transformation is not instantaneous, but gives
rise to intermediate mixed systems "with an endless variety of forms characteristic of a transitional epoch". Lenin states that it is difficult to
discern the lines of demarcation between different systems during the
transitional stage, but suggests that a key element is who owns the implements of agricultural production. The increasing incidence of peasant
workers under the otrabotki system who do not own implements, draught
animals, etc., is an indication of the emergence of wage laborers. The
otrabotki system declines because of the following reasons: (i) the
polarization of the peasantry in which the implement-owning middle peasantry
progressively disappears and is replaced by well-to-do peasants and dispossessed proletarians, neither of which is suited to the otrabotki type
of labor arrangement which calls for a type of peasant able to carry on
production independently, but at the same time dependent on account of
the need for land.

Lenin illustrates the process of transformation of landlord
farming with a detailed account of Engelhardt's farm from which the main

logic of the process may be extracted. The initial condition was otrabotki. Productivity was low. Technology was obsolete, the condition of
the soil was poor, and the same is true for cattle raising. The remuneration of laborers is low because productivity is low. Engelhardt introduces the following changes: (i) switch to production of flax, which is
more profitable than grain, (ii) the landlord himself acquires personal,
non-land means of production, purchasing horses, harness, carts, ploughs
and harrows. He begins direct participation in the production process with
help from a combination of regular hired workers and job hire for specific
jobs under a more productive system of piece-wages, (iii) there is consequently an increase in the intensity of production and in the degree of
monetization; (iv) from flax and specific operations, the incidence of
wage work spreads gradually to other crops and operations. In a similar
fashion, technological change gradually diffuses through the farm. One
crop requires some new type of implement. This necessitates a new type
of horse, a new type of laborer, a new system of labor, in progressive
sequence. Thus, a capitalist farm is created. The switch to production
for profit creates the basic dynamic of transformation in this case.

The third aspect of change studied by Lenin is the growth of commercial agriculture. Increasingly, agriculture becomes commercial, profit-
oriented and entrepreneurial. This is especially true for the landlord
farms and the larger 'Group (a)' peasants, though in the latter case, it
is not as transparent since the peasants often do not hire labor in as
great amounts. With respect to the growth of commodity production, agriculture "by its very nature" follows a different process than industry.
In this case, specialization does not proceed as smoothly or as completely
as in industry. Establishments do not quite split up, each with a special-

ized product, but instead farms specialize relatively, concentrating on one major crop, with others adapting around it. The growth of commercial agriculture once again expands the home market for capitalism. With commercialization grows the demand for the products of industry--machinery, consumption goods--as well as for labor power. The growth of commercial agriculture greatly aids the extension and intensification of 'capitalist contradictions' in agriculture, but in the very same process, accelerates the process of change. Agriculture becomes integrated with the world market and therefore open to international competition. This forces various changes in agriculture, "compelled willy-nilly, on pain of ruin". Among these, labor relations and techniques adjust.[19] Meanwile, with the repeated crises of capitalism, this aids the expropriation of the small peasantry and speeds up disintegration.

The development of capitalism in agriculture, Lenin asserts, does not require any special form of land relations. Instead, capital by drawing agriculture into its dominion, is able to <u>create</u> a system corresponding to it in <u>essence</u>, despite differences in legal forms of land tenure.

We may summarize the methodology used by Lenin as follows: The initial step is to identify the broad process of transformation--the formation of a home market for capitalism. The succeeding steps are to trace out the implications of this for agriculture in terms of a few key interconnected subprocesses. These are explained with reference to empirical data, which makes the analysis concrete. At each stage, the <u>interconnections</u> between the disintegration of the peasantry, the transformation of landlord farming, and the growth of commercial agriculture, are emphasized and elaborated, thereby establishing the unity of the total process. The great strength of Lenin's study derives from the <u>analytical description</u>

which it provides of agrarian structure and transformation. Particularly
striking is the characterization of peasant economy as a polarized structure.

The chief weakness of Lenin's analysis, however, lies in his
inability to clearly specify the mechanisms of transformation. There is
the appearance of an axiomatic character about the emergence and development of capitalism in agriculture. It is for this reason that he is often
interpreted as having discovered a "law" of development of capitalism in
agriculture.[20] It seems fair to state that Lenin simply assumes that the
capitalist form is capable of achieving dominance because of its superior
productivity and efficiency. As regards the mechanisms by which transformation is brought about, a close reading suggests that in Lenin's view this
is ultimately connected with the growth of monetization of the rural economy
and of competition in exchange. In other words, once the market develops,
the emergence of capitalism is fairly spontaneous. In particular, we may
note that Lenin does not ascribe any special role to technical innovations
and to the growth of industrial capitalism in generating change.

Kautsky on 'The Agrarian Question'[21]

Kautsky's study, based upon the experience of Western Europe,
attempts to generalize and arrive at the 'laws' of development of agriculture under capitalism. The object of study is "all the changes which agriculture experiences under the dominance of capitalist production. . . . and
in what ways capital [is] taking hold of agriculture, revolutionizing it,
smashing the old forms of production. . .and establishing new forms which
must succeed". In his treatment, Kautsky tries to answer several questions. What is the principal mechanism--'motor force'--underlying agrarian
transformation? According to Kautsky, this is the growth of industry.

Kautsky also attempts to explain why capitalism proceeds differently in agriculture and assumes different forms compared to industry. In particular, he focusses on the co-existence and mutual interrelation between the big and small farms, and also on the process of proletarianization of the peasantry.

In general, capitalism develops first in industry in the towns. It then gradually "modifies" the character of agricultural production. The growth of communications systems breaks down the insularity of the countryside. Competition from industrial products dissolves the peasants' domestic industry. This increases the degree of monetization and market dependence of the peasants. In a parallel development, the form of _rent_ is changed to money by the landlord. With the increasing role of money comes the growth of the financial intermediaries--usurers and merchants. Thus, an avenue for expropriation is created as market crises occur. Finally, as land grows scarce, peasants begin to engage in subsidiary paid occupations. Thus, even before the _form_ of production is capitalist, the mere growth of monetization, commercialization induces important changes. Capitalism becomes possible in agriculture with the decline of feudal property and the gradual establishment of generalized private property in land. This is made possible by the rise of the urban bourgeoisie to economic and political dominance and the carrying out of legal and juridical reforms in the countryside. In the course of this, "peasants were deprived both of serfdom and the better part of their land". The intervention ends the "feudal impasse" of agriculture with its low productivity, underutilized land and agrarian crises.

During the 19th century, agriculture is modernized. Technical improvements in livestock raising and in grain production, the adoption of more rational cropping patterns and most important, the introduction of modern machinery take place. The character of modern agriculture, states Kautsky, is capitalist, being based on individual ownership of land and the commodity character of its products. Kautsky ignores the process of transition--the variety of transitional forms of labor relations, but emphasizes instead the process of <u>accumulation</u> of capital in agriculture. The process of accumulation is seen by him in terms of the relative development of small and large <u>holdings</u>, in contrast to Lenin, who was concerned with the formation of <u>classes</u>.

The penetration of capital creates a <u>technical gulf</u> between small and large holdings. The larger holdings are superior in commanding a larger proportion of the cultivated acreage. Also, they are in a better situation with respect to the realization of <u>economies of scale</u>. For example, they are better able to mechanize and use electricity. Some machines simply cannot be used profitably below a certain size of farm. Similarly, a more efficient allocation is possible for labor, draught animals, and there is easier access to credit and product markets. The small farms are unable to mechanize or to obtain sufficient credit at low rates and remain technologically backward. Under the pressure of competition and the need to meet cash needs, the peasant increases the intensity of utilization of family labor, both on farm and for off-farm work. Thus, <u>two types</u> of holdings are created--one geared to production for the market, and the other to household subsistence--both of which are subordinated to the market.[22]

The evolution of big and small farms is conditioned by the process of accumulation. Capitalism is characterized by two "broad movements"-- accumulation and centralization of capital. But in agriculture, because of the centrality of land, centralization is synonymous with centralization of holdings, which should be contiguous. This is more difficult under the bourgeois form of property where acquisition is chiefly through default, and also because small farm units have "enormous reserves of resistance". This accounts for the continued co-existence of big and small farms. Also, as land resources grow scarce, even in capitalist agriculture the mode of cultivation shifts from extensive to intensive, which permits the increase in the scale of output on farms of smaller acreage. Thus, with this shift, land loses in importance as a measure of capitalist scale of production. This again has implications for the co-existence of big and small farms. But even in the case where centralization of holdings has taken place-- the large holdings known as latifundia--small holdings (minifundia) per- sist in order to assure the supply of labor on the large farm. Thus, Kautsky concludes that the "triumph of the big over the small" runs into limits and is not smooth. In addition, he asserts that there is a mutual connection between them through labor exchange and argues that the real basis of survival of the small holding is non-competition with the large holding.

With regard to proletarianization, Kautsky traces it to: (i) the destruction of home industry of peasants through competition; (ii) the shrinking land base and the necessity of supplementary work. The selling off of peasant land is more rapid when alternative employment opportuni- ties exist. But the growth in industrial employment possibilities creates a "rural exodus" to the towns which, however, creates a labor problem for capitalist agriculture. This can be resolved either by further mechaniza- tion or by allotting more land to the peasants. Hence an "alternating rhythm" of growth and decline in small farms is possible.

Kautsky also stresses the role of international competition in the process of development. His observations are very similar to Lenin's and need not be discussed at length. Basically, it lowers rents, weakens the landlords, and forces adoption of new crops and techniques. Finally, it directs capital from agriculture increasingly to agricultural industries which process imported agricultural products--sugar factories, starch works, etc.

The usefulness of Kautsky's analysis lies in his locating the mechanism of transformation--the growth of capitalist industry and the introduction of technical innovation in agriculture. His analysis of the coexistence, interrelations and dynamic of development of big and small farms is insightful. But the chief drawback of his approach is the neglect of the process of transformation, i.e., the creation of intermediate organizational forms, and the assumption of sharply defined new forms. The other feature of Kautsky's treatment of the problem is his neglect of the social aspect of change--the changing relations of production, the emergence of new social groups in the agrarian system.

I.3.   The Approach of This Study

The basic objective of this study is to provide an analysis of a set of concrete phenomena connected with Indian agriculture. But our analytical discussion touches upon several theoretical issues raised by the authors we have discussed above. Our basic methodology has already been outlined in an earlier section. To recapitulate the main features: (i) The central theoretical tool is the reproduction process. (ii) The analysis contains the following elements: First, we identify and analyze the pre-existent economic structure in terms of the conditions of repro-

duction of the units of production. Second, we identify and analyze the
mechanisms of transformation in each historical phase. These mechanisms
are related to the development of capitalism in a specific context. Third,
we analyze the evolution of the agrarian system in relation to these
mechanisms of transformation. The nature of this evolution is governed
by the conditions of reproduction.

Our theoretical position with respect to the development of agriculture is that there is no general "law" of transformation valid across
different countries and periods of history. Instead, there are processes
of change with similarities and differences between them which have to do
with the specificities of structure and mechanisms of transformation. However, certain general features are common to most. The development of
capitalism has played a crucial role in generating the mechanisms of transformation and further, in many (though not all) historical instances, these
have been connected with the development of industry. But there are great
differences in the precise mechanisms between Europe and the 'Third World'
economies and even within the latter group itself. Among other things,
the structure of capitalism itself has been altering historically--levels
of technology, patterns of international co-ordination and markets have
all changed. This is not to imply that the problem cannot be studied
systematically, but that historical specificity should be integral to the
analysis. This is what we have tried to do with respect to India.

In our study, mechanisms of transformation are of two types:
(i) political-legal mechanisms enacted through the state. These deal
with reforms in the system of land ownership, land tenure, taxation;
(ii) economic mechanisms, which operate through altering economic incentives.[23] These include changes in the structure of prices, and also ele-

ments of state policy which manipulate the economic environment of production without legal coercion by expanding marketing opportunities and possibilities for technological change.

The difference in the character of these mechanisms is quite striking in the two historical phases which we study here. In the colonial phase (for Bengal), the extraction of agricultural surplus (taxation and rent), the introduction of private property in land, play a key role. In the modern period, the stimulation of agricultural production and marketing through the type (ii) mechanism is far more important. These differences correspond to the character of capitalist development in the Indian economy. The development of industry in the urban areas during the latter phase accounts for the shift in the relative importance of the latter mechanism.

The process of agrarian change itself is viewed as a transformation of the process of reproduction. Two types of change occur: Social and economic relations of production change, transforming the social basis of agricultural production. New classes of producers and new types of economic relations, motivated by a new logic of economic motivation, are brought into existence. And second, there is an alteration in the role of various material elements, e.g., land, money, in the process of production and distribution. In Chapter II, we study the transformation from the village community system to a landlord-intermediary-sharecropper system (the 'colonial agrarian system'). In Chapters III and IV, we analyze the transformation from a differentiated agrarian system containing a complex of elements--landlords, tenant-cultivators and owner-cultivators of varying economic position--to a new system in which polarization within agriculture takes on increasingly a capitalist character. Change occurs because the conditions of reproduction are altered and because the conditions for new forms of reproduction are created.

A key concept which we utilize in our discussion of reproduction
is that of 'viability'. This has already been discussed above. This provides us with a way of differentiating between alternative states of reproduction conditions confronting a given production unit. Non-viability
creates the precondition for <u>dependent</u> relations of production, i.e.,
transfer of labor-power. Viability and non-viability of reproduction conditions contain very different <u>propensities</u> with respect to change. This
explains the very different response to the mechanisms of transformation.
This is essentially the way in which we analyze the differential development of the peasantry in Chapters III and IV. Here, the relations of production <u>between</u> viable and non-viable cultivators are transformed as the
logic of production of the former group changes towards production for
profit.[24] In Chapter II, by contrast, the viable-nonviable distinction
<u>among</u> the cultivators is not significant. What is central here is the
shifting of the broad <u>mass</u> of cultivators to a non-viable condition by
expropriation from land and the establishment of relations of production
between non-viable <u>cultivators</u> and <u>non-cultivating</u> landlords and intermediaries.

Our discussion in the remainder of the study touches upon various
issues of general interest. In Chapter II, we deal critically with the
neoclassical explanation of surplus labor. We then attempt to explain the
emergence of surplus agricultural population in Bengal principally as the
consequence of retrogression of the productive forces in the economic environment obtaining in the colonial system, in conjunction with the non-development of alternatives to agricultural employment. The counter position
of these two distinct methodological approaches to the same problem pro-

vides a useful illustration of the differences between them, and we
argue, demonstrates the relative superiority of our approach in explaining the phenomena of surplus agricultural population. Also, while the
retrogression of productive forces in Bengal agriculture has often been
noted by Indian economic historians, to our knowledge a complete,
systematic and theoretical explanation of this subject is not available.
We believe our treatment in Chapter II to be a first step in this direction, but we have left the task itself as a project for future research.
In this study, we have confined ourselves to extracting the main elements
for an explanation. In this chapter, the main objective is to establish
the basis for the emergence of surplus agricultural population. After
having done so, we examine the evidence on population growth and refute
a possible alternative explanation of surplus agricultural population in
terms of purely demographic trends.

In Chapter III, we present a theoretical conceptualization of a
differentiated agrarian structure, using the notion of viability. We
analyze empirical evidence of the mid-1950's from the Farm Management Surveys and other sources. We examine also empirical material on modes of
tenancy and sociological studies on agrarian hierarchy. We conclude that
the most useful theoretical formulation of differentiation at any point
in time is through the concept of conditions of reproduction. The observed
cross-sectional variations in the quantitative aspects of production (e.g.,
labor intensity, productivity, market-participation) are explained in these
terms.

We also present a model analyzing the 'perverse' reaction of the
non-viable cultivator to a change in the price of the product. This marks
a new formulation of the old problem of the price elasticity of 'marketed

surplus'.

In Chapter IV, our analysis of the implications of the penetration of capital offers an interpretation of agrarian development since independence. It contrasts in its approach with some of the leading trends in the Indian economic literature on the subject, specifically the debate on the 'mode of production' in Indian agriculture. Our approach, rather than setting out to label the agrarian system as 'capitalist' or 'pre-capitalist', is to study directly the process of change itself. The main focus of Chapter IV is to study the interrelation between change-inducing mechanisms (such as agrarian investments, adoption of the new 'green re-volution' technology), and the agrarian economic structure, i.e., a pattern of differential development among the agriculturists which has been occurring in India in the modern period. Here, it is worth noting the contrast with the European and Russian situations analyzed by Lenin and Kautsky in relation to <u>technological change</u> in agriculture. While Kautsky and Lenin have emphasized <u>mechanization</u> of farming and more efficient allocation of labor, technological progress in India is associated with innovations in <u>seed</u> and <u>fertilizer</u> (the 'green revolution'). In Europe and Russia this appears to have been <u>induced</u> by the process of transformation itself, e.g., labor shortage. In India, with the 'green revolution', technical innovation serves to <u>monetize</u> the production process and thereby becomes a key <u>change-inducing</u> mechanism. Moreover, the connection between technological change and the labor process is not as straightforward when it is of the seed-fertilizer type as it is with labor-saving mechanization.

We may note some interesting aspects of the Indian case which emerge from our analysis of the empirical material. The first observation relates to the invalidity of the usual assumptions made in the ahistorical literature regarding phases of agricultural development. 'Backward' agriculture is neither static nor is it a simple system of poor peasant family farms. We notice that backward agriculture is itself the result of historical development and the same is true of the privately-owned family farm. Further, the small farm is not necessarily isolated, but is linked by economic relations. This point is, of course, not novel. Yet it is often overlooked. The second observation is about the non-homogeneity of the agrarian production structure analyzed in Chapter III. Here, the parallels between the Indian situation in the 1950's and the Russian case analyzed by Lenin are striking. We notice the co-existence of landlord farms and family farming, and within the latter, a similar type of polarization. Third, we note the specifics of the relation between industry and agriculture. The development of industry in India does create conditions for the transformation of agriculture, as in Russia and Europe. It accelerates the extension of the market and of monetization. It aids in the decline of rural crafts and artisan industry. It supports the development of new agricultural technology, although here, the relation between national and international capital is important. In short, industry creates the conditions for the deeper penetration of capital. However, in India the pace of industrial accumulation is slow not only in the towns, but also we do not have the development of rural-based, agriculture-related industry as in Europe and Russia. Consequently, alternative opportunities for employment do not emerge as significantly. There is no migration on a scale sufficient to create labor shortage in agriculture. This contrasts with the rural exodus analyzed by Kautsky. This retards the pace of proletarianization in agriculture. Agricultural wage labor is not remunerative and peasant farms, despite non-viability, tend to persist. Fourth,

the adoption of new technology has some interesting features. As in Lenin's
and Kautsky's description, we find that new technology is not uniformly
adopted across production units. This intensifies differentiation. But
there are differences. Because of its form, i.e., seed-fertilizer-based
rather than mechanization, technological innovation does not affect the
system in quite the same way. Its adoption has less to do with the size
of the farm and economies of scale. More crucial in this case is the uneven availability of finance. In fact, the larger the farm, the heavier
the capital requirement for innovation. This is one reason why there is
a trend towards intensive farming and the emergence of medium-sized capitalist farms. Notice the contrast with Kautsky's observation of the dynamic
between large and small farms. The other consequence is that because technical innovation is not related as directly as in mechanization with the
reorganization of the labor process, it is possible for innovation to be
incorporated within the structure of landlord-tenant relations. We observe in many instances the emergence of new forms of tenancy in which
the landlord advances a portion of the costs of new inputs. But this is
likely to be transitional because the increased investment of capital leads
naturally to greater involvement by the landlord in the production process.
Evidence of this is increased bookkeeping and supervision. We may also
observe that while in Europe technological progress came under pressure
from overseas competition and was associated with a cheapening of the price
of agricultural products, the opposite is true in India. Finally, we may
note the far greater role of the state in agrarian transformation than
seems to have been the case in Europe and Russia.

I.4.   Conclusion

In this chapter we have explained the content of this study from the viewpoint of both subject matter and methodology employed. In addition, we have critically reviewed the major strands of the literature relevant to this field and attempted to situate this particular study in perspective. We have examined both the ahistorical and some historical approaches and outlined the similarities and differences in theoretical conceptualization and logic between these other works and our study. The succeeding chapters take up the task of analyzing the specific experience of agrarian transformation in India.

FOOTNOTES - CHAPTER I

1. This is studied in detail in Chapter III. We note, among other things, the U-shaped relationship between the degree of market participation and the size of operational holdings, i.e., the degree of market participation is high for the smallest farms; it falls and then rises with the size of farm.

2. W. A. Lewis (1954), J. C. H. Fei and G. Ranis (1964), D. W. Jorgenson (1961), (1967)

3. This controversy and its resolution in the neoclassical literature is dealt with in Chapter II. Sen (1966) freed disguised unemployment from zero marginal productivity by distinguishing between surplus labor from surplus laborers.

4. See Mellor (1966),(1967)

5. Mellor identifies technological change in agriculture very closely with the introduction of inorganic fertilizer. This contrasts with the form of technological change, viz. farm mechanization, which was associated with agricultural development in Europe and the U.S. during the 19th century. The emphasis on fertilizer is connected with the so-called "green revolution" strategy which has been adopted by governments in several underdeveloped countries, including India, in recent years. The introduction of this strategy has been backed by the foreign aid policies of the U.S. and the loan policies of international agencies, such as IBRD. For a discussion, see H. Cleaver (1972).

6. Mellor (1967), p. 49, (1976), p. 63.

7. Mellor (1966), p. 224.

8. This is not surprising given that the empirical material in many of Mellor's studies is drawn from Indian agriculture.

9. See W. Ladejinsky (1970), P. Bardhan (1970), H. Cleaver (1972), among others.

10. For the clearest and one of the earliest expositions, see Amartya Sen (1966). See also Mellor (1966), Sen (1975), among others.

11. This is discussed in some detail in Chapter II.

12. The formulation, which by now is quite familiar, is essentially to consider jointly the production and consumption behavior of an egalitarian farm household (assumed to be a 'typical' peasant household). The mathematical formulation is given in Chapter II, Section 3.

13 Lenin (1974), Kautsky (1970). Our discussion of Kautsky is based on the translation of sections of Kautsky's work by J. Banaji (1976).

14 This covers the period between 1861 to 1899 when the first edition of Lenin's work appeared.

15 We may note that this is quite the opposite of what has happened in India. The relative lack of growth of non-farm employment has tended, if anything, to make agriculture the relatively more important occupation for many rural proletarians.

16 This is noteworthy in relation to the treatment of the peasantry as a homogeneous category in the approaches we have discussed above. Our study shares with Lenin the position that we must distinguish between different categories of agriculturists.

17 Lenin (1974), p. 185.

18 "Diametrically opposite" because pure wage labor is based upon the fact that workers are not in possession of the means of production, whereas "otrabotki" is the arrangement whereby peasants are allotted land for independent cultivation in exchange for labor services.

19 Lenin (1974), pp. 318-319. The notion that technological change is adopted under compulsion is interesting and consistent with thinking in terms of the process of reproduction. The idea here contrasts with the neoclassical formulation in terms of profitability of innovation and rational behavior. Profitability is a necessary condition, but it may not be as effective as the pressure of competition, in inducing technological change.

20 See, for example, N. K. Chandra (1974), R. K. Sau (1976).

21 Based on translation and summary by J. Banaji (1976).

22 Kautsky concentrates on the nature of the holdings rather than the related phenomenon of the split between the two types of peasantry.

23 These two types of mechanisms are not necessarily mutually exclusive or independent. Obviously, the activities of the state have an impact on the structure of economic incentives. The distinction is simply in the nature of implementation--political coercion vis-à-vis pecuniary and voluntary inducements.

24 As already stated above, the usefulness of making the viability-nonviability distinction lies in its enabling us to greatly simplify the complex of highly diverse social groupings, hierarchies, tenancy and labor relations which exist in India's agrarian economy. A meaningful classification of different types of agriculturists in terms of these usual categories--landlord-tenant, worker-nonworker, wage earner-profit earner, etc., is not possible. We argue that what is essential is the condition of reproduction of these agriculturists, and our distinction is made on this very basis.

CHAPTER II

AGRARIAN CHANGE IN THE COLONIAL PERIOD:
THE EMERGENCE OF SURPLUS AGRICULTURAL POPULATION
IN GREATER BENGAL (1793-1947)

II.1. Introduction

The structure of Indian agriculture, both of society and of the
system of production, underwent important transformations during the 19th
century. In the immediately preceding period, significant political
changes had occurred on the subcontinent--the disintegration of the Moghal
Empire and the establishment and consolidation of British imperialism.
Indeed, there was a close connection between the nature of agrarian transformation and the economic basis of the colonial relationship between
India and Britain. In this chapter, we analyze the process of transformation in the northeastern Greater Bengal region in the period 1793-1947.
We have confined our discussion to this geographical region for two
reasons: (a) the need to keep the discussion tractable since there were
differences in the historical sequence and specific forms of the colonial
relationship between various regions; (b) the case of Greater Bengal has
certain striking features which make it an interesting subject of study
in its own right.

The major changes that took place in agrarian Bengal included
the following events. The village community system collapsed. Private
property in land was legally established and enforced by the state. The
independent, self-working, self-sufficient mode of farming by peasant

families declined in importance. New types of social and economic relations emerged and grew dominant in agriculture in the form of a rent-receiving class of rural landlords and intermediaries vis-à-vis a class
of petty tenants. The latter half of the period witnessed the commercialization of agriculture and the increase of agricultural exports. At
the same time, there was a remarkable stagnation and even retrogression
in the forces of production as evidenced by declining productivity.
Moreover, there were declines in the extent of cultivated acreage in the
face of growing population size.

In this chapter we study the process of agrarian transformation
in colonial Bengal with particular reference to one aspect, namely the
emergence of surplus agricultural population. We attempt to explain the
phenomenon by tracing its development within the process of historical
evolution of the agrarian economy. Our argument, elaborated in the following pages, is that surplus agricultural population or 'relative overpopulation' occurred as a consequence of (a) the process of expropriation,
(b) the stagnation and retrogression of the productive forces, and (c) the
non-development of alternative opportunities for employment. Each of these
can be shown to stem from the nature of the social reproduction process
which evolved in the colonial economy of Greater Bengal.

There are several reasons why this analysis may be useful. The
first is as a theoretical analysis of a concrete process of underdevelopment.
Thus, underdevelopment itself may be explained and understood as the product of a process of transformation and not simply as a set of primitive
characteristics of an economy, the latter being the common practice of
much of modern development literature. The historical experience of underdeveloped countries of the modern world has been varied and we may observe

different types of underdeveloped structures. For example, the 'labor surplus economy', the 'plantation economy', the 'enclave economy',--to name a few of the most discussed types--have emerged in the course of the world-wide expansion of capitalism. It is hoped that from an historical, concrete analysis of alternative particular cases, a more general theory of underdevelopment will emerge.

The notion of surplus agricultural population plays an important role in the literature of economic development. Our analysis aims to provide an explanation of the phenomenon, based upon an historical method of analysis which we have explained in Chapter I. Our analysis and methodology, which is rooted in the historical analysis of the evolution of economic structure, stands in contrast to some of the standard discussions of the subject. In order to highlight this contrast and to demonstrate the superiority of an historical analysis, the first half of the chapter presents a detailed critique of conventional explanations of surplus labor in agriculture. In particular, we concentrate on the neoclassical explanation as contained in two studies by Amartya Sen (1966, 1975). The former work, recognized generally as a classic on the subject, is perhaps the best example of the application of neoclassical method to the problem. The latter study contains refinement, restatement and further elaboration of the initial framework. The sharpness and clarity of Sen's presentations constitute additional reasons for their being selected for specific discussion of method. A critical analysis of neoclassical method is important and useful in itself. But a consideration of the historical evidence from a concrete example provides for a richer critique and a sharper presentation of the differences between ahistorical and historical analysis, particularly in the nature of theoretical explanation of the same phenomenon. For this reason, we have combined within a single chapter our critique and the historical analysis of relative overpopulation in agriculture.

Finally, the historical evolution of the agrarian structure in colonial Bengal was associated with and dominated by the development of capitalism in the region. In this respect, the situation is similar to numerous other cases. However, there are obvious and sharp differences between the Bengal case and that, say, of English agriculture, which also experienced the expropriation of the peasantry during the transition to capitalism. Also, the nature of the transformation in the colonial period in Bengal differs significantly from the process occurring in the modern period (after independence) in India, which we analyze in Chapters III and IV. These differences may be attributed in large measure to the specific nature of colonial capitalism and the forms of social reproduction associated with it. This chapter, because it analyzes the latter aspect, may be useful toward an understanding of these differences in the impact of capitalism, although this is not its central purpose.

The structure of the chapter is as follows: Section II.2. discusses the development of the conventional literature prior to Sen (1966). Section II.3. presents a critical discussion of Sen (1966), (1975). Section II.4. outlines the alternative formulation, and Section II.5. deals with the emergence of relative overpopulation in the agriculture of Bengal as an illustration of the historical method.

II.2. Conventional Discussions of Surplus Labor

The concept of 'surplus labor' has enjoyed considerable prominence in the literature of economic development. During the 1950's, the notion

was associated with growth models for a class of less developed economies--
so-called 'labor surplus' economies. The postulate of a labor surplus came
to be associated with another concept--the 'dual economy', and the development of dual economies became a subject of extensive discussion in the
development literature. These postulates rest on the notion of economies
with agricultural sectors containing a surplus population, with the implication that a withdrawal of laborers from agriculture would lead to no
fall in the output of agriculture. The surplus population was of two
types: (1) those actually unemployed, and (2) those in 'disguised unemployment'.[1]

The assumption of surplus labor or of 'unlimited supplies of
labor' was a starting point for theories of dualistic growth. This postulate had an immediate corollary: subsistence wage rates[2] and infinite
supply elasticity (at those wage rates) for labor in capitalist industry.
According to the theories proposed by Lewis (1954), and Ranis and Fei (1964),
the 'labor surplus' phase consists of a reallocation of surplus agricultural
laborers, whose contribution to output may have been zero or negligible, to
industry where they become productive members of the labor force. Once surplus labor is exhausted, these models suggest a different rule for labor
supply price to capitalist industry, viz., the marginal product of labor
in agriculture. The central focus of this tradition being capitalist growth
in less developed economies, the concept of surplus labor in these models
merely serve to justify assumptions regarding the supply curve for wage
labor to industry.

However, assuming a labor surplus in agriculture constitutes a
statement about the system of production in the agrarian sector. In the
conventional interpretation of this postulate, the marginal productivity

of labor in agriculture, within a certain range, is zero. This immediately poses a paradox in neoclassical theory, especially when surplus labor is assumed to be in a 'disguised unemployment' form. The paradox emerges from the apparent irrationality of disguised unemployment: (1) peasants engaged in work(involving disutility) when marginal benefits (marginal productivity of work) are zero, appears irrational; (2) the inability of the production system to absorb a section of the population through the mechanism of substitutability in techniques. Issues such as these gave rise to a large literature,[3] the proponents of the notion seeking to provide theoretical justification for zero marginal productivity. Lewis, whose concern is with the capitalist wage, dismissed the problem:

> "Whether marginal productivity is zero or negligible or not is not, however, of fundamental importance to our analysis. The price of labour, in these economies, is a wage at the subsistence level".[4]

Others, such as Eckaus (1955) and Georgescu-Roegen (1960), provide explanations for zero marginal productivity of agricultural labor based on conditions of production. Eckaus suggested a technical barrier to substitutability as the explanation. An upper bound on the labor-capital ratio prevents a complete absorption of the excess labor force--the problem is thus related to a shortage of capital in agriculture. Georgescu-Roegen's argument is based on an institutional characterization. He suggests that under a feudal organization of agriculture, serfs (under pressure for subsistence consumption) maximize gross production, i.e., apply labor, ceteris paribus, until the point is reached where the marginal product of labor equals zero. These studies, predating Sen (1966), are typical in the implicit identification of disguised unemployment with zero marginal productivity of labor. The attention on productivity in these works (even in

the institutional arguments of Georgescu-Roegen) is technical and mechanical, and they contain no discussion of the historical evolution of conditions of production.

II.3.   Amartya Sen on Surplus Labor

In the context of the preceding discussion, Sen's work is notable
because it proposes a model in which the neoclassical paradoxes surrounding 'disguised unemployment' are resolved. A central theme of this treatment of the problem is that surplus labor or disguised unemployment does
not depend on a zero value for the marginal product of labor. As an explanation of disguised unemployment, the debate over zero marginal productivity
is, as a consequence, no longer relevant. Sen poses the problem in the
framework of rational allocation of effort within a typical peasant household. He argues that given a particular structure of preference between
work and income, rational decision-making is consistent with disguised unemployment.

Let us consider this formulation more closely. The model presented in the initial article is of an egalitarian peasant household which
maximizes utility. Let

x = individual share of work,

q = individual share of output,

L = total volume of household labor hours applied to production,

Q = total output,

$U(q)$ = the typical individual's utility function,

$V(x)$ = the typical individual's disutility function,

$Q(L)$ = the production function relating output to labor-hours.

It is assumed that $V'(x) > 0$, $Q'(L) > 0$, $Q''(L) < 0$. The condition for utility maximization leads to the following rule for the allocation of work effort, where marginal benefits from work equal the marginal disutility of work for the typical member of the peasant household.

$$Q'(L).U'(q) = V'(x)^5 \qquad (1)$$

Rearranging terms, we have

$$Q'(L) = V'(x)/U'(q) = \beta \qquad (2)$$

The interpretation of the equilibrium condition is that the marginal product of labor on the peasant farm equals β, the 'real cost of labor', which is given by the 'individual rate of indifferent substitution between income and labor'. In applying this model to the problem of surplus labor, Sen draws a clear distinction between laborers as units of population, and labor-hours, the measure of technical labor input. The volume of output is, of course, a function of total labor input and is not uniquely related to the size of population, N. In other words, $L = x.N$, and $Q = Q(L)$. Surplus labor exists when the withdrawal of some members of the workforce does not alter the total amount of labor input applied in agricultural production. In terms of the equilibrium condition (2) above, the invariance of the 'real cost of labor', β, within a given range, is sufficient for the existence of surplus labor. This implies that when some members of the workforce are removed from agricultural production, the amount of work performed by each of the remaining individual workers, x, rises; their share of consumption rises correspondingly, but the total amount of labor input, L, does not change. If N' is the size of the remaining workforce and x' the corresponding equilibrium share of effort, a constant β implies that in the new equilibrium $x'N' = L$. The model presupposes a situation where all laborers are not fully employed in terms of their capacity for work.

More specifically, x is less than x* where x* is a critical amount of
work, beyond which the marginal disutility of work increases. It is
clear that in this model, the constancy of β does not imply a zero marginal product of labor. Instead, it is a statement about the nature of
preference schedules. As Sen puts it:

> "The existence of surplus labor depends, in this model,
> therefore, on the marginal utility schedule and the
> marginal disutility schedule being flat in the relevant
> region".[6]

With the help of this model, Sen derives a number of striking conclusions,
some of which are summarized below:

(1) Surplus labor is consistent with rational allocative behavior.

(2) Surplus labor is independent of whether or not the marginal productivity
of labor is zero. It does not require that β = 0, but only that β be
constant within a range.

(3) Surplus labor may exist even under technologies which permit any
degree of substitutability between labor time and other factors.

Sen explains the basis of a constant 'real labor cost' thus:

> "Of the two [assumptions], perhaps the assumption of a
> flat marginal disutility schedule up to a critical
> value is less objectionable. The flatness of the
> schedule of marginal utility of income until a certain
> standard of living is reached may be thought of as
> more dubious. However, near the so-called level of
> subsistence, when the end of having a 'decent' standard
> of living has not yet been achieved, such non-diminution
> of the desire to earn more income may not be implausible.
> This is a verifiable question, and more empirical work
> is called for to settle it".[7]

It is clear that the key theoretical concept in this model is
that of 'real labor cost', on which the argument turns--its constancy implying the existence of disguised unemployment. However, the concept merely
describes a psychological condition--the subjective marginal trade-off be-

tween income and leisure for a typical peasant. Sen's contribution is important within the context of neoclassical method, or, as Sen terms it, the 'rational behavioral approach'. He removes a lacuna within the theory by constructing a model in which surplus labor and rationality are mutually consistent, and his answer is that for this to hold, the relevant utility and disutility schedules must be flat. However, if this is to be an explanation of the concrete, historical phenomenon of disguised unemployment, the relationship between 'real cost of labor' and material, objective conditions must be firmly established. It is fair to state that Sen (1966) does not achieve this, if only because he does not attempt it.

In his book on employment policy, Sen (1975) presents a modified version of his earlier model. This version is interesting on account of a new element in the 'real cost of labor'. We shall argue that the concept is still subjective. The model is as follows. Let the marginal supply price (measured in terms of output) of labor hours to the household by a typical peasant be constant, denoted by z. Then $S(x)$, the total compensation for x hours of work is given by

$$S(x) = z.x \qquad (3)$$

where x is less than or equal to x^*, the critical amount of work beyond which the marginal disutility of work rises. In equilibrium, for a rational allocation of labor, the "required compensation per unit of work" is equated by the typical peasant to his marginal return from work. Assuming egalitarian distribution, the amount of additional output going to the peasant as a reward for extra work is simply his (equal) share of the marginal product. But a novel element is introduced in the valuation of the marginal product. Sen argues that since the producing unit is a peasant household, or cooperative, each individual displays an attitude and values

somewhat deviant from the standard homo oeconomicus. Specifically, each
member of the household places a positive value not only on his or her
own consumption, but also on the share going to others. The degree of
'concern' is measured by h per unit of self-consumed output, where h lies
between 0 and 1. If α is the proportion of additional output accruing
to a peasant, the equilibrium condition may be written as:

$$z = Q'(L)[\alpha + (1-\alpha)h] \qquad (4)$$

subject to x less than or equal to x*. The right-hand side of equation (4)
is the marginal benefit from work obtained by weighting the marginal physical product of labor by the appropriate measures of 'share' and 'concern'.
Rearranging terms in (4), we get

$$Q'(L) = z/[\alpha + (1-\alpha) h] = \beta' \qquad (5)$$

β' is the 'real cost of labor' in this model and is a function of z, α and
h, and as before, the invariance of β' implies the existence of surplus
labor. Thus again, the marginal product of labor equals, in equilibrium,
the 'real cost of labor'. The difference here is that the latter is now
measured in terms of output. At first sight, it might appear that this is
a more objective formulation than the one adopted in the first model. It
is easy to see that this is not really the case, the difference being entirely in the units adopted and not in theoretical substance. It is still
the case that z and h are determined by the underlying utility structure.
Sen does not explicitly discuss how the marginal supply of effort, z, is
determined in this model, but one may infer that the subjective equilibrium
model is what he has in mind. He only suggests, somewhat imprecisely,
that the value of z depends on the 'degree of alienation' associated with
each mode of employment.

> "At one extreme is the case of the cooperative being
> one big family and at the other is the case in
> which members treat their work simply as jobs to be
> done to earn some income. The value of z will
> depend on the appropriate assumption".[8]

Similarly, the value of the 'concern' parameter, h, is determined by the
"values and social consciousness of the society in question". The allu-
sion here to the fact that individual values and preference structures may
be socially conditioned and determined is interesting since it represents
a clear break with neoclassical orthodoxy. In the latter, individual
tastes are simply 'given' from outside the theory.[9] The central point,
however, is that the explanation provided by Sen is ultimately a subjective
one, relying as it does on psychological conditions like attitudes towards
work or distribution. He grants that values and attitudes are socially
moulded by relations of production. Yet, in the absence of any systematic,
empirically grounded theory relating modes of employment with individual
attitudes and utility structures, individualist approaches to such problems must remain content, as Sen's does, with casual intuitive statements.[10]
As far as the specific problem of surplus labor is concerned, the argument
turns on the constancy of β'. Given the relative stability of individual
shares and the degree of 'concern', surplus labor exists as long as the
marginal supply price of labor by the individual, z, is constant. Whereas
the magnitude of the value of z might depend, as Sen suggests, on the degree
of 'alienation', its constancy is however presumably still equivalent to
invariance of the marginal trade-off between the disutility of work and the
utility of its returns within the relevant range. In other words, as far
as the explanation of disguised unemployment is concerned, the new model is
essentially equivalent to the old.[11]

We would argue that the application of neoclassical logic or the 'rational behavioral method' to the problem of surplus labor leads to explanations which are unsatisfactory if the problem one is interested in is the understanding of a concrete phenomenon. From this point of view, the question is why surplus agricultural labor or disguised unemployment comes to exist within certain agrarian systems. This is an objective and historical question, the answer to which can come from an investigation of objective and historic conditions. It hardly needs pointing out that the question which the 'rational behavioral' method would raise is of an entirely different order. Here it is not a matter of explanation, but of internal consistency. The question here instead is, "How can surplus labor and utility maximization be mutually consistent?" Sen's answer to this question is, not surprisingly, in terms of properties of utility and disutility schedules, namely their 'flatness'. But in the absence of thorough knowledge about these schedules in actuality, this exercise for all its clarity and sharpness cannot be an explanation of the historical phenomenon. This is not to imply that peasants do not make choices, but that the framework of choice theory is not adequate since it does not focus on the core of the problem. The invariance of the 'real cost of labor' is a state of mind; as such, it is a mere projection on the psychological plane of the objective circumstances in which choice is made. And it is by reference to these objective circumstances that Sen justifies his argument, as in the statement quoted above.[12] Thus, the magnitude and variation of the 'real labor cost' reflects social organization, the state of technology, the distribution and utilization of the means of production. When it is further recognized that these objective circumstances are not random but emerge in the course of analyzable historical processes operating at the level of the system as a whole, the case is extremely strong for an explanation of these very objective conditions which lie at the root of the phenomenon in question. The riddle of consistency between the phenomenon of disguised unemployment and rational economic behavior, despite its intellectual challenge and its internal significance for neoclassical pre-occupation, is nevertheless somewhat irrelevant on this score. The main problem with the conventional discussion of surplus labor is, in other words, in the type of questions it sets out to answer.

A pervasive feature of non-historical economic approaches is their bias towards concepts defined in mechanical terms. Pertinent to this discussion, for instance, is the definition of surplus labor--"that part of the labor force in [the] peasant economy which can be removed without reducing the total amount of output produced, even when the amount of other factors is not changed".[13] Whether or not this is an operationally meaningful definition depends on the empirical plausibility of a ceteris paribus removal of a portion of the labor force. It need hardly be pointed out that historical processes seldom operate in a ceteris paribus manner, but are associated with significant changes in the distribution of means of production and even in the structure of the social organization of production. The process of rural-urban migration, which is most often the implicit mechanism of 'removal' of agricultural workers, is such an historical process.[14] Thus, this mechanical notion makes attempts to confront empirical reality in these terms highly problematic. Sen would probably concur on this point for in discussing the problem of measuring surplus labor to test for its existence, he notes:

> "The empirical part of the debate is particularly difficult
> to settle, for two separate reasons. First, it is not easy
> to find an actual case of a withdrawal of part of the labor

> force with other things remaining the same. Typically
> such a withdrawal would take place side by side with
> other changes. Furthermore, the type of withdrawal
> one is concerned with takes place in response to
> economic incentives and other types of withdrawal may
> be quite different. For example, sudden death through
> epidemics would not give relevant information on
> this question..."[15]

We would stress the fact that even when economic incentives are involved,

the process of migration and proletarianization of the peasantry is seldom

a simple quantitative response to a price signal, but one which is closely

interwoven with changes in land distribution, property rules and in economic

structure in agrarian systems. When one takes the longer view, the pre-

supposition of a ceteris paribus withdrawal of a labor force proves to be

an abstraction of doubtful value. This damages the scientific status of

the conventional surplus labor concept and of theories which stem from it.

Consider the assumed equivalence between surplus labor and subsistence

industrial wages in the Lewis-Ranis-Fei models. While it is clear that

the existence of surplus labor in agriculture plays a role in the deter-

mination of industrial wage-rates through rural-urban migration and the

'reserve army' of the unemployed, one must recognize that actual wage

rates are affected by other factors as well.[16] Thus, surplus labor, it

may be argued, is not a sufficient condition for subsistence wages in

industry. These shortcomings of the traditional concept of surplus labor

stem from its static, ahistorical character and undermine its analytical

usefulness. Sen himself expresses his dissatisfaction thus:

> "It is easy to overestimate the importance of the
> problem of surplus labor. . . Some conclusions
> that are drawn with the assumption of surplus
> labor can be drawn just as easily without the
> assumption. Even for those problems where the
> existence of a surplus makes a genuine difference,
> much will depend on the size of the surplus and

the _extent_ of the response once the surplus is exhausted.
If the latter response is very weak, the consequences
may be similar to those of surplus labor".[17]

II.4. An Alternative Formulation

It might be stated at the outset that our reformulation marks

a transition, not merely to an alternative 'model', but to an analytical

system that is methodologically distinct, an historical method of analysis.

Trite as it may seem, it is useful to bear in mind that a different

theoretical system poses very different sets of questions in the analysis

of the same 'reality', i.e., questions which are appropriate to the

internal logic of the theory.

The concept of 'surplus labor', while pertinent to the 'rational

behavioral method', is essentially non-historical, together with the nexus

of theoretical problems in which it is embedded. For our purpose, we shall

define a new concept, the purpose of which is to represent an _historical_

condition of the agricultural system which we shall call relative over-

population. Recall that 'surplus labor' implicitly deals with potential

migration or the possibility of (physical) withdrawal of a portion of the

agricultural labor force. But, as Marx noted in his discussion of European

rural-urban migration in the formation of an industrial proletariat:

> "... the constant flow towards the towns presupposes,
> in the country itself, a constant latent surplus popu-
> lation, the extent of which becomes evident only when
> its channels of outlet open to exceptional width.
> The agricultural laborer is therefore reduced to the
> minimum of wages, and always stands with one foot
> already in the swamp of pauperism."[18]

The _process of emergence_ of what Marx terms 'latent surplus population' in

a somewhat different context is the object of our study in this chapter.

Thus, 'relative overpopulation' is a more general concept as compared with 'surplus labor'. The former refers to the historical preconditions of 'surplus labor'. However, the case of migrant proletarianization from agriculture is just one (and not the only) form of its expression.[19]

Relative overpopulation in an agrarian system denotes the secular incapacity of agriculture to absorb the agrarian population in productive activity. It is the result of a prior process of historical evolution by which relative overpopulation emerges. We consider the process of social reproduction of the agrarian system in the relevant historical period. Thinking in these terms implies:

(a) Taking account of the various forms of social connectedness within the system. In this manner, we deal directly with the objective basis of economic behavior which corresponds to the socio-economic relations of production;

(b) Examining the state and evolution of the productive forces, i.e., the level of technology and the condition and degree of utilization of the means of production, corresponding to (a) above.

It is assumed that the employment capacity of social labor within a system is determined by the joint configuration of forces and relations and production.

The forms in which relative overpopulation in agriculture manifests itself may be varied. It may take the form of large-scale migration of labor on the one hand, and on the other, it may be reflected in open unemployment or immiserization in the countryside. It may reflect itself in high man-land ratios on small farms. These variations depend upon the overall nature of the economic transformation through which relative overpopulation is generated. In the case of Bengal, we shall find that during the course of the colonial period, the economic evolution of agriculture is characterized by:

1) long-run stagnation or decay of the forces of production in agriculture; insignificant increase or an actual decrease in agricultural productivity; absence of technical innovation; deterioration of the means of production over time;

2) the emergence of unequal relations in agricultural production, e.g., landlord-intermediaries-share tenant, supervisory farmer-landless laborer, etc. These are related to prior transformations in forms of property and concentration of ownership and control of agricultural means of production, primarily land. It reflects the loss of control over the means of production by large sections of the peasantry;

3) the progressive immiserization of the agricultural population, poverty, rural unemployment and increasing man-land ratios in the small peasant farms.

In the historical discussion, we shall try to show that the specific nature of (1) and (2) above leads to (3), the latter being the specific form taken by relative overpopulation in colonial Bengal. Our aim will be to show that the development of the agrarian system was conditioned by a major transformation in the relations of production. The latter in turn was itself induced by the operation of political and economic mechanisms associated with the peculiar form of interaction between colonial capitalism and the pre-existent socio-economic structure.

The logic of our explanation runs as follows: relative overpopulation emerges from a three-fold set of developments. First, the collapse of the pre-existent system of self-sufficient peasant cultivation through a protracted political-economic process of expropriation. During this process, the bulk of the peasantry is deprived of possession of the major part

of their land. This simultaneously lays the foundation for a new type--
landlord-intermediaries -petty-tenant--relations of production. Second,
the conditions of social reproduction emerging under these conditions
were such as to lead to a long-run stagnation and retrogression in the
productive forces in agriculture. Third, the non-development of alternative employment opportunities outside agricultural production within the
colonial economic system, i.e.,the limited development of industry.

We therefore analyze empirically the development of each of these
features and relate them to the dynamic of colonial development. This type
of development observed in Bengal stands in sharp contrast to the transformation of agriculture in England. In the latter case, despite expropriation and the enclosure movement, a prosperous commercial agriculture
subsequently emerged. The difference lies in the colonial pattern of
capitalist development in Bengal, with its consequences for the economic
role played by the colonial state, and the international economic relationship between Bengal and Britain.

Finally, we examine the role of population growth in relation to
the phenomenon of relative overpopulation. Clearly, the demographic explanation in terms of the growth of numbers of population, given fixed land
resources, may seem to provide an alternative explanation to the one presented here. We therefore analyze trends in population growth, agricultural
production and land utilization in the period for which such data are
available, in order to determine whether the alternative demographic explanation is plausible and sufficient to explain relative overpopulation in
Bengal. Our conclusion is that in the particular period of history in
which relative overpopulation played a secondary role as an exacerbating
and intensifying influence, rather than being the ultimate and dominant

cause of the phenomenon.

The logic of the formulation of the problem in terms of an historical process of relative overpopulation may be illustrated in a schematic fashion by means of a diagram. The arrows indicate directions of influence. (See Figure II.1)

II.5. Relative Overpopulation in Agrarian Bengal

Our analysis focuses on the eastern region of India--Greater Bengal (the area now divided into the Indian states of West Bengal, Bihar and Orissa, and Bangladesh). The choice of region is in part to keep the discussion tractable. The essentials of the Bengal experience are likely to have features common to the rest of India. As an integral part of British India, Bengal was not fundamentally different from the rest of India with regard to rural society and village economy. On the other hand, the emergence of overpopulation was comparatively sharp in Bengal. British power was first consolidated there and the Land Revenue Settlement in the region was of the zamindari type (settlement with landlords) as opposed to the ryotwari settlement of southern India. The exceptionally fertile quality of much of its agricultural land prior to 1800 is attested to by travellers.[20] Yet by the turn of the 20th century, yields were declining and by 1931, the area had a very high number of persons dependent on agriculture--769 persons per square mile of cultivated land.[21] It therefore provides an appropriate example to study, and indeed, India is the classic example of a labor surplus economy.

Our purpose here is not to present a new interpretation of the economic history of agrarian Bengal, but rather to elaborate on specific aspects of its historic development which bear on relative overpopulation.

Figure II.1.

Relative Overpopulation in Bengal, 1793-1947

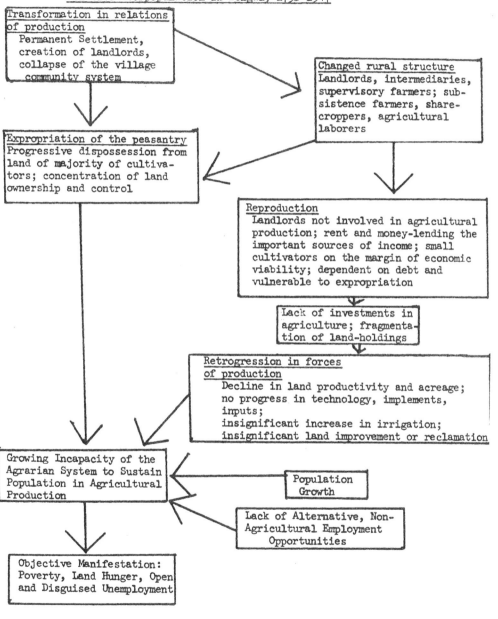

In other words, it is to explain theoretically this process in Bengal.

The historical information analyzed and presented here is derived from well-known works on Indian economic history dealing with the British period, and other sources.[22] These are the broad outlines of events: Relative overpopulation in the region developed during the latter half of the period of British colonial rule (1765-1947). During this period, especially beginning with 1793 when the land revenue system was reorganized, the agrarian structure of Bengal underwent a fundamental transformation. The essence of this change was the breakdown of the pre-existent system of agriculture and rural organization--the so-called 'village community system', and its replacement by a new form marked by unequal relations of production. Specifically, the colonial form in Bengal was characterized by a growing polarization--never quite completed--between landlords, intermediaries and supervisory farmers, on the one hand, and petty sharecropping tenants and agricultural laborers on the other. The process of transition involving expropriation of the peasantry, occurred over an extended period marked by brief intervals of rapid change during agrarian crises. The new relations of production brought about a drastic intensification of surplus extraction. Little or no improvement or innovation in agricultural technology took place. In the long run, i.e., by the fourth quarter of the 19th century, a pattern of stagnation and decay in the conditions of production emerged, as manifested, for example, in declining yields per acre. Throughout the period, a protracted process of expropriation occurred which created large-scale loss of control over land and also brought about fragmentation and subdivision of small holdings. With the growth of population, these conditions were intensified during the succeeding decades. Our investigation ends with Indian independence.

Bengal was partitioned and the subsequent situation was greatly affected
by the large-scale immigration of refugees. The abolition of the zamindari
system by the new government formally ended the colonial land system in 1948.

II.5.(a) The Pre-existent Agrarian System

The village community system which prevailed in Bengal and elsewhere in India at the time of the British conquest was one of great anti-
quity, with remarkable stability over centuries despite political upheavals.
Agricultural production was carried out by self-sufficient cultivators,
using plots of land over which they had usufructuary rights on a hereditary
basis. The land was owned communally by the whole village and plots could
not be bought or sold or otherwise transferred on a private basis. Each
village community was administered by a headman, assisted by a local village council composed of village elders or leading householders. These
village communities also contained their own weavers, potters, carpenters,
oil-pressers, goldsmiths, etc., and this accounted for the high degree of
economic autonomy of these villages for they did not engage in 'external'
trading, except to a minimal degree. Marx noted the self-sufficiency,
internal balance of agriculture and non-agricultural production and the
peculiar division of labor of this agrarian system and to this he attributed its longevity:

> "Those small and extremely ancient communities...are based on
> possession in common of the land, on the blending of agri-
> culture and handicrafts, and on the unalterable division of
> labor.... Occupying areas from 100 to several thousand acres,
> each forms a compact whole producing all it requires. The
> chief part of the products is destined for direct use by the
> community itself and does not take the form of a commodity...
> The constitution of these communities varies in different
> parts of India. In those of the simplest form, the land is
> tilled in common, and the produce divided among the members.

At the same time spinning and weaving are carried out by
each family as subsidiary industries. Side by side
with the masses thus occupied with one and the same work,
we find the 'chief inhabitant', who is judge, police and
tax-gatherer in one; the book-keeper who keeps the
accounts of the tillage and registers everything thereto;
another official who proscribes criminals, protects
strangers travelling through and escorts them to the
next village; the boundary man who guards the boundaries
against neighbouring communities; the water overseer who
distributes water from the common tanks for irrigation;
the brahmin who conducts the religious services; the
schoolmaster who on the sand teaches the children reading
and writing; the calendar-brahmin or astrologer who makes
known the lucky or unlucky time for seed time or harvest
and for every other kind of agricultural work; a smith
and a carpenter who make and repair all the agricultural
implements; the potter who makes all the pottery in the
village; the barber, the washerman who washes clothes,
the silversmith, here and there the poet.... The whole
mechanism discloses a systematic division of labour;
but a division like that in manufacture is impossible
since the smith and the carpenter etc., find an unchanging market".[23]

The village communities were, however, subordinate to the local monarchs

and paid a conventional fixed proportion of output (usually one-sixth)

as tax to the state, which was collectively paid. Responsibility for

tax collection at the local level was in the hands of the village coun-

cils, so that the autonomy of operation of these village communities was

fairly complete. The Moslem rulers, who commanded extensive empires,

introduced a revenue system whereby revenue collectors were given charge

over large areas. Nonetheless, these collectors were merely state officials

who had no direct rights of ownership and control over the land in their

charge, beyond the collection of revenue for the emperor. Moghal rule did

not alter in any basic way the system of production under the village com-

munity system because the relationship with the state remained essentially

'external' and in no way generated internal contradictions within the

structure. Population size in relation to land was very low, and since

virgin land was available in plenty (until late into the 19th century),
there was no barrier to the extensive expansion of the form of agriculture.
Within the village itself, the predominant form of agricultural production was for subsistence by households having direct control over the
means of production. Consequently, the relations of production characteristic of this form were independent, i.e., were marked by the lack of
dominance of one group over another on the basis of monopoly of control
over land. The "self-working, self-possessing and self-sufficient type
of a cultivator represented the characteristic form of production relations prevalent in the agrarian economy of those days".[24] To summarize,
the principal elements of the agrarian system in existence in Bengal at
the time of British seizure of power were the following:

1) Communal ownership of land by the village; land was not privately
owned, nor could it be freely bought and sold by individuals;

2) Production was done by self-sufficient cultivators on plots allotted
for use by the community, for the purpose of subsistence; relations of
production were 'independent';

3) The village community was an autonomous unit, meeting its consumption
through internal division of labor;

4) The fiscal relation between agricultural producers and the state preserved the autonomy of the village. Taxes were settled collectively at
the level of the village community itself, without administrative intervention by the state in the collection of revenue within the village;

5) Virgin land was in plentiful supply.

II.5.(b) Transition to a Colonial System of Agriculture

The British East India Company assumed the civil administration of the 'subah' of Bengal (comprising Bengal, Bihar and Orissa) in 1765. In 1793, the rulers introduced a new system of land revenue collection in the region, known as the Permanent Zamindari Settlement, the consequences of which were the dissolution of the village community system and the gradual development of a new agrarian structure. We shall call this the colonial system of agriculture. The reasons underlying the introduction of the new land system were several. First, the stabilization and system-atization of the land revenue administration with a view to "securing the largest possible revenue. For it was basically from these sums that British consolidation and conquest in India were financed".[25] Second, the conscious creation of a privileged class among the indigenous popu-lation which would serve as vassal, ally and intermediary between the foreign rulers and the masses.[26] The essential features of the Permanent Settlement were:

1) The conversion of the previous revenue collectors of the Moghal admin-istration into landlords, with proprietory rights over large tracts of land. These zamindars, as they were called, were made responsible for the collection and payment of tax revenues. The sum, extremely high by compar-ison with that paid to the Moghal state, was fixed in perpetuity--"per-manently settled".[27] The zamindars were to keep a fixed portion (ten percent) of their collection as a commission. In addition, they were granted widespread powers of distraint, including arrest, and confisca-tion of the property of tax defaulters;

2) The legal establishment of private property in land and of unrestricted possibility of the transfer of land through purchase and sale.

These features of the new land system served as important pre-conditions for the breakdown of the village communities, the progressive expropriation of land from the peasantry and the emergence of new relations of production in Bengal agriculture.

The economic mechanism underlying expropriation of the peasantry was essentially the increasing burden of tax and rent extraction which became the hallmark of the system. As already alluded to, the revenue demand of the British administration was extremely high as compared to that of the Moghals. In the critical phase following the Permanent Settlement, the severity of the land revenue demands led, in fact, to many cases where even some zamindars, apparently unwilling to resort to the violent methods of extraction now necessary, were ruined and replaced by a "new type of sharks and rapacious businessmen who were ready to stick at nothing... in order to pay their quota and fill their pockets".[28] The sale of zamindari lands on default and their purchase by urban merchants and moneylenders, helped to create a class of city dwelling, absentee landlords, who were quite removed from agricultural operations, and interested exclusively in rental incomes. With the possibility of unrestricted sub-letting, a whole new process of 'subinfeudation' took hold whereby layers of rent-receiving intermediaries were gradually created in Bengal.

> "Permanent undertenures, known as patni tenures, were created in large numbers, and extensive tracts were leased out on long terms.... The practice of granting undertenures has steadily continued, until at the present day but a small proportion of the permanently settled area of Bengal remains in the direct possession of the zamindars. In these alienations, the zamindars made far better terms for themselves than the Government was able to make for itself in 1793.... The process of

subinfeudation...has not terminated with patnidars
and izaradars. Darpatnis, dar-izaradars, and
even further subordinate tenures have been created
in large numbers".[29]

As a natural consequence of the rising importance of rent as a major form
of income, the magnitude of rents increased in quantity both absolutely
and, in all probability, relative to agricultural output as well. While
at the time of the settlement the total revenue collection was Rs. 40
million (10% or Rs. 4 million going to zamindars), by 1900 the landlords
were able to collect a total of Rs. 165 million, i.e., retain Rs. 125
million after meeting the land revenue demand of Rs. 40 million. This
figure does not include various illegal extractions.[30] These trends were
made possible quite simply by rackrenting of the actual cultivators of
land, testimony to which is the fact that during the 19th century, "the
entire period is marked by continual agrarian unrest".[31]

The growing immiserization of the peasantry under these conditions opened the way for their progressive expropriation from land.
Especially during periods of harvest failures, the peasantry were driven
to debt-finance from rural moneylenders at usurious interest rates in
order to meet their consumption requirements and rent and tax exactions.
Such was the case, for instance, after the famine of 1876-77. Many of
these peasants were not in a position to repay and lost their land through
mortgage and sale on default of debt obligations. The phase of expropriation through the debt attachment cycles was bound up with a new develop-
ment--the growing commercialization of agriculture. After 1850, with the
ascendancy of industrial capitalism in Britain, there was a change in the
composition of colonial trade, particularly a partial shift towards production and export of cash crops from Bengal, e.g., jute, opium and indigo.
The finance of the production of these non-food crops brought about increased

monetization of production and cash dependence of the peasantry even for subsistence purchases, and the importance of rural moneylenders in the agrarian scene. The trend towards market reliance apparently led to declining stocks of food-grains and a greater vulnerability to droughts and market crises. At the same time, the price of land rose rapidly, raising the possibility of gainful speculation by moneylenders.[32] The process of expropriation continued throughout the 19th century into the 20th century and progressively intensified, as is evident from the figures on sale and mortgage of land shown in Table II.1. It is clear that the plots alienated were small parcels since the average price of each sale was diminishing when land prices were rising.

Table II.1

Documents Registered on Sale and Mortgage of Land, (1930-43)

Year	Number Registered (in 1000's)		Average Value per Document (in Rs.)	
	Sold	Mortgaged	Sold	Mortgaged
1930	25	51	292	182
1931	22	37	250	173
1932	24	34	217	162
1933	25	31	208	158
1934	30	35	183	129
1935	32	34	181	141
1936	34	35	179	137
1937	33	30	182	133
1938	41	16	178	175
1939	65	15	163	140
1940	65	15	163	140
1941	87	15	158	120
1942	88	10	172	110
1943	169	18	187	106

Source: Mukherjee (1957), p. 39, from official records of the Bengal Government.

The figures also reveal the rising proportion of parcels sold to mortgaged-- an indication of the intensification of expropriation when small peasants

are compelled to sell out instead of first mortgaging their holdings.
The dramatically high figure for 1943 reflects the impact of the Bengal
famine. The dispossession from the principal means of production spelt
the end of the prior agrarian system as objective preconditions of independent
production by self-working, self-possessing and self-sufficient cultivators
were no longer present. Whereas the Land Revenue Commission (1938) declared the minimum size of an 'economic' holding to be 5 acres, a sample
survey of 19,599 rural households in Bengal conducted by the Commission
found that 74.6% of these owned holdings less than 5 acres. Another sample
survey of 80,000 households conducted by the Indian Statistical Institute
(1944-45) indicated that an even higher proportion (88.5%) owned less than 5
acre holdings.[33] The process of subdivision and fragmentation of holdings
had actually begun much earlier.

> "The typical problems of modern Indian agriculture--
> subdivision, fragmentation, rural indebtedness--
> arose in the 19th century, long before there was
> any pressure of population on land".[34]

The obverse of this process was the creation of a new structure of relations
of production--the landless laborers and petty landowners who subsist as
sharecropping tenants, on one end of the spectrum, and landlords who lease
out land, and 'supervisory' farmers with holdings cultivated by hired
workers on the other end. In the middle, a class of independent, self-
sufficient cultivators still managed to survive, but over time, with
every crisis their numbers declined.[35]

II.5.(c) Transformation of Social Structure and Economic Relations

The collapse of the village community system, as we have noted
already, was accompanied by a profound transformation of the social struc-

ture and of economic relations in agriculture. These changes were to have
a significant determining effect on relative overpopulation. Hence, it
is necessary to understand the extent and content of these changes more
precisely. These transformations occurred simultaneously at two distinct
levels--(a) the system of production and distribution at the point of production, and (b) within the zamindari system itself, i.e., the social composition and internal relations between the rent receivers cum tax collectors. These two facets of change arose ultimately from the same source--
the reorganization of the revenue system--and were therefore interconnected.

Distribution System Within the Village Communities Before 1793

The organic unity of the village community, particularly with respect to the fiscal relation between the village and the state prior to
1793, has already been noted. It had a collective responsibility in the
payment of taxes. We should observe next the main features of the internal
distribution system that prevailed in pre-British agriculture. The village
was a closed unit with rights and obligations of its own. Its social composition was made up of extended or joint family groups and castes whose
legal and economic relations were interfamilial rather than interpersonal.
While it is true that in depicting these relations, the notions of property
rights, alienability and market relationship are not applicable, it has
been pointed out that the village communities by and large were not com-
munistic in the sense of everything being held and used in common.[36]
Rather, different families or groups had different types of rights and re-
sponsibilities. Even within a single village, caste groups maintained their
separate styles of life and conduct. In agricultural production, different
families separately worked their individual plots of land, which had been

allocated to them by the community, and over which they possessed permanent usufructuary rights.

Despite the fact that cultivation was carried out by individual
families separately, the distribution of the crop was a _communal_ process.[37]
The division of the crop was carried out in various stages--from the
standing crop, on the threshing floor, and from the heap of grain set aside
for the village tax revenue. The process of distribution was entirely
public and took place (except for the part distributed from the standing
crop) on the threshing floor directly after harvest in the presence of all
the assembled villagers. The shares going to different families were
decided and the tax was set aside. The actual distribution was a fairly
intricate and complex process of apportioning out the produce. We shall
not describe it in detail here but confine ourselves to its main features.[38]
The distribution was carried out in separate steps in which grain was ladled
out from different heaps, corresponding to the different cultivating families.
At no point was it necessary to know the magnitude of the total product in
any heap--distribution by following fixed formulae was carried on till each
heap was exhausted. More important, distribution was not based on any
simple fractional quota accruing to different groups. There were various
deductions at each stage, some expressed in fractional terms and some in
absolute terms. And the actual proportions could vary from year to year
with the size of the harvest. The shares received by different groups
of cultivating families in any given year would depend on the number, size
and distribution of cultivators' holdings, the number, size and distribution
of ploughs, of bullocks, of farm workers, as well as of the gross produce.
The non-cultivating workers of the village, e.g., the blacksmith, the
carpenter, etc., would all be paid at this time, the contribution of each

cultivator depending on the number of ploughs he possessed. There was no bargaining or payment for specific services.

The most important features of this distribution, from our point of view, were the existence of a multiplicity of arrangements to ensure a minimum income for all and also to tend towards equalization of incomes among families. Fixed quantities going to village workers assured them a basic minimum, even if the harvest was small. Deductions by each culti-vating family in the shape of harvesting a fixed acreage, prior to bringing in all the crop for public distribution, played a role analogous to the income tax exemptions of modern times and was progressive in its incidence. Other schemes of equalization of incomes included the practice of contri-buting a fixed proportion of output of several crops by all families to a common heap and subsequently redistributing equally from it. Thus, there existed a variety of built-in mechanisms to share output and risks evenly throughout the village population which effectively ruled out the inten-sification of social and economic differentiation among the cultivating families as long as the social unity of the village communities persisted. On the other hand, we should note that because the work of tilling was carried out by the family and separate plots (which varied in size and perhaps also in fertility) were held by different families, the potential for differentiation was always present.

Zamindars Prior to the Permanent Settlement

The zamindari system developed during the Moghal period. The agri-cultural surplus collected in taxes was shared between the emperor, his nobles and the zamindars. There were constant struggles between the zamindars and the imperial government. However, under Akbar the zamindars were integrated more closely into the imperial administration, and at the same time, their rebellious tendencies were controlled. It is important to note that there were in existence, even in Moghal times, different categories of zamindars. Among these we may distinguish autonomous chieftains and intermediary zamindars.[39] These categories existed in the same territory and moreover were not mutually exclusive. They differed with respect to their origins and status. The first group were originally the hereditary autonomous rulers who were politically subdued by the Moghals. The second category were various types of intermediaries who collected revenues and paid them to the autonomous chieftains or to the imperial treasury directly. These came to be the backbone of the Moghal land revenue system and were responsible for the maintenance of law and order.

There were differences of detail between different regions of Moghal India with respect to the structure of the zamindari system. In Bengal,[40] the zamindars at the top of the social scale were tribute paying, independent or semi-independent chieftains who had become subordinate allies of the emperor, retaining their administrative autonomy. Another group was created by the Moghal administration and made hereditary revenue farmers with full administrative authority. By 1750, a functionally homogeneous amalgam of these two groups had been created. These were officials with effective administrative control over various specified areas whose positions depended on the payment of a stipulated revenue.

In addition to the zamindars, there were other categories such as the talukdars, a subset of which had attained a status comparable to the zamindars by 1793. The majority of the talukdars were initially intermediaries who were granted specific regions for revenue collection by the zamindars, to whom they turned over the revenue. In certain cases, over

time the talukdars paid directly to the imperial treasury. These were the
"independent" talukdars who, in effect, were no different from zamindars
and by the 1790's, they were a significant proportion of all talukdars.
At the time of the Permanent Settlement, the Company settled the terms of
revenue with the zamindars, the "independent" talukdars, and with certain
other talukdars who were made independent at the time of the Settlement.
These groups were designated as "proprietors" during the Settlement.

The Agrarian System after 1793

Two crucial changes took place in the agrarian system of Bengal
during the 19th and early 20th centuries. One was the rapid pace of subinfeudation, i.e., the creation of vast numbers of intermediary tenures.
These subtenures appear to have proliferated and created an exceedingly
complex maze of de facto and de jure rights of landed income. This created
an extreme form of a break between the ownership of land and the productive
activity being carried out on it. Apparently, those who owned land very
often did not know what land it was they owned, and those who cultivated
the land very often did not know the title or estate of their landlords.[41]
The second remarkable development in the colonial system was the emergence
of various types of petty sharecropping tenants in place of the former independent cultivator all across Bengal, particularly after 1890. Both these
developments altered in a fundamental way the conditions under which production and distribution took place.

Subinfeudation

The process of subinfeudation began with the "proprietors", i.e.,
the zamindars and the independent talukdars, leasing out portions of their
estates and thereby creating a subclass of landlords. These new sublandlords

in turn created similar subclasses by releasing out their portions. The
process did not end there, but was further extended along the same lines.
In this fashion, an extremely complex network of landed interests was
created by the end of the 19th century.[42] The patterns of subinfeudation
varied somewhat over the regions. In some districts, like Bakarganj,
the number of "landlords", i.e., rent-receivers, per square mile averaged
170, and it was not abnormal to have 20 grades of intermediaries interven-
ing between the producer and the zamindar.[43] It is possible, however, to
obtain a simplified picture by focussing on the nature of some of the main
types of subtenures. We have already discussed the original type of sub-
tenure--the 'taluks'--granted by the zamindars. There were, of course,
several types of talukdars. Other types of grants included "izaras" which
were leases on land given for a fixed term of years, with the izaradar
having no claim to the land beyond the period. On the other hand, the
izaradar had the right to create subtenures. There were also the "patni"
tenures which were granted by zamindars to persons on payment of a fixed
sum, usually large, which then gave the patnidar a right to a portion of
the rent. Again, there were the "karsha" tenures granted on payments of
certain sums to cultivators, which bestowed occupancy rights to them on
land in their possession. In other words, there were types of subtenures,
each with its own particular terms and conditions, which carried differences
in social status and income. Despite the existence of gradations of tenure,
we should note that these varieties of tenure did not fall into a neat
hierarchical pattern. A single landlord might simultaneously have held
different lands under different types of leases. There were even some instances of a landlord re-acquiring a portion of his land from his own sub-
lessee on an undertenure in order to plant commercial crops. Nonetheless,

there existed a spectrum of tenure holders from wealthy large estate-holding zamindars to the petty landlord.

The type of subtenures discussed so far were created by the leasing out of zamindari estates in various stages. However, there was a parallel but somewhat different type of evolution, viz., the emergence of "jotedars", "chukanidars" and similar undertenures. The difference here was that the jotedars rose from the ranks of the cultivators themselves. They were able apparently to purchase small plots from other small cultivators and thus represented an upward mobile group among the peasants. However, the jotedars themselves frequently leased out portions of their jotes to subtenants--"chukanidars"--who in turn followed a similar pattern, and indeed there were several further grades to which this was extended. These were the so-called "under-ryoti" tenancies--the term ryot meaning cultivator. This development should not surprise us, given our analysis of the nature of cultivation on family plots under the village community system. Once the social organization of the village communities disintegrated and private property and alienability with respect to land were legally recognized, the latent possibilities of differentiation among the peasantry became actualized. However, over time petty landlords came from groups other than the better-off cultivators, viz., the members of the trading classes.

What accounts for the proliferation of subtenures within the agrarian system? Several reasons may be advanced for the proliferation of undertenures which, together, contribute towards an explanation:[44]
(a) For the facilitation of administration and revenue collection on scattered zamindari estates;
(b) Some undertenures, e.g., the patni tenures, were created because of

financial difficulties of the zamindars. These could be acquired on payment of a large fixed sum of money to the zamindar, in return for which
the person acquired a portion of the rent. The creation of these undertenures marked a diminution in status, as well as potential future income
for the zamindars, but they did not have alternative sources of generating
liquid sums to pay off debts and commitments to the Company or urban moneylenders;

(c) From the point of view of persons acquiring subtenures, an important
consideration was the acquisition of the "landlord" status for a price,
quite apart from the provision of a steady income;

(d) A motive similar to (c) was present to some extent even in the case
of the ryots and under-ryots. But here certain other factors were also at
work. Under conditions of unchanging labor-intensive methods of production and rising costs of cultivation,[45] ryots with larger than subsistence
holdings adopted the practice of cultivating only a small portion of their
land with family labor and either leasing to under-ryots or to sharecroppers. Clearly the small extent of (money-) capital accumulation in
these strata was a determining factor in the pattern, as was the absence
of labor saving innovations. Further, the practice of subletting to petty
sharecroppers and under-ryots was due to the higher exploitability of the
latter. Evidence for this may be found in comparative rent schedules for
different types of tenants. The smaller, most insecure, tenants with
the smallest holdings also paid much higher rents per acre than the ryots.
Average rents moved inversely in general with size of holdings.

Economic Relations at the Point of Production

Towards the end of the 19th century and with increasing frequency
thereafter, the real work of agricultural cultivation was carried out by

"bhagchasis" (literally meaning sharecroppers) who worked the lands under
jotedars and the chukanidars. There were variations between regions as
to the precise shares and with regard to different crops—the shares depending on which party supplied the inputs(manure and seed) or in what proportions they were shared. It depended also on whether or not the cultivator required advances for subsistence and on the quality of the land leased.

There were several conditions associated with this process. On
the one hand, these petty sharecroppers were subject to enhanced rents
because of their economic vulnerability. This was also legally permissible
since, under the Bengal Tenancy Act, only the ryots were recognized as
cultivators and protected. This did not apply to the under-ryots and hence,
the rents from the latter could be raised. They could also be evicted at
will. But many ryots were not really cultivators at all, being in fact
moneylenders who had acquired ryoti lands, and who never touched the plough.
Rackrenting became commonplace. On the other hand, throughout this period,
as we have noted earlier, a process of expropriation was taking place
through the debt attachment cycle. This meant that a steady supply of
landless peasants who were potential sharecroppers was being created. The
process was thus self-reinforcing.

There still remained some self-cultivating peasants. These worked
their (medium-sized) holdings, which were either owned or over which they
possessed occupancy rights, with the help of family labor and some hired
labor. But they diminished proportionately in number and became rather a
small fraction. Because of the confusion over the terminology regarding
"ryots"—which came to include non-cultivating landlords, on the one hand,
and on the other, included tiny plot-owning cultivators who partly worked
for others—it is difficult to accurately estimate their numbers. An

approximate idea of their relative numbers may be obtained from Table II.4, (p. 108).

II.5.(d) Evolution of Forces of Production in the Colonial System

Under the new form of social reproduction, the progress of agricultural expansion took a particular form--consistent with its methods of economic existence and surplus appropriation. As previously noted, agricultural land in Bengal was annually enriched by alluvial deposits and naturally highly fertile. As long as virgin land existed, there was no resource barrier to the extensive expansion of this form. It is likely that output increased, keeping pace with population, through the third quarter of the 19th century, broken by periods of famine or epidemic. Over the longer run, however, with the gradual exhaustion of good land, a remarkable process of decay in the productive forces set in.

The problem was rooted in the character and bias of the utilization of surplus associated with the colonial system. There was little or no investment in land improvement. The surplus at the point of production was siphoned off from the actual cultivators in the form of taxes and rent, leaving little at their immediate disposal. For the direct producers, this meant, on the one hand, increasing monetization of activities, and on the other, an exclusive preoccupation with the basic problem of survival. Consequently, they could afford little time or resources to investment in land improvement or innovations. Under conditions in which the communal character of village society was disintegrating and cash-dependence was rising, mobilization and coordination of efforts to make large-scale improvements in land were not possible without monetary resources, which the peasants did not possess. The pattern of utilization of investible resources was determined by the conditions of economic existence of the rent-receiving classes and the budgetary policies of the colonial government. It is a matter of record that neither of these two dominant groups utilized resources drawn from the land in productive investment in agriculture to any significant degree. The zamindars, who were absentee landlords, did not concern themselves with actual production and invested very little or nothing in land improvement, irrigation, or land reclamation. It was apparently felt that these were unwarranted given the natural fertility of the soil.[46] However, as we have shown below, this attitude of the zamindars and other intermediaries is best understood in relation to their objective conditions of economic reproduction. The same neglect of agriculture is true of the budgetary expenditures of the government, which were biased towards military expenditures and the railways. While land revenue made up the bulk of the government's tax receipts, expenditures on irrigation were uniformly low by comparison with the size of land revenue and with other items of state expenditure.[47] This manner of utilization of surplus, together with the expropriation of actual cultivators and accompanied by the subdivision and fragmentation of holdings described earlier, led to the eventual stagnation and decay of the forces of production and laid the foundations for relative overpopulation.

Reasons for the Lack of Agrarian Investments under the Zamindari System

What explains the fact that little or no investment in land improvement took place under the zamindari system? The answer lies in the extreme degree of separation between "proprietorship" and production which grew up within the system. To put the matter simply, the actual cultivators of land, being economically at the margin of subsistence, did not

have accumulations of investible funds. Nor did they have the incentive
in most cases, since they were insecure tenants at will. To understand
why the landlords did not invest in land improvements, we need to look
more closely at the way in which rents were distributed between different
categories of landlords.

As we have noted above, there were several grades of landlords who
obtained a share of the rent from the same piece of land. Further, any
given landlord often held different portions of his holdings under different
types of tenure. The class of landlords was not homogeneous, there being
great differences between them with regard to status, economic background
and level of income. The large landlords--the zamindars and independent
talukdars--were traditionally non-cultivators and remained so for more
than a century after the Permanent Settlement, when they were recognized
as "proprietors". Thus, in Bakarganj, only 1% of owned land was held by
this group for personal occupation. Of this, a minute fraction, amounting to
0.18% of owned land, was cultivated. Practically all the rest was leased
to rent-paying tenants. A large number of them were absentee landlords,
but even if physically present on the estate, they had no connection with
cultivation.[48] Income from rent was fairly substantial and as long as
the tax revenue was paid regularly, their property was secure. They were
under no competitive pressure to maximize returns from land. Further,
within the general context of the colonial economy, there was neither an
expanding market for an expanding domestic urban economy,[49] nor an expanding export market for agricultural products through 1850 at least, as
the East India Company did not export traditional agricultural products
from India. It was at a later stage, after the industrial revolution had
taken firm hold in England, that certain agricultural products were exported

from India. Therefore, initially the objective conditions for a transformation of the economic reproduction of the zamindars from non-producing
receivers of rent and collectors of revenue to entrepreneurial agricultural
producers, were not present. And by the late 19th century, the structure
of subinfeudation had already emerged. Many of these sub-landlords had,
in fact, long-term, hereditary tenures and this made it objectively difficult for the "proprietors" to make the aforementioned transition.

Why did the intermediary landlords not invest? There were several
reasons which may have accounted for this. One factor was the nature of
the distribution of rent. Often it was the case that the zamindar leased
only a specific proportion of the rental income and not a specific piece
of land--a practice that was extended through various layers to which these
intermediaries leased in turn.[50] Not only did this lead to greater exploitation of the actual cultivator who had to pay separate dues and special
charges (nazars, salamis) to a host of different landlords, but it also
rendered investment unlikely. Basically, it now required collusion and
agreement among all the rent receivers to invest, since the returns for
investment would have to be shared by all the receivers of rent, and no
single one of them was willing to invest in isolation.[51] This was com-
pounded by differences in social status among the various intermediaries,
and there were social antagonisms among them, which made collaborative
investments unlikely.

It should be noted that not all of the intermediary landlords were
wealthy and few of them were "proprietors" of land. Essentially, they came
from groups for whom a major motivation in acquiring leases was advance-
ment of social status to that of landlord. The majority of petty landlords
were not wealthy and were in no financial position to invest, even in such

cases where they held tenure to a specific piece of land. The return on
these tenures was very meager and they changed hands with great frequency.[52]
This reflected an unwillingness to commit investible resources in land.
On those lands over which a hierarchy of rent receivers cum revenue collectors had control, there was an additional problem. No intermediary along
the line could be certain that he would be able to obtain the full extent
of incremental returns on any investment from those below him, as enhance-
ment of rents would be resisted across the chain of intermediaries, even
if the actual producer was too weak to put up effective resistance. They
could not maintain, as did the zamindars, armed rent and revenue collecting
personnel.

Some ownership holdings were acquired by members of the moneylending and trading classes in the course of the expropriation process.
These were traditionally non-cultivators. Agriculture for these people
remained only a part of the total economic operations. Rather than enter
into agriculture as capitalist producers, they tended to hold land for
speculative purposes in the most liquid form. For this reason, they leased
only to the poorest sharecroppers who were evictable on short notice.
When they did invest in agriculture in the latter part of the 19th century,
it was not on land improvement or new technology, but rather in the financing of certain cash crops such as jute and indigo, under the sharecropping
system.

Thus, the internal economic relations within the zamindari system,
together with the range of economic opportunities available to the moneyed
groups within the zamindari system, accounted for the lack of investments
in Bengal agriculture. These reasons help explain why, despite the establishment of private property and the conversion of land into a commodity,

despite expropriation of the bulk of cultivators, despite the creation of a multiplicity of "landlords", agricultural capitalism did not emerge in colonial Bengal as it had in England. Instead there was a marked decay of the productive forces.

Decline in the Productivity of Agriculture

There were three aspects to the process of the decline of agricultural productivity. First, the absence of technical improvement in the form of agricultural implements. The proportion of wooden ploughs to iron ploughs, for instance, remained very high. The use of machines, such as oil engines and electric pump tubewells, was negligible even in 1940. There was some growth in the use of better seeds, but in 1922-33, only 1.9% of all crop acreage in India was under improved seeds, rising to 11.1% in 1938-39. Chemical fertilizers were practically unknown. Taken together, these reflect a picture of technical stagnation in agricultural production, especially for foodcrops throughout the 19th century and the first four and a half decades of the 20th.[53] Second, and more important, was the gradual decline in the productivity of the land. Trends in the productivity of land between 1891 and 1947 are presented in Table II.2. Adequate information prior to this period is not available.

Table II.2.: Trends in Rates of Change of Yields Per Acre in Agricultural Production, Greater Bengal, 1891-1947,* (percent per year)

	1891-1901	1896-1906	1901-1911	1906-1916	1911-1921	1916-1926	1921-1931	1926-1936	1931-1941	1936-1946	Average
All crops	0.56	-0.61	0.07	0.29	-0.97	-0.81	0.73	-0.30	-1.44	-0.90	-0.34
Food grains	0.23	-0.75	-0.02	0.10	-1.00	-1.10	0.29	-0.73	-1.92	-0.59	-0.55
Nonfood grains	1.54	0.07	0.49	0.84	-0.67	0.49	1.06	2.33	-0.52	0.24	0.59

*Trends are measured as annual rates of change for 10 overlapping 'reference decades' covering the 56-year period.

Source: Blyn (1966), Appendix Table 5B, p. 331, and Table 7.4, p. 165.

The trends were negative for 'all-crops' and particularly for the group 'foodgrains'. The average rates of change in yield per acre in Greater Bengal were -0.34% per year for all crops and -0.55% for foodgrains for the 56-year period, amounting to a 16% decrease in yield per acre for all-crops over the whole period. The trend in non-foodgrains' yield per acre was positive throughout, but the all-crop trend was dominated by food-grains, which accounted for over 85% of all crop acreage. For foodgrains, the decline in yield per acre tended to accelerate over the period. While the rate was -0.55% per year for the whole period, the figure for 1891-1916 was -0.11% and for 1921-1946 it was -0.74% per year. This was reflected in the all-crop figures--the decline over 1921-46 was -0.48% per year. For rice, the single most important crop in the region, the average rate of change in yield per acre for the 56-year period was -0.49% per year. The evidence on decaying productivity of land during this period is thus quite striking. Third, and still more remarkable, there was a reduction in acreage cultivated in relation to population growth. During this period, in Greater Bengal over 3 million acres of land went out of cultivation. The average rate of change in acreage for the total period was -0.06% per year. For foodgrains as a whole, there was a zero trend, but for rice, the rate of decline in acreage was about equal to the all-crop average. (The arithmetic rate of decline in rice acreage was 52,000 acres /year in 1891-1947). It is therefore clear that trends on yield per acre cannot be explained in Ricardian terms, i.e., through the gradual inclusion of submarginal lands into cultivation. In fact, over this 56-year period, acreage and yield per acre both declined. All crop and food-grains production thus diminished in absolute terms.

What were the reasons for this deterioration in the productivity
of land? A firm answer to this question must await further research.
However, several reasons flow from the conditions of production and surplus utilization within the colonial system. One factor was the destruction through disrepair of the ancient system of canal irrigation maintained
in prior (pre-British) times by the state. During British rule, these
canals, at once vital to irrigation, drainage and transport, were "suf-
fered to fall into dilapidation" and became "innumerable small destructive
rivers of the delta region, constantly changing their course".[54] As a
result, some areas lost fertility of soil or were turned to jungle. In
West-Central Bengal apparently, careless construction of railway embank-
ments contributed to the destruction of natural irrigation and drainage
by cutting off the annual supply of soil-enriching, loam-bearing Ganges
water and caused inundation, leaving the affected areas poorly drained
and malaria infested. Consequently, they became unproductive. However,
the region affected by railway construction in this manner was relatively
small, amounting to only about 6% of total cultivated area in Greater
Bengal.[55] In any case, the level of irrigation in Greater Bengal as a
whole remained low. Between 1908 and 1946, the percentage of irrigated
land to cultivated land was within 13.3% to 15.0%,[56] a fact which may be
attributed to the small public expenditures of the state on irrigation.
At the local, and no less important, level the attitudes of zamindars and
other absentee landlords were responsible for the lack of improvement in
irrigation.

But quite apart from the question of falling yields per acre,
agrarian decay with regard to the productive forces was manifested in the
dwindling of acreage cultivated in the face of rising population size. The

character of land utilization within the colonial system was such as to exclude from cultivation potentially cultivable land which called for reclamation expenditures or some investment. This was not forthcoming, as we have seen, from the state, the zamindars, the intermediary tenure holders, or the rackrented peasant producers. It was observed as early as 1879:

> "There are extensive areas of good waste land covered
> with jungle in various parts of the country, which
> might be reclaimed and rendered suitable for culti-
> vation; but for that object capital must be employed,
> and the people have little to spare".[57]

In view of the evidence, there is little reason to doubt that throughout the period, the level of utilization of cultivable land was below potential. The average acreage of land under various uses showed some changes between 1907 and 1946. There was a 3.3 million acre decline in land under cultivation. Acreage in major and minor crops individually diminished. The category 'forest' increased by 4.5 million acres. Quite remarkable is the fact that there was a substantial increase in fallow land by 2.4 million acres. This is also borne out by figures showing the ratio of fallow land to land "generally cultivated", i.e., net sown area plus fallow, which went up from an average figure of 16.0% for 1897-1921 to one of 24.3% for 1921-46.[58] It is not possible to attribute these changes in land utilization to variations in 'natural' factors. It seems likely that this was in part related to the ongoing process of expropriation. The mechanism for the alienation of land from small peasants was through indebtedness--mortgage--sale to moneylenders. Throughout this period, the price of land was rising, making speculative holding of land (by money-lenders) profitable. It is plausible that under these conditions, portions of these lands remained unutilized and were reflected in the statistics as 'fallow'. To summarize: During the period, particularly from the closing decade of the 19th century and continuing into the first four and a half decades of the 20th century, the forces of production in the agriculture of Bengal underwent a marked stagnation and deterioration. Three inter-related aspects of this process were located:

1) Stagnation in implements, inputs and techniques in agriculture;

2) Deterioration in the productivity of land (yield per acre);

3) Incomplete utilization of potentially cultivable land and the contraction in acreage under cultivation at a time when population was growing. All three aspects are traceable to the degree and form of the extraction and utilization of agricultural surplus in the colonial system. These, in turn, stem from the relations of production in agriculture and the revenue and expenditure policies of the colonial state. The third aspect may be a reflection of the ongoing process of expropriation of land throughout this period. This historical configuration of forces and relations of production and the developing contradiction provides the basis of relative overpopulation in Bengal.

II.5.(e) Population Size and Relative Overpopulation

Census figures for population in India are available from 1871. It is estimated that prior to 1870, India's population was roughly constant in the range of 100 to 125 million for 1600-1800. After 1871, the population began to rise, recording an average annual growth rate of 0.6% between 1871 and 1941. This was not excessive for the period, being below the world average (0.69%) for 1850 to 1940.[59] Underlying the aggregate figure, however, there is substantial regional variation within India. The population of Greater Bengal in 1891 was 74.01 million and in 1941 it stood at 100 million. The average trend rate of growth for the period 1891-1946 was 0.65% per year, but barring a decade of virtual stagnation (1911-1921), the rates of growth by decade accelerated, rising from 0.47% per year (1891-1901) to 1.00% per year (1931-41).[60] This paper does not concern itself with the explanation of these trends. Here we examine the relationship between population size and trends and relative overpopulation. Our main conclusion is that population growth served to exacerbate the material conditions of production of the cultivators, and thereby to intensify relative overpopulation. In other words, population played a secondary role in the total process and was not the root cause. That lay in the decaying conditions of production which had emerged, independent of population trends.

There are two aspects to population change--changes in size, i.e., population growth, and the other, density in relation to land area. Moreover, the density of population per unit of area itself may be viewed in different ways: One is the density measuring the average concentration of population in a region. This relates to the question of the numbers of people engaged in rural occupations as opposed to urban occupations. The other is to view density more specifically in relation to the utilization of agricultural land, which leads to the question of cultivated acreage and trends in farm size. It is commonly believed that population size and acreage under the plough in any given agricultural system move in the same direction and consequently, if agricultural population rises, so should the area cultivated, as long as land is available. It is also generally supposed that when population size expands in a given region, density also moves upwards throughout the region. However, the evidence in Bengal stands in opposition to these expectations. See Table II.3, where trends in population and acreage are compared on the basis of Blyn's estimates.

Table II.3.: Trends in Rates of Change of Population
and All-Crop Acreage, Greater Bengal,
1891-1947,* (percent per year)

	1891-1901	1896-1906	1901-1911	1906-1916	1911-1921	1916-1926	1921-1931	1926-1936	1931-1941	1936-1946	Average
Population	0.47	0.54	0.61	0.61	0.05	0.25	0.86	0.93	1.00	1.15	0.65
Acreage	-0.33	-0.45	0.05	0.03	-0.42	-0.61	-0.23	-0.06	0.21	1.20	-0.66

*See note to Table II.2.

Source: Blyn (1966), Appendix Table 5B. P. 331, and
Table 6.2, p. 131.

We notice that while for each of the ten reference decades the average
annual growth rate of population was positive, the rate for all-crop acreage
was negative for six and below 0.05% for two others. Only in one, the
last decade 1936-46, did it exceed the rate for population. For the
period 1891-1946 as a whole, all-crop acreage fell; the rate of change was
-0.06% per year, while that for population was 0.65%. The picture of a
given area of arable land which was being gradually occupied by a growing
population, progressively bringing marginal lands under cultivation, is
quite contrary to the facts. Instead, we observe a contraction of actual
acreage, together with falling yields per acre. It is therefore clear
that a simplistic explanation, based on population growth, is not adequate
for dealing with the facts of the case. Earlier we suggested some reasons
for the contraction of acreage. Geddes (1937) provides some useful information on population trends for Bengal Province (which accounted for over 55%
of the population of Greater Bengal). Over the period 1872-1931, the
picture that emerges is one of remarkable diversity between different regions
within the province in terms of population growth. Some areas, particularly
in the fertile, well-watered eastern and southern river plain and delta,

recorded very high increases in population--by 100% in the 60-year period.
But elsewhere there was slower growth, with a wide range of variation. In
fact, some tracts in Central Bengal actually registered declines by 10%.[61]
Not surprisingly, the density of rural population measured in 1931 showed
a divergent pattern: the fertile eastern river plain and delta, showing
the highest density (900/square mile) as compared with the average (640/
square mile) for the rural Bengal plain.[62] Despite the wide range of
variation, however, it appears that declines in acreage cultivated were
not localized to any particular tract but fairly general.[63] These were
not exclusively or closely associated with density or population growth
as such. More information is needed on Bihar and Orissa for firm conclusions about Greater Bengal as a whole, though densities in Bihar were
comparable.

These facts make it plausible that trends in population were of
secondary importance to the evolution of Bengal agriculture, as compared
with the degree and manner of utilization of land and its proper maintenance over time. Our earlier arguments relate the latter to the evolution of the forces of production--irrigation, land reclamation, etc. As
we have seen throughout the period under study, there was land available
which was potentially cultivable, but which nevertheless was not brought
under cultivation.[64]

II.5.(f) The Non-Availability of Alternative Employment Opportunities

The growth of population did contribute to the intensification
of contradiction within the agrarian economy by making less cultivated
land available per head of rural population. But in this, too, its role
must be seen in conjunction with other factors. The other contributory

factor was the lack of non-agricultural occupations. Given the overall
nature of colonial economic development, the growth in urban employment
opportunities was meager and as a result, the proportion of rural to total
population remained very high, being 93% for Bengal in 1931, while two-
thirds of the urban population was concentrated around Calcutta. Not all
members of the rural population were agriculturists, but a very high
percentage was, being wholly or largely dependent on agriculture for their
livelihood. Much has been written on the decline of Indian handicrafts,
first as a consequence of exploitation of artisans by the East India Company, and later because of competition from English manufactures.[65] Fresh
historical evidence on the decline of traditional industries, especially
cotton textiles in Gangetic Bihar, is presented by Bagchi (1976), the
data pertaining to the period 1809-1913. Bagchi finds that the number of
persons" dependent on secondary industry" (i.e., employed in non-agricultural production and exclusive of pure traders) fell not only relative to
total population from 18.6% to 8.5%, but also in absolute terms.[66] This
lends strong support to the earlier contentions of Indian historians and
qualitative accounts of official publications published in the 1870's.
Bagchi also argues that this phenomenon was not restricted to Bihar alone,
but also to the rest of Greater Bengal and indeed to most of colonial India.
We need not enter into an explanation of the causes of this decline here,
except to note that this was due largely to a loss in the producers'
domestic markets in competition with English cotton manufactures, in the
promotion of which the state was an active agent. While traditional manufactures declined, large numbers of the artisanry were thrown out of employment. At the same time, the development of modern industry was practically
absent until the 1870's and, in relation to the labor force, negligible

thereafter.[67] Thus, there was not only a lack of alternative opportunities for agricultural producers who were being progressively expropriated, but even those who had been employed in non-agricultural occupations found themselves driven to seek agricultural occupations.

Taken together, all three trends--declining acreage, lack of non-agricultural occupations, and population growth--were manifested as the "pressure of population on the land". The per capita availability of land, measured as acres of agricultural land per person dependent on land, fell from 2.23 to 1.9 during 1890-1940 for the area of Permanent Zamindari Settlement.[68] For Bengal, "the number of acres cultivated per cultivator" fell from 3.1 to 2.1 between 1921-1931.[69] Figures for average availability of land do not adequately reveal the actual resource position of cultivators because of the inequality of land distribution. Various estimates of percentages of total households under different size-classes of holdings are given in Table II.4.

Table II.4.: Landholdings of Agrarian Households in Bengal, 1939

Size of Holding	Millions of Households
>5 acres	2
2-5 acres	2
<2 acres	3.5
Total number engaged mainly in cultivation	7.5
Bargadars (sharecroppers)	1
Agricultural wage laborers	2

Source: B. M. Bhatia, Famines in India, p. 319, citing Famine Inquiry Commission Report on Bengal.

The Land Revenue Commission (1940) declared five acres to be the minimum 'economic' size in the sense of producing enough to fully support an average family. But in 1939, around 75% of households had holdings below five acres,

and over 46% had holdings below two acres.[70] Conditions worsened after the
1943 famine. In the light of these tendencies, we might suppose population growth contributed to the acceleration of the expropriation process.
With non-viable holdings, the economic pressure to obtain the means of
subsistence must have driven the peasant households to depend on consumption loans, petty tenancy and other economic relations, which were at
once exploitative and increased their vulnerability to expropriation. But
it must be remembered that falling acreage and yields per acre, and fragmentation of landholdings had begun to be evident in the late 19th or early
20th century, prior to the period in which population size, density or
growth rate attained significant magnitudes.

II.6.   Conclusion

This chapter began with a criticism of the neoclassical (rational
behavioral) analysis of surplus labor in agriculture. The main points
of the criticism were:

1) This analysis, which resolves the problem of consistency between subjective rationality and disguised unemployment, does not provide an explanation of the actual phenomenon. The historical existence of surplus labor
needs to be explained in terms of its objective basis;

2) The neoclassical conception is itself historically non-operational (and
empirically problematic) because 'labor withdrawal' is a process not usefully
conceived in ceteris paribus terms.

The second part of the chapter attempted the analysis of surplus
agricultural population by viewing it in terms of an historical process of
development of the agricultural system, whereby the objective conditions
for the existence of surplus population are created. To this end, a method

of historical analysis was elaborated and utilized with concrete reference
to Bengal. Our conceptualization of surplus agricultural population was
in terms of a condition in which the bulk of peasant households are unable
to fully use their labor power with the means of production at their
direct disposal, i.e., their owned landholdings. This inability arises
from two aspects of their production conditions:

1) the size of landholdings in relation to household size;

2) the conditions of forces of production which determine productivity.
These two aspects of production conditions, therefore, needed to be explained in the concrete case of Bengal. The first stage of the explanation
traced the reasons for loss of land and diminution of landholdings of the
majority of actual cultivators. This period (1793-1947) was seen as one
of the formation of a colonial system of agriculture, displacing the village community system in Bengal. The size of landholdings of the majority
of cultivators diminished progressively through a prolonged process of
expropriation which was self-reinforcing. The second step was to analyze
the process of the arrest and retrogression of the productive forces in
agriculture, i.e., its 'underdevelopment'. It was shown to arise within
the process of evolution from the fact that:

1) the economic reproduction of landowners and other non-producing intermediary rent earners, did not require capital investments in land improvement. Moreover, the nature of the internal relations of rent distribution
within the zamindari system discouraged investment. Therefore, it was not
forthcoming; this was also reinforced by the fiscal policies of the state; and

2) the expropriation of peasant households was effected through their immiserization, marginalization and increased vulnerability to agrarian crises.
They existed on the brink of economic viability, in debt, leading to mort-

gage and sale of land. Hence, they were unable to improve the productive forces. These affect both the social form of labor utilization, as well as the character of land utilization in the system.

Relative overpopulation was sharpened and intensified by population growth which, in conjunction with the lack of non-agricultural employment opportunities and the decline in total cultivated acreage, contributed to the trends toward fragmentation and subdivision of holdings, i.e., increasing expropriation. Some households were converted into landless laborers. Among those which retained land, the majority of cultivating households came to possess holdings below the minimum economic size for the average family. This explains why there was pervasive land hunger and why there was more labor power available than there was work on the farm, i.e., why there was disguised unemployment.

FOOTNOTES - CHAPTER II

1   For a survey of the literature on 'disguised unemployment' and extensive bibliography, see Kao, Anschel and Eicher (1964). 'Disguised unemployment' is said to exist when the withdrawal of apparently employed agricultural workers from production, ceteris paribus, does not lead to a fall in output.

2   Given by the average productivity of labor in agriculture.

3   See Kao, Anschel and Eicher (1964) and Sen (1966) for a discussion of the debate on disguised unemployment.

4   Lewis (1954), p. 403.

5   This may be derived as follows:

The egalitarian peasant household maximizes its welfare, e.g., we maximize $Z = N [U(q) - V(x)]$
with respect to the total family labor allocation L, where
$q' = \dfrac{Q}{N}$, $x = \dfrac{L}{N}$, and $Q = Q(L)$.

We have $\dfrac{dZ}{dL} = N [U'(q) \cdot \dfrac{dq}{dL} \cdot - V'(x) \cdot \dfrac{dx}{dL}]$.

In this expression on the right-hand side, $\dfrac{dq}{dL} = \dfrac{Q'(L)}{N}$, $\dfrac{dx}{dL} = \dfrac{1}{N}$.
Hence,

$$\dfrac{dZ}{dL} = \cancel{\dfrac{N}{N}} [U'(q) \cdot Q'(L) - V'(x)].$$

For a first order extremum, $U'(q) \cdot Q'(L) - V'(x) = 0$

i.e., $Q'(L) \cdot U'(q) = V'(x)$
A check on the second order condition reveals that this yields a maximum: $\dfrac{d^2 Z}{dL^2} = U'(q) \cdot Q''(L) < 0$, since $U'(q) > 0$, $Q''(L) < 0$.

6   Sen (1966), p. 429, italics in original.

7   *Ibid.*, p. 430.

8   Sen (1975), p. 26.

9   For some forceful criticisms of the weakness of 'individualist' economic theory in providing scientific explanations of phenomena, see Foley (1975). See also Althusser's essay, Chapter 7, Althusser and Balibar (1970) for a deeper epistemological critique.

10   In view of the overall structure and ramifications of general equilibrium theory, it seems extremely doubtful whether the aforementioned scientific task can be attempted by neoclassical economists without seriously damaging the foundations of the theory. The dilemma here is that if individual utilities are

shown to be determined by objective social conditions, the entire utility apparatus loses explanatory power for most problems since its mediation becomes unnecessarily circuitous. As a further consequence, the basis of neoclassical welfare economics is shaken. On this latter point, see Sen (1973).

11 To avoid misunderstanding, we should explain that Sen (1975) does not intend to supply a new theory of surplus labor. The novel features in the expression for 'real labor cost' permit Sen to compare alternative agrarian 'modes of employment' by associating, on intuitive reasoning, different ranges of α and h with each 'mode'.

12 See Footnote 7, above.

13 Sen (1966), p. 428.

14 For an excellent discussion of proletarianization as a historical process in the case of Rhodesia, see Arrighi (1970).

15 Sen (1975), p. 35.

16 Sen (1975), pp. 53-55, gives five reasons why a 'wage-gap' between agricultural and industrial employment may exist. Among these are labor legislation and union pressure, and employers' incentive for paying high wages, e.g., reduced turnover of laborers.

17 Sen (1966), p. 432. Emphasis in original.

18 Marx (1967), p. 642.

19 This is not to suggest that rural-urban migration is not an appropriate subject for historical analysis. But here we are concerned primarily with the agrarian system itself, rather than labor supply for industrial employment. In this historical case and period, rural-urban migration for industrial employment did not occur on any significant scale.

20 Raychaudhuri (1968), p. 83.

21 Davis (1951), p. 22, Table 5.

22 The following studies have been particularly useful in providing information and analysis: Ramkrishna Mukherjee (1957), (1974), Radhakumud Mukherjee (1933),R. C. Dutt (1950),R. P. Dutt (1949), Thorner and Thorner (1962), Raychaudhuri (1968),Chandra (1968), Blyn (1966), Neale (1957), Frykenberg (1969), Bagchi (1975), Davis (1951)and Geddes (1937),(1946). Specific references are noted in the text.

23 Marx (1967), pp. 357-358.

24   Mukherjee (1957), p. 21.

25   Thorner and Thorner (1962), p. 53.

26   "If security was wanting against popular tumult or revolution, I
      should say that the Permanent Settlement, though a failure in
      many other respects and important essentials, has this great
      advantage at least, of having created a vast body of rich,
      landed proprietors deeply interested in the continuance of
      British Dominion and having complete command over the mass of
      the people." Bentinck, Governor-General of India, speech,
      November 8, 1829, quoted in Mukherjee (1957), p. 32.

27   Land revenue in Bengal in the last year of Moghal administration,
      (1764-65), was L818,000. Under the Permanent Settlement (1793)
      it was raised to L3,091,000. See Dutt (1949), pp. 187-191.

28   Dutt (1949), p. 216. See also Dutt (1950), Volume I.

29   D. J. McNeile, "Memorandum on the Revenue Administration of the
      Lower Provinces of Bengal", Government Publication, Calcutta,
      1873, quoted in Mukherjee (1957), p. 35.

30   Mukherjee (1957), p. 35. There was no relaxation of land revenue
      collection, even during the famine years. For figures, see
      Chandra (1968), p. 67.

31   Raychaudhuri (1968), p. 89.

32   Thorner and Thorner (1962), p. 54.

33   Mukherjee (1957), using sample survey data for 1946, classifies the
      rural society of Bengal into three broad classes: Class I -
      landlords and 'supervisory farmers' (4% of households);
      Class II - self-sufficient peasants, artisans and traders (42%
      of households); and Class III - sharecroppers, agricultural
      laborers, menial employees and others (54% of households).
      Class II is probably an overestimate of 'self-sufficient'
      peasants since it includes tenants who derive most of their
      income from direct cultivation.

34   Raychaudhuri (1968), p. 89.

35   "Many bargadars (sharecroppers) are the original tenants who have
      lost their lands in the civil courts for failure to pay their
      rent or other liabilities.... It is bound up with the commer-
      cialization of land.... Free transferability has tended and must
      tend to facilitate the transfer of raiyati (peasant) lands into
      the hands of mahajans (moneylenders) and non-agriculturists, with
      the result that the number of rackrented bargadars and under-
      raiyats is going u by leaps and bounds". Land Revenue Commis-
      sion, Report (1940),pp. 67-71.

36   See W. C. Neale (1957), p. 228. Our discussion of distribution within
      the village community draws upon this study.

37   It was carried out in public before the assembled gathering of all
      villagers. There were no private arrangements on payment for
      specific services. See Neale, op. cit., p. 224.

38   For a detailed discussion, see Neale, op. cit., pp. 223-233, where
      he gives a summary of an eyewitness account of a British colonial
      administrator, W. C. Bennet. Though this account does not relate
      specifically to a Bengal village, it seems very likely that
      the system was not too different. Neale himself regards it as
      'typical' for India.

39   For an account of the zamindari system under the Moghals, see
      S. Nural Hasan (1969). Hasan's treatment concentrates on the
      Northern and Western regions of India. He distinguishes a third
      category, 'primary zamindars', which does not appear to have
      existed in Bengal during the Moghal period.

40   See T. Raychaudhuri (1969), pp. 164-166. Raychaudhuri gives an
      account of the Bakarganj district, Eastern Bengal. The study
      contains useful information on the zamindari system in Bengal.

41   Raychaudhuri (1969), p. 163.

42   See Radhakumud Mukherjee (1933), Chapter VII, for a detailed discus-
      sion.

43   T. Raychaudhuri (1969), p. 167.

44   See Radhakumud Mukherjee (1933), Chapter VII, and T. Raychaudhuri (1969).

45   Radhakumud Mukherjee (1933), Chapter VII.

46   Mukherjee (1957), p. 34, quotes P. N. Driver, Problems of the Zamin-
      dari and Land Revenue Reconstruction in India, (1949), in support.

47   This was consistent with the overall nature of the imperialist
      economic relationship and the growing importance of exports of
      minerals and agricultural raw materials from India after 1850.
      State expenditures (all-India) on irrigation were consistently
      lower than 5% of land revenue between 1876-1901. At the same
      time, expenditures on railways were usually between 400-500%
      higher than on irrigation. See Chandra (1968), pp. 67-68.

48   The absentee character of the Bengal landlord has been noted by many
      writers. See Ramkrishna Mukherjee (1957), Radhakumud Mukherjee
      (1933), R. P. Dutt (1949) and T. Raychaudhuri (1969), among
      others. Raychaudhuri's article contains a rare account of the
      actual administrative structure and operation of some zamindari
      estates in Bakarganj.

49   There is a large literature in Indian economic history on this ques-
      tion. It has been argued that not only was there no expansion
      of industrial activity during the 18th and 19th centuries, but
      there was a net decline--"de-industrialization". For a recent
      discussion which also contains fresh empirical evidence in favor
      of this view and for references to the literature, see Bagchi (1976).

50   Mukherjee (1933), Chapter VII.

51   Ignoring for the moment the possibility of antagonism among the
      landlords, the logical possibility of little investment may be
      seen in terms of the game-theoretic model of "isolation paradox",
      which demonstrates the inoptimality of individualistic action.
      Applied in this context, the argument would be as follows:
      Assume that investment by any single landlord is advantageous
      to him and to other landlords and each faces two avenues of
      action--to invest or not to invest. Given that each would pre-
      fer the rest of the landlords to invest in land improvement
      rather than himself, the result of individualistic action would
      lead to the typical landlord not investing. The reason is that
      the landlord in choosing his action (in isolation) would find
      not investing to be a preferred strategy, given that the others
      are investing, as well as that others are not investing. The
      problem is posed as a "two-person non-zero-sum non-cooperative
      game". For a discussion, see Sen (1968), Chapter VIII, Appendix.

52   Mukherjee (1933), Chapter VII.

53   Blyn (1966), pp. 195, 203; Mukherjee (1957), p. 2.

54   Dutt (1949), pp. 176-178, cites W. Wilcocks, "Lectures on the Ancient
      System of Irrigation in Bengal and Its Application to Modern
      Problems", 1931.

55   Geddes (1937), pp. 360, 368; Blyn (1966), pp. 138-140, 157-158.

56   Blyn (1966), Table 8.3, p. 187.

57   Report of Sir J. Caird to the Secretary of State for India, 1879.
      This view was corroborated by the Royal Commission on Agricul-
      ture (1928) which maintained that the categories--"cultivable
      waste other than fallow" and "land not available for cultivation"
      (which in government statistics made up together 32% of the total
      surveyed area of Bengal), contained potentially cultivable
      areas. For figures, see Mukherjee (1957), p. 36, and Blyn
      (1966), p. 129, Table 6.1.

58   Blyn (1966), p. 134, Table 6.3; p. 187, Table 8.3.

59   Davis (1951), Chapter 4. This was, of course, much lower than the
      rates for England and other industrialized countries.

60   Blyn (1966), p. 326, Appendix Table 4D; p. 331, Appendix Table 5B.

61   Geddes (1937), p. 348, Figure 2.

62   Ibid., p. 346, Figure 1.

63   Blyn (1966), pp. 138-140; 157-158.

64   The natural quality of the soil does not appear to have been too
      different between regions of the Bengal plain. Once forests
      were cleared and land reclaimed, the average acre of cultivated
      land was capable of supporting similar numbers of population
      across areas of varying densities of settlement. See Geddes
      (1937), pp. 355-356.

65   See Dutt (1950), Volume I, Chapters 14 and 15; Mukherjee (1974),
      Chapter 5.

66   See Bagchi (1976), Tables I and II, pp. 139-140.

67   See Ibid., pp. 138-145, for a discussion.

68   Davis (1951), pp. 207-208.

69   Mukherjee (1957), p. 38.

70   Famine Enquiry Commission, The Report on Bengal, Government Publi-
      cation, Calcutta, 1945.

CHAPTER III

AGRARIAN STRUCTURE, CONDITIONS OF PRODUCTION,
PEASANT ECONOMIC ACTIVITY AND MARKET PARTICIPATION
IN INDIA, 1950-1970

III.1.   Introduction

An analysis of Indian agriculture in the modern period must confront many interesting and important issues. In this chapter and in
Chapter IV, our study focusses on the period since independence. The
analytical and empirical literature on this subject is vast, compared
with the colonial period. A much larger quantity of information (though
not always complete or fully reliable) is available for this period from
government statistical publications and private surveys. We have, therefore, found it possible to expand our domain of analysis to Indian agriculture as a whole for this period. The division of tasks between Chapters III and IV is as follows: In Chapter III, we analyze the structure
of Indian agriculture, abstracting from the problem of change. Our objective is primarily to theoretically grasp the nature of differentiation
among agriculturists and to explain their consequences for variations in
patterns of economic activity. In Chapter IV, we concentrate our attention
on the process of agrarian transformation which has been occurring and on
explaining it in the context of the agrarian structure analyzed in Chapter III and in relation to different mechanisms of transformation. Historically, the process of change has been more rapid since the mid-1960's,
being associated with the 'green revolution'. On the other hand, our analysis

of structure in Chapter III is based to a large extent on data pertaining to the mid-1950's. Thus, there is implicit a temporal sequence between the analyses in Chapters III and IV.

We noted in Chapter I that in the economic development literature concerning agriculture, the broad tendency has been to conceptualize agrarian economies of underdeveloped countries as consisting of a homogeneous category of peasant households who cultivate on the basis of family labor. In practice, this has led to the analysis of peasant economic activity by means of abstract theoretical models of 'typical' or representative peasant households. However, by contrast, empirical studies and anthropological or sociological research in many countries, including India, have revealed marked differences within agrarian society and economy in terms of landholding, consumption and income levels, wealth and status. Quite apart from questions of methodology, this would lead one to doubt the appropriateness of the above characterization. Examining the empirical evidence in India, we find that the Indian peasantry is best understood not as a homogeneous category of peasant households, but indeed as quite the opposite. There exist marked differences between them which make them fundamentally distinct in terms of the basic logic of their economic activity. These differences are not only qualitative, but are reflected also in quantitative variations in productive activity.

What would constitute an adequate theoretical abstraction in analyzing India's agrarian structure during this period? We attempt to answer this question in this chapter in the context of this study. We have two main objectives. First, to provide a theoretical basis for analyzing differentiation among the peasantry. This is achieved through the concept of reproduction. The differentiation itself is, of course,

the result of prior historical evolution of the agrarian system. Moreover, it is not static, but constantly changing. Nonetheless, it is
possible to grasp the essential features of this differentiation during a
relatively short, stable period. This analysis is useful in laying the
theoretical groundwork for the analysis of differential development of
the peasantry, which is undertaken in Chapter IV. It is useful also in
its own right in contributing towards a systematic understanding of the
agrarian social formation in India.

As is well known among researchers in this field, the superficial
appearance of Indian agriculture, in terms of regional variety, organizational structures of production, concrete relations of production, terms
and conditions of distribution, social and economic hierarchy among the
population, is exceedingly complex. This poses an analytical challenge
in arriving at meaningful categories through which the essential features
of differentiation may be perceived. Quantitative information on the distribution of landholdings and consumption levels, while reflecting patterns
of inequality, in and of itself is of limited value in this regard. Differentiation in terms of functional categories such as landlords, tenants,
owner-cultivators, and agricultural laborers, is also not very meaningful.
Quite apart from problems raised by regional variations, these categories
do not quite correspond systematically with the economic and social position of agriculturalists. For example, the term 'tenant' represents a
rather mixed bag. On the one hand, there are petty, insecure, often landless sharecroppers and tenants-at-will; on the other hand, there are large,
landed tenants who are substantial farmers with intermediate types of
'tenants' in between. A further difficulty arises because a large number
of agriculturalists would not fit any of these 'pure categories', but in

fact combine two or more functions. Our method of differentiation in terms of the <u>conditions of reproduction</u> provides a simple yet direct way of conceptualizing essential differences from the viewpoint of economic analysis, which is also helpful in understanding agrarian change.

The main idea explored here is that the basis of differentiation among the peasantry is in the degree of ownership and control over land, which is the principal means of production in agriculture. The criterion used is that of '<u>viability</u>' of the production unit, i.e., whether the degree of control over the means of production is more than sufficient, just sufficient, or less than sufficient to sustain the subsistence requirements of the cultivating household. The conditions of reproduction confronting these groups are different. The resource position of the peasant household influences (1) the objectives or purpose of agricultural production, (2) the nature of the labor process and the relations of production underlying production, and therefore, (3) the character and extent of market involvement.

The <u>second</u> objective of this chapter is to analyze and interpret some aspects of peasant economic activity in the light of our treatment of differentiation. We focus on the nature and extent of market participation by different categories of agriculturists, particularly in relation to the marketing of agricultural output. A topic which has received some attention in the empirical literature in India is the so-called 'perverse' response of marketed surplus of foodgrain to price changes, i.e., estimated empirical elasticities have been negative or low. We re-examine the issue and present an explanation based on our analysis of agrarian structure. A simple analytical model is presented in this connection, which differs from previous explanations in not being based on subjective equilibrium, but instead on the conditions of reproduction and relations of production of the non-viable peasantry.

The structure of this chapter is as follows: In Section III.1 we examine the evidence regarding the distribution of land ownership, operational holdings and consumption levels. Section III.2 presents a summary of the evidence on variations across size classes of operational holdings with reference to quantitative indicators of production activity, viz., productivity and resource utilization. These two sections establish the empirical grounds for the idea that the Indian agrarian structure is non-homogeneous, i.e., differentiated. In Section III.4 we examine the nature of agrarian social hierarchy and also land relations, i.e., tenancy. In Section III. 5 we develop our basic theoretical argument regarding conditions of production as a criterion of differentiation. The concept of viability is defined and explained. The agrarian structure is perceived in terms of the _polarity_ of viability and non-viability and within this, a spectrum in terms of the degree of viability. This characterization is supported on the basis of the available evidence on the patterns of market participation by size class of holdings. The implications of the analysis in III.5 for the understanding of the nature of agrarian relations of production and exchange are discussed in Section III.6. In Section III.7 we analyze the short-run price responsiveness of agricultural marketed output. The evidence is examined and interpreted in the light of our theoretical analysis of differentiation. A simple theoretical model, demonstrating the possibility of negative price response to a price rise in the case of a non-viable peasant under special assumptions, is also presented. Section III.8 concludes the chapter with a summary.

III.2.   Land Ownership, Operational Holdings and Consumption Levels

Let us consider first the differences in terms of the ownership
of means of agricultural production which form the objective basis of
agrarian social and economic hierarchy.   Table III.1 shows the pattern of
land ownership in Indian agriculture.   We notice that it is highly unequal
between land-owning households.   The bottom 30% own only 0.54% of the
total area, the bottom 80% own 31.55% of area, while the top 3% own about
28% of the total area.   What is more important from the point of view of
economic existence, the average size of holdings for a very large portion
of land-owning households is very small.   About 30% of these households
have ownership holdings of only 0.09 acres, and 72% of households own
average holdings of under 5 acres.   This excludes households owning no
land or holdings of less than 0.005 acres.

Table III.1: Distribution of Land-Owning Households
and Area Owned (1960-61)

Size Class of Ownership (Acres)	% of Total Households	Area Owned as % of Total	Average Size of Holdings (Acres)
up to 0.49*	29.70	0.54	0.09
0.50 - 0.99	7.15	1.05	0.73
1.00 - 2.49	17.94	6.00	1.66
2.50 - 4.99	17.16	12.39	3.58
5.00 - 7.49	9.39	11.57	6.12
7.50 - 9.99	5.17	8.97	8.61
10.00 -12.49	3.61	8.04	11.06
12.50 -14.99	2.15	5.93	13.71
15.00 -19.99	2.80	9.66	17.13
20.00 -24.99	1.71	7.60	22.08
25.00 -29.99	0.97	5.33	27.22
30.00 -49.99	1.57	11.79	37.27
50.00 -and above	0.66	11.13	80.96
Total	100.00	100.00	4.98

*excludes households owning no land or less than 0.005 acres.
Source: B.S. Minhas, "Rural Poverty, Land Distribution and Development Strategy: Facts and Policy", Economic Development Institute, IBRD, Sept. 1970, mimeo, Table 5.

Because of the practice of leasing of land, widespread among
all classes of cultivators, actual cultivation by households does not
coincide with ownership holdings. The unit of cultivation, known in
official statistics as operational holding, is more relevant in the analysis of agricultural production. The pattern of distribution of population
and cultivated area by size class of operational holding is given in
Table III.2. Here, too, we notice the same pattern of inequality--large
numbers of households operate small proportions of the total area and
the size of the operational holdings is very small. A small fraction of
households operate a large proportion of total area and their holdings are
larger in size. Nearly 74% of the households have operational holdings
below 5 acres, accounting for 19% of the total operated area. At the
upper end of the spectrum, 3.2% of households operate farms larger than 25
acres, accounting for slightly over 30% of the area. In the intermediate
range, about 19% of households operate 34% of area in 5-15 acre farms,
while 4% of households operate holdings between 15-25 acres in size,
amounting to 16.6% of area.

While these figures are highly aggregative and the productivity
of an acre of land shows variations across different regions in India,
they nevertheless serve to portray a reasonably accurate picture of the
extent of inequality in land distribution and of cultivated acreage, which
holds true for all parts of Indian agriculture in spite of regional variations. The patterns of inequality in terms of the possession of the means
of production carries over to other (non-human) means of production as well,
namely, draught cattle, which are the principal source of power during
ploughing, harvesting, irrigation and transport. They are also the source

of animal fertilizer and an accumulable asset. A majority of small cultivators own one bullock or **none**, while a pair is the relevant unit.[1]

Table III.2: Households, Population and Operated
Area by Size Class (1960-61)

Size of Opera- tional Hold- ings (Acres)	Number of Households (000)	Average Size of Household	% of Popu- lation	Operated Area (000 Acres)	% of Area
up to 2.5	40,205	4.19	48.23	21,811	6.71
2.5 - 5.0	11,153	5.46	17.43	39,546	12.17
5.0 - 10.0	9,369	6.19	16.59	64,819	19.95
10.0 - 15.0	3,748	6.80	7.29	45,012	13.85
15.0 - 20.0	1,752	6.90	3.46	30,601	9.42
20.0 - 25.0	1,042	7.01	2.09	23,403	7.20
25.0 - 30.0	653	7.34	1.37	17,974	5.53
30.0 - 50.0	1,089	7.54	2.35	42,201	12.99
50.0 and above	494	8.35	1.18	39,602	12.19
Total	69,505	5.03	100.00	324,969	100.00

Source: Utsa Patnaik, "Contribution to the Output and Marketable Surplus of Agricultural Products by Cultivating
Groups in India, 1960-61", Economic and Political
Weekly, Vol. X, No. 52, December 1975, Table 1,
p. A-91

Given the nature of distribution of land and other physical
(non-human) means of production, it is not surprising that the distribution of income and levels of consumption and living are also unequal.
Tables III.3 and III.4 give figures for the distribution of income and
consumption in rural India, which is largely agricultural, so that these
are reasonably accurate for the cultivating population as well.

Table III.3 : Distribution of Income and Consumption in Rural India

A: Disposable Personal Income by Group of Households, NCAER Data (1964-65)			B: Percentage Share in Total Consumption by Decile Groups, NSS Data (1968-69)	
Decile Groups of Households from Bottom (%)	Share in Total Income (%)	Average Annual Income per Household (Rs)	Decile Group of Population from Bottom (%)	Share in Total Consumption (%)
0 - 10	3.01	412	0 - 10	3.29
10 - 20	4.38	599	10 - 20	4.79
20 - 30	5.39	734	20 - 30	5.87
30 - 40	6.40	872	30 - 40	6.90
40 - 50	7.42	1014	40 - 50	7.98
50 - 60	8.34	1136	50 - 60	9.19
60 - 70	9.56	1302	60 - 70	10.63
70 - 80	10.85	1479	70 - 80	12.50
80 - 90	13.75	1871	80 - 90	15.37
90 -100	30.90	4213	90 -100	23.48
Total	100.00	1364	Bottom 20%	8.08
			Top 20%	38.85

Source: P.K. Bardhan, "The Pattern of Income Distribution in India - A Review", 1972, mimeo, Tables 2 and 5

Table III.4: Distribution of Households, Persons and
Consumption by Expenditure Class,
1960-61

Monthly per capita Expenditure Class (Rs)	Percentage Share of		
	Households	Persons	Total Consumption
0 - 8	5.46	6.38	1.94
8 - 11	10.23	11.95	5.34
11 - 13	9.19	9.88	5.58
13 - 15	9.85	9.82	6.44
15 - 18	13.97	13.79	10.58
18 - 21	12.13	11.44	10.39
21 - 24	9.44	9.03	9.47
24 - 28	8.27	7.72	9.25
28 - 34	8.14	7.66	11.00
34 - 43	6.19	5.93	10.47
43 - 55	3.66	3.12	6.95
55 and above	3.47	3.28	12.59
Total	100.00	100.00	100.00

Source: A. Vaidyanathan, "Some Aspects of Inequalities in
Living Standards in Rural India", 1972, mimeo,
Table 2

Disparities in income and living standards among rural households has
been the subject of a large literature and does not require further elaboration here. We merely note that these inequalities are rather striking.
The poorest 10% account for only 3.29% of total consumption, and the rich-
est 10% for 25% to 30% of the total. The per capita consumption of the
top decile is nearly 8 to 9 times that of the poorest. This pattern has

tended, if anything, to have worsened over the late 1950's and 1960's. The distribution of per capita consumption expenditure is, however, less uneven than that of the ownership of land, partly as a result of more intensive cultivation of small farms, partly because of the more even distribution of milch cattle, which provides subsidiary income and consumption, and also as a result of family size, which tends to be higher among larger farmers.[2]

III.3.   Cross-sectional Variation in Productivity and Resource Utilization

With the appearance of the farm-management surveys under the auspices of the Government of India, much empirical information concerning the operating characteristics of Indian agriculture became available, especially relating to the mid-fifties. These have since provided material for empirical and theoretical discussion on Indian agriculture. Six typical agricultural regions were selected and sample surveys were conducted with the 'operational holding' as the ultimate unit of inquiry. Detailed information regarding returns and costs incurred, of production of individual and total crops, utilization of labor, bullock power and other inputs, is presented by size-class of holdings. In measuring costs and returns of farming, the procedure adopted was to use imputed prices for resources and outputs when these were not purchased or sold, to yield a unified valuation for costs and returns analogous to that of capitalist farms. This enabled the FMS to arrive at figures for 'farm business income' and 'profit' for farming operations.

It was observed on the basis of these survey reports that:[3]
(1) the 'profitability' of agriculture increases with the size of holding,

'profitability' being measured by the excess (or deficit) of the value of
output over costs, including the imputed value of labor. Further, much
of Indian agriculture under these calculations showed losses;
(2) the productivity, measured as the value of output per acre, decreases
with the size of holding.

Observation (2) above is generally interpreted to mean that small farms
were relatively more 'efficient' and became the subject of extensive discussion, particularly in the context of land reforms. Empirical investigations seeking to examine the validity of these observations in other
cases were attempted. A variety of theoretical explanations were also
offered. Despite some controversy, it appears from econometric tests
that the observation of an inverse relationship between yield per acre and
size of holdings is a generally valid hypothesis.[4] Indices for yield per
acre by size of operational holding are shown in Table III.5.

Table III.5: Variation in Yields per Acre by Size Class
of Operational Holdings

Size Class of Operational Holdings (acres)	Index of Yield per Acre (50+ acres = 100)	
	1954-55	1954-57
0 - 5	219.5	170.6
5 - 10	180.8	145.2
10 - 15	127.5	118.0
15 - 20	116.8	114.6
20 - 25	107.3	104.7
25 - 30	105.3	106.6
30 - 35	99.5	107.2
50 and above	100.0	100.0

Source: FMS data compiled by Utsa Patnaik, "Contribution to the
Output and Marketable Surplus of Agricultural Products,
1960-61", Economic and Political Weekly, December 1975,
Table A

In a recent study, K. Bharadwaj (1974) has re-examined the evidence
of the FMS reports. She has attempted to econometrically test the relationship between size of operational holdings, resource utilization, productivity

and cropping patterns. Her work provides a very useful summary of the patterns of quantitative variations over size classes of farms and some important insights. On the basis of this and other studies, it is possible to make the following additional general observations about Indian agriculture:

(3) Physical yields per acre for individual crops do not bear any particular relationship to the size of operational holdings.[5]

(4) The intensity of <u>land utilization</u> in terms of frequency of cropping generally varies inversely with the size of operational holding, though this is not true systematically or in all cases.

(5) For total crop production, the intensity of <u>labor utilization</u>, as measured by labor-days per acre, <u>declines</u> with the size of operational holdings. The selection of labor intensive crops and multiple cropping underlie the variation of labor intensity. Also, the <u>proportion</u> of <u>work</u> on <u>crop production</u> is <u>positively</u> associated with the size of holding. Table III.6 gives indices for total labor utilization per acre by size of holding in various regions.

(6) The utilization of <u>bullock power</u> per acre declines with the size of holdings, as does the ratio of hired to owned bullock power.

(7) The level of <u>irrigation</u>, which permits multiple cropping, higher yields per unit cost, and a more varied crop composition, is higher on smaller farms as compared to the larger farms.

(8) The <u>cropping pattern</u> shows some interesting variations. The very small farms tend to devote a higher proportion of area to cash crops, while the next larger farms tend to concentrate relatively on subsistence production. Still larger farms tend to produce a diverse crop mix, including vegetables, while the biggest farms have a varying pattern--in poorly irrigated regions

they favor low-valued sturdy crops, but in well-irrigated regions, they devote large proportions of area to lucrative cash crops.

Table III.6: Variations in Labor Utilization by Size
Class of Holdings (1956-57)

Size of Operational Holdings (acres)	Index of Labor Input per Acre		
	Uttar Pradesh	West Bengal	Madras
0 - 1.0	N.A.	153.2	411.0
1.0 - 2.4	195.2	141.7	
2.5 - 4.9	200.4	129.6	275.5
5.0 - 7.4	131.6	115.0	224.1
7.5 - 9.9	128.1	93.6	209.0
10.0 -14.9	103.8	116.2	179.6
15 and above	100.0	100.0	100.0
	Punjab	Bombay	Madhya Pradesh
1.0 - 4.9	315.2	382.1	234.9
5.0 - 9.9	231.6	281.5	173.8
10.0 -14.9	195.1	189.4	143.7
15.0 -29.9	157.0	151.7	124.5
30.0 -49.9	126.2	123.8	120.1
50 and above	100.0	100.0	100.0

Source: FMS data compiled by Sakuntala Mehra, "Surplus Labor in Indian Agriculture", Indian Economic Review, April 1966 (N.S.)

Thus we find that there are systematic variations within farms of different size groups in the quantitative aspects of production-- in terms of the intensity of the utilization of labor, land, irrigation and other inputs; in terms of the value of yield per acre and the composition of crops planted. These patterns appear to hold across different and distant regions of agrarian India. These findings, along with the patterns of distribution noted in Section III.2, provide strong reasons to believe that the structure of Indian agriculture is not homogeneous and that theoretical discussions which implicitly assume homogeneity of cultivating groups are, therefore, likely to be inadequate.

III.4.   Agrarian Hierarchy and Land Relations during 1950-1961[6]

Quantitative variations in agricultural production configurations are only one aspect of the differentiation among the peasantry.
The highly uneven nature of land distribution is at the foundation of
social differentiation and of unequal social relations of production in
agriculture. Indian agrarian social structure is notoriously complex and
because of diversities in historical experience, differences in village
society and culture between regions, generalizations about social structure must be treated with caution. Especially in societies in which land
is 'scarce', i.e., large sections of the agricultural population are landless or own very little land, the ownership of land forms the basis of
social cleavages. Land ownership implies not only better material standards
of living, but a dominant position in the relations of production--the
control over the livelihood of others. In general, a two-fold hierarchy
may be said to exist: First, the difference between the landed and the
landless; and second, between the land-owning households themselves. It
would seem logical that landownership might provide the basis for analyzing
differentiation.

In India, however, a clear-cut division between the landlords
and the landless as the two 'classes' of agriculturists, does not provide
an accurate characterization. There exists an ambiguous category of marginal landlords--'more or less' self-supporting peasants, owning small
parcels of land which are cultivated 'mainly' by family labor. Ownership
of land also is not a complete criterion because of tenancy. However,
tenancy itself is highly variable since there is a whole spectrum of
tenants--from very large tenants who are almost equivalent to landowners

in status, to small tenants who are almost equivalent to landless laborers.
Further, all groups of farmers utilize hired labor in varying degrees.
Within the agrarian society itself, there exist categories of the 'class'
type in terms of which individuals actually perceive themselves, e.g.,
zamindar, talukdar, jotedar, adhiyar, mahindar, etc., many of which are
presumed to connote economic divisions. However, these vary from one
region to another, and the terms have their origin in the language of
the colonial land revenue administration. In spite of the fact that the
peasantry tend to identify themselves by such terms, these are not very
satisfactory as categories of differentiation. This is because of the
fact that here too, there are great variations in objective conditions
of the same category between regions, and even between districts within
the same region. For example, the 'jotedar' in Bengal carries a greatly
varied significance in different regions in Bengal. The 'jotedar' is a
lowly sharecropper in Burdwan district, but is a 'substantial' farmer in
North Bengal, and in pockets such as 24 Parganas. Interestingly, these
differences are traceable historically to the differential impact of the
land settlements of 1793. The jotedars are 'big' farmers in areas where
the zamindars (landlords) were nonexistent and revenue settlements were
made with them. Yet 'jotedars' do have a distinct social identity, but
it is one which cannot be derived in mechanical fashion from either size
of holding or role in production, nor from 'cultural' factors such as
caste or lifestyle.

Tenancy

An alternative aspect of hierarchy is in terms of the work pro-
cess--the division of labor. But here too, it is not possible to draw a

distinction at the concrete level between 'working' and 'non-working',
or between 'working' and 'exploiting' peasants. The reason is that most
agriculturists participate in some form or other in direct agricultural
production, and that all farmers, big and small, owners or tenants, employ hired wage workers. We shall discuss the work process in more
analytical detail later, but at present we note that there are difficulties in using it as a descriptive criterion for differentiation without
reference to its role in the conditions of reproduction for the system
as a whole. At the root of relations of exploitation and economic domination over the labor process is land--ownership and degree of control
over land. This translates itself into unequal land relations--tenancy
contracts and land tenure. As mentioned earlier, the nature of tenancy
contracts and conditions of land tenure in India is remarkably hetero-
geneous. Tenancy, therefore, by itself is not a useful criterion for
differentiation. Broadly speaking, there are three types of tenurial
contracts--fixed rent paid in cash, fixed rent paid in kind, and sharecropping. Within each category there are broad variations with respect
to the actual quantitative terms of distribution and in the sharing of
inputs. There are variations across regions as well. According to the
FMS reports, in which information on tenurial relations is very scanty,
it appears as if the ratio of owned to cultivated area does not vary in
any systematic fashion with the size of operational holding. The ratio
appears to be clustered around 0.80, and varies within a range of 0.66
and 0.90.[7] Land reform legislation, which attempted to impose ceilings
on landholding and to improve the security and share of small tenants, has
led to widespread increase of concealment of the actual conditions of land
tenure and terms of land lease and because of this, comprehensive and

reliable information on land contracts is not available either from government or private publications. Bearing these reservations in mind, we note (on the basis of FMS) the following quantitative impressions. For Punjab, about 30% of the land is under non-owner cultivation. In West Bengal, 40% of farms rely on land under sharecropping with 50:50 shares and no rights on the land for the tenant. In Bombay too, the prevalent share is 50:50. In Uttar Pradesh, 74% of area is under Bhumidari, which provides only occupancy rights where the tenant is liable to eviction; and 24% of area is under Sirdari, which allows the cultivator freedom from eviction and right of transfer. In all these reports, there is an element of over-estimation of 'owner-cultivated' farms. There are great variations in the types of tenancy and in terms and conditions of contracts. There are cash rent, fixed produce rent, share produce rent as the major types. The rates of rent vary considerably between different categories of tenants, and also between regions. In addition, there are variations between crops.[8]

It is clear that the simple fact of tenancy is no criterion by itself of a meaningful differentiation of the peasantry. As far as the social hierarchy of agriculture is concerned, we may concur with Beteille's classification. In descending order, these are: landlords, owner-cultivators, tenants, sharecroppers, and agricultural laborers. The dividing line between these categories may not in practice be sharply drawn because the peasants may often be a blend of contiguous categories, combining functions.

The nature and variation of tenancy contracts is a subject of increasing attention among Indian economists in recent times. Most of these studies are localized at the village level. A few, such as Bardhan

(1976), seek to generalize at a more aggregative level. Bardhan's econometric investigations are quite interesting and he also brings together
much useful empirical information. Using data aggregated at the level of
states, he examines the relationship between the percentage of cultivated
area under tenancy and a number of variables, among which are measures of
land quality (irrigation levels, soil fertility), the labor-intensity of
the crops harvested, the extent of unemployment facing landless households,
the proportion of total leased-in area in which the tenant can be evicted
at will. He finds a positive, statistically significant relation between
the proportion of area under tenancy contracts and the variables reflecting land quality, the proportion of cropped area under labor-intensive
crops, and the level of agricultural unemployment for landless laborers.
He finds a negative, statistically significant relationship between the
proportion of area under tenancy contracts and the proportion of total
leased-in area under tenants-at-will. Particularly interesting in view
of its significance for relations of production, is the association of
tenancy with labor intensity and with the influence of the rate of unemployment.[9] Bardhan's regression equation uses cross-section, state-level
data from the early 1950's, some of which are presented in Table III.7.

We notice that the percentage of cultivated area under tenancy
varies from 6.22 (in Saurashtra and Kutch) to 43.54 (in Assam). The percentage of leased-in area worked by insecure tenants, evictable at will,
varies in the range of 16.08 (in Madhya Pradesh) to 66.32 (in Bihar)--
the simple average figure being 40.56%. The percentage of total leased-out
area accounted for by non-cultivating landlords is highest in the state
of Kashmir (75.38%), followed by Andhra (68.97%) and the lowest in Travan-
core and Cochin (3.85%). In examining the form of tenancy, Bardhan's re-

Table III.7: Aspects of Tenancy by States, India (1950-54)

States	(1)	(2)	(3)	(4)	(5)	(6)
Uttar Pradesh	11.38	31.46	63.34	28.90	61	54.17
Bihar	12.39	17.15	66.32	55.72	63	68.47
Orissa	12.58	40.37	48.89	64.55	54	60.28
West Bengal	25.43	47.54	58.47	78.49	81	89.57
Assam	43.54	4.64	19.37	76.02	56	22.64
Andhra Pradesh	19.07	68.97	54.54	29.15	NA	43.05
Madras	27.53	21.93	40.64	38.15	60	21.54
Mysore	16.37	51.94	47.01	33.13	65	24.72
Travancore-Cochin	23.63	3.85	30.00	30.24	61	9.70
Bombay	26.81	28.82	23.01	9.18	45	48.95
Saurashtra	6.22	25.69	26.20	0.93	84	18.13
Madhya Pradesh	18.61	26.88	16.08	27.06	37	64.03
Madhya Bharat	19.54	6.81	46.32	2.34	57	37.06
Hyderabad	18.04	57.20	40.77	7.18	57	40.11
Vindhya Pradesh	21.33	9.00	41.49	28.08	68	17.91
Rajasthan	20.92	17.98	39.05	5.14	57	23.21
Punjab	40.42	49.52	48.09	9.09	59	76.89
PEPSU	37.71	32.88	28.37	3.92	66	56.25
Jammu-Kashmir	22.17	75.38	33.29	29.37	NA	67.31

Explanation: (1) % of cultivated area under tenancy
(2) % of leased-out area accounted for by non-cultivating households
(3) % of leased-in area under tenants who may be evicted at will
(4) % of area under labor-intensive crops
(5) % of total borrowing for household expenses by small cultivators
(6) Area under sharecropping as % of area under sharecropping and fixed-rate tenancy

Source: P. K. Bardhan, "Variations in the Extent and Forms of Agricultural Tenancy: An Analysis of Indian Data Across Regions and Over Time", 1976, University of California, Berkeley, mimeo

sults indicate that the proportion of sharecropping--as measured by the ratio of the area under sharecropping to area under fixed rate tenancy plus sharecropping--are positively associated with the labor-intensity of cropping pattern, with agricultural wage rates for hired laborers, with the percentage of leased-in area by insecure tenants-at-will, and with the proportion of leased-out area accounted for by non-cultivating land-lords. Repeating this exercise for data from the early 1960's, Bardhan finds once again a positive, significant association between the relative extent of sharecropping and labor-intensity of cropping, agricultural wage rates and an additional variable--the percentage of all cash loans borrowed by rural households from landlords and agriculturist money-lenders--which measures the relative importance of the debtor-creditor relationship between landlord and tenant.

The character of tenant cultivation and the nature of the tenant-landlord relations depends on the economic position and conditions of existence of the tenant. The majority of landless rural households lease in some land. In many states, while the majority of tenants are landed, these are typically or mostly small farmers. There are other states, however, where the typical tenant is a large farmer. The geographical pattern seems to be that in West, Central and Northwest India, the typical tenant is the large farmer, operating farms in excess of 15 acres, e.g., 50% or more of total leased-in area in Punjab and Gujerat. In Eastern and Southern India, the typical tenant is a small farmer. In 1953-54, 40% or more of the tenanted area was accounted for by below 5 acre sized farms in Uttar Pradesh, Bihar, Orissa, Madras and Travancore-Cochin. In 1960-61, Assam and Kerala join the list of states. Bardhan's econometric analysis reveals once more a significant, positive relationship between the area cultivated by small tenants and labor-intensity of crops, as well as the degree of agricultural unemployment. Thus, the pattern is quite striking: we find tenancy always associated with work-intensive cultivation and the pressure of unemployment. It immediately suggests that tenancy, in the case of the small tenant, is an unequal, dependent relationship, analogous to the putting-out system in the sense of relative freedom from supervision of the work-process.

This impression is supported by micro-studies--surveys conducted at the village level.[10] Tenancy is an unequal relationship where tenants are small, and is often accompanied by an element of **labor rent** as well, and reinforced through the mechanism of usury. Labor services, as well as the supply of such items as firewood, accompany the lease of land. By and large, the bigger landlords tend to lease to the small tenant, presumably since the ability to extract regular payments of rent and enforce evictions on the part of the large landlords is high. However, even in a localized area, there are variations of detail in the terms and conditions of tenancy in terms of shares of output, by-products, and of costs.

To summarize our discussion in this section, we may note that the evidence on agrarian social hierarchy and land relations tend to confirm our conclusions of the preceding sections regarding differentiation. We see moreover that there are qualitative dimensions to this differentiation which are reflected in social hierarchy and the character of tenancy relations. However, for the purposes of a meaningful theoretical categorization, it is not possible to use purely functional categories because large numbers of actual cultivators are 'mixed' types which combine functions. And within any category itself, e.g., tenancy, is included a very wide diversity of economic agents. It seems clear, however, that at the root of social and economic cleavages is the degree of control over land, especially under current historical conditions of land scarcity and property rules. This possibility is explored theoretically in the next section.

III.5. Conditions of Production and the Character of Market Participation

Given the uneven nature of access to means of production and the variation in the terms and conditions of land relations, the objective con-

ditions of production confronting the agricultural cultivators are very
different. These differences affect the nature of market participation and
of the work process in agriculture. We may consider two aspects of the
conditions of production--_internal_ and _external_. The first refers to
'viability' of the farm and, in general, the extent of availability of
land and other means of production. The second aspect ·refers to the environment of economic relations, terms of exchanging labor, credit, outputs
and inputs.

The notion of 'viability' is fundamental in appreciating the
different qualitative bases of agricultural production between farms.
In general, viability is not an absolute concept, but is meaningful only
in the context of the economic logic of the system of production as a
whole. For example, under conditions of capitalism, economic viability
is connected with the ability to generate an average rate of profit
realizable in money. But in agriculture, especially Indian agriculture
in this period, where the logic of profitability is by no means universal
and the role of money itself is partial, the idea of viability must be
situated in its proper context. And failure to meet the criteria of
viability in this case also has a different consequence. Rather than a
cessation of production--as in the case of an unprofitable capitalist firm
'going out of business'--production may still continue, but with a transformed character. This possibility adds a certain richness and analytical
challenge to the theoretical understanding of agrarian behavior.

Historically, the basic purpose of agricultural production in
India on the part of the majority of cultivators has been the direct production of the items of subsistence. This is also the case at the present
time. The vast majority of cultivating households and of operational hold-

ings, if not the major portion of cultivated area, is devoted to direct subsistence production. A critical aspect of viability--a fundamental dividing line--consists of whether or not the means of production controlled by a cultivating household is sufficient for meeting its subsistence requirements. This idea is often discussed in the Indian literature on land reform as the 'minimum feasible holding.' A certain size of operational holding, given the size of the household, may be regarded as being an adequate size from this point of view. But a minimum feasible size can only be indicative because the net productivity of an operational holding from the viewpoint of cultivating households depends on soil quality, on the proportion of area which is owned, on family size, as well as on the terms and conditions of tenancy. Ignoring such complications for the moment, let us focus on the size of operational holdings. It is generally regarded that the minimum feasible size of holding (assuming an average household size) in India is between 5 and 10 acres. The Land Revenue Commission (1940) declared 5 acres to be the minimum size of farm to provide an adequate consumption standard for the average household. Khusro (1973) discusses three separate considerations:

(1) the provision of a 'reasonable standard of living'

(2) adequate employment for a family of average size, and

(3) technically efficient in the employment of the draught power of a pair of bullocks (plough-unit).

These three are not always mutually consistent. Examining data for the mid-1950's, Khusro considers the minimum size under criterion (1), a "farm which provides farm business income of Rs 1200 per annum" to be above 10 acres in all cases, and suggests an approximate all-India average of 15 acres. By this reckoning, 89.54% of the cultivating population are

engaged in farms below the minimum feasible size, accounting for 52.68%
of cultivated area in India in 1960-61. In terms of the criterion of providing adequate utilization of family labor on the household farm--"on
which three-quarters of the total labor comes from the family itself and
permanent [hired] labor accounts for no more than 10% of the total"--
Khusro finds 7.5 acres as the size below which household labor is underemployed and 10 acres as the minimum size for which it is adequately employed, as the average sizes for India as a whole. Thus, approximately 74%
of the cultivating population operate holdings which are not large enough
to provide adequate employment for household labor on the family farm.
Khusro's estimate of the minimum (average) plough-unit is also around 7.5
acres. These figures are necessarily somewhat arbitrary, but they very
clearly indicate the strikingly high proportion of agricultural households
for which independent household production for the purpose of meeting its
subsistence requirements by family cultivation alone is not a possibility.
If the norm of subsistence production--the traditional, 'natural' aim of
household agriculture--is considered, between three-quarters and nine-
tenths of the cultivating population (excluding landless laborers) and
between a third and a half of the area cultivated, are engaged in agricultural production under conditions which are not 'viable'. This non-viability
affects the basis of economic relations and in particular, the character
of market participation of these cultivators. It affects the labor-intensity
of production and the composition of cropping.

It has been observed that the character of agrarian markets in
India is 'imperfect'. Usually the discussions tend to note deviations from
the perfectly competitive 'norm'. Indeed, certain important markets--to
the extent these can be called markets at all--are localized and contain a

personal element. Such is the case for land-lease and credit from village
sources. In such cases, prices, i.e., the rent for land and interest
rates, are conventionally fixed and not subject to a bidding process. Instead, subjective evaluations of credit worthiness or the security with
which rent and interest payments will be made are crucial in the allocation process. To be sure, the markets for credit are 'fragmented', allowing differential rates of interest to coexist--the economically weaker,
small peasantry paying higher, usurious rates and typically without access
to cheaper sources of state credit. Bharadwaj has remarked on the 'interlocked' character of agrarian markets. Since the landlord often combines
the functions of lessor of land, supplier of credit for household or production purposes, employer of hired labor on his 'self-cultivated' farm,
and merchant for the final product the household wishes to sell--the markets
for land, credit, labor and output are not independent. The small cultivator's range of feasible choice in any particular market is effectively
curtailed--prices and quantities confronting him become interlocked as a
result of the monopoly power of the landlord-cum-moneylender-cum-merchant-
cum-employer.

The significance of this lies in the consequence that the economic
existence of the weaker party--the non-viable household--becomes closely
bound up with and controlled by the economic decisions of the stronger
party in the relationship. This is analogous to the wage-worker-capitalist
relationship, as perceived by Marx, with the difference that the wage
earner has a greater degree of freedom in switching employers, while the
non-viable household retains a higher degree of control over the work
process itself. In both cases, dependence in the relations of production
arises from the lack of sufficient control over the means of production

relative to subsistence requirements. However, in the case of the wage
worker under capitalism, the separation from the means of production is
more extreme compared to the non-viable peasant household.

Partial Monetization and its Implications

In discussing the 'non-capitalist' character of the agrarian
market, it is useful to appreciate the role of money in this economic
environment. Monetization of the rural economy and of agriculture is
an on-going process, begun during the colonial period. As a process, it
is closely associated with the structural evolution of the system, with
the encroachment of capitalism into Indian agriculture. At the present
time, the process is incomplete. Not all exchange is carried out through
the medium of money; the lease of land involves predominantly shares or
kind rent. Even wages are often paid in kind, and so are the rural traders
and artisanry. Exact figures on the extent of monetization of exchange in
the village economy are not known. What is clear is that calculations exclusively in terms of money returns realized do not form the basis of
economic rationale within the system of production, except perhaps for a
narrow fringe. This is despite the fact that the overwhelming majority
of the peasantry does, and indeed must, partake in exchange within the
agrarian economy.

The partial character of monetization in the agrarian economy
finds reflection in statistical data on agricultural production in forms
which, at first sight, appear puzzling, e.g., the 'unprofitability' of
agriculture. FMS reports evaluate crop production completely at market
prices (imputing such values for inputs which are either not purchased or
not exchanged against money, and outputs not sold). We referred earlier

to Sen's observation regarding the 'net-losses' of many peasant farms,
which is plausible given the partial role of money in this framework.
Unfortunately, the practice of the FMS of lumping together monetized and
non-monetized aspects of crop production in order to arrive at unified
measures of costs and returns, makes it impossible to obtain a sharper empirical picture of this duality. Further, the use of imputed market prices
for household labor, imputed rent on owned land, and imputed charges on
owned implements, distorts the actual objective conditions of production.
We must rely on indirect evidence, bearing in mind the imperfect correspondence between exchange in general and exchange in terms of money. Noting
the negative profitability of many farms, several authors have questioned
the 'rationality' of economic behavior of Indian peasants. However, quite
apart from the fact that this basis of evaluation is itself incorrect in
the context of a semi-monetized economy, it is very probable that the
monetized part of agricultural operations yields a positive return, i.e.,
cash returns exceed cash costs in all farms.[11]

Considering an alternative (somewhat approximate) indicator, we
find that for most states, crop production is a 'rational' activity. The
FMS provides a measure--'farm business income'--which is equal to the 'value
of gross output' minus 'cost A2'. The latter, 'cost A2', equals the sum
of cash and kind expenditures incurred in (i) hiring human labor, (ii) purchasing seeds, manure and other inputs, (iii) payment of land revenue,
irrigation and other charges, (iv) depreciation charges on fixed assets,
interest on crop loans, and (v) rent on leased-in land. 'Farm business
income' is thus a measure of the returns to 'owned resources', i.e., family
labor, owned land and owned 'capital'. The FMS also provides a measure--
'retained cost'--which is the total of imputed costs of 'owned resources',

the imputation being at the 'market' wages, rent and interest rates. Thus, the ratio of 'farm business income' to 'retained cost' is a measure of the comparative opportunity cost of the utilization of 'owned resources' in agricultural production, as opposed to direct sale of 'owned resources', i.e., selling household labor power for wages, renting out owned land, or earning interest incomes. Computing these ratios for each size class of farms for the various states, we find that in most cases, it has a value higher than unity. This is an indication of the 'rationality' of agricultural production, quite apart from long-term considerations of security and independence of 'self-cultivation'. Over size classes, the value of the ratio tended in general to rise. Table III.8 shows figures for the ratio by size class in various states in the mid-1950's. In the few cases where 'irrationality' occurs, this is mostly in the smallest size classes of operational holdings, as in Bombay, Madras, Punjab and Uttar Pradesh. The sole exception to the general pattern is Andhra Pradesh where the variation of the ratio (farm business income/retained cost) has a U-shape, being close to unity at the extreme size classes of holdings.[12]

The partial role played by the monetized market in the agrarian economy raises certain interesting issues about the appropriate theoretical characterization of peasant economic behavior. The popular practice among economists is to formulate the problem in terms of rational allocative behavior. Recognizing that the calculus in terms of money is inadequate within the framework, the tendency in general has been to follow the tradition set by Chayanov[13] and consider peasant behavior in terms of subjective equilibrium between the disutility--'toil and trouble' of work and the utility of consumption--the end-product of economic activity. Essentially, this implies ignoring market rationality altogether, which is seen as

Table III.8: Ratio of 'Farm Business Income' to 'Retained Cost' for Different States by Size Class of Holding, (1954-57)

Size of Operational Holdings (acres)	FBI/RC	Size of Operational Holdings (acres)	FBI/RC
Andhra		Madhya Pradesh	
Below 1.25	1.017	Below 5	1.410
1.26 - 2.50	0.820	5 - 10	1.227
2.51 - 5.00	0.960	10 - 15	1.600
5.01 - 7.50	0.787	15 - 20	1.460
7.51 -10.00	0.679	20 - 30	1.800
10.01 -15.00	0.862	30 - 40	1.679
15.01 -20.00	0.961	40 - 50	1.925
20.00 and above	0.999	50 and above	1.896
Bombay		West Bengal	
Below 5	0.608	0 - 1.25	1.078
5 - 10	1.003	1.25 - 2.50	1.258
10 - 15	0.813	2.50 - 3.75	1.353
15 - 20	1.448	3.75 - 5.00	1.277
20 - 25	1.035	5.00 - 7.50	1.749
25 - 30	1.476	7.50 -10.00	1.747
30 - 50	1.374	10.00 -15.00	1.861
50 and above	1.301	15 and above	1.451
Madras		Punjab	
Below 2.5	0.558	Below 5	0.684
2.5 - 5.0	1.561	5 - 10	0.873
5.0 - 7.5	1.419	10 - 15	0.857
7.5 - 10.0	1.597	15 - 20	1.124
10.0 - 15.0	1.388	20 and above	1.137
15.0 - 20.0	0.829		
20.0 - 25.0	0.917		
25 and above	1.774		

Source: FMS data; see A. M. Khusro, Economics of Land Reform and Farm Size in India, Table 33

irrelevant, and instead of price, which is an externally determined objective category, we have a subjective valuation of labor and output. This, for example, is the theoretical approach followed by Amartya Sen in his work on peasant behavior.[14] In a peasant farm, as distinct from a capitalist farm, the logic of economic behavior is derived from a cost benefit calculation in which utility is maximized. A crucial element in the calculation which determines the intensity of labor application is 'real labor cost'--the marginal tradeoff between work and consumption. Explaining variations in yield per acre as size of operational holdings changes-- the inverse relation referred to earlier--Sen postulates a dualism between peasant farms, which predominate among smaller holdings, and capitalist farms, which are more numerous among the larger holdings. The capitalist farms rely on wage labor; hence, the price of labor to them is the wage rate. For the peasant farms, the wage rate is not relevant, but the 'real cost of labor'is the relevant 'price'. It is suggested that this will, in general, be lower than the market wage rate because the peasant would prefer work on the family farm to the alienating experience of working for another. This assumption, in turn, explains a higher intensity of work effort on the smaller peasant farms and therefore explains the higher yields per acre, compared to the larger farms.

However, there are several problems with such a theoretical approach. Most important in this connection is the problem which arises from seeking to generalize the notion of rationality beyond the logic of market evaluations. It goes to the other extreme and effectively ignores actual exchange relations in the agrarian economy. As we have seen, production and exchange relations are a crucial aspect of economic behavior even, and especially, for the smaller farms, because they are necessary to subsistence. The implicit dualism between an independent and a dependent production process simply on the basis of whether or not wage labor is utilized is not altogether appropriate as an abstraction in view of what we have seen regarding the 'viability' of the bulk of the smaller farms. Also, of course, actual production often combines wage

labor with family labor. Thus, it may not provide the correct explanation
for observed patterns of labor intensity. An alternative might be the
variation of the degree of exploitation--the demanding terms of tenancy
associated with the lease of land in small parcels, the threat of eviction under conditions of competitive pressure from the existing landless
peasantry. The 'real labor cost' logic does not permit us to analyze
the nature of the agrarian market and agrarian exchange in general, even
though it is correct in rejecting the notion of market rationality in the
peasant economy. A theoretical issue of some importance is involved here.
Utility analysis of the peasant household attempts to preserve the
'rational allocation' method in a more general context. It attempts also
to provide a universal economic logic--maximization of household utility
or welfare--for the entire gamut of cultivating households, regardless of
economic differences (qualitative and quantitative) between them. But
this very universality makes the method overly general by ignoring fundamental differences in the conditions of production and forms of reproduction between agriculturists. The technique of introducing variations, as
Sen does, in 'real labor cost' merely shifts the burden of the explanation. It immediately raises the problem of explaining the variations of
'real labor cost'. If we abandon the simple dualism between wage labor
based and family labor based farms, which Sen postulates, this becomes an
arbitrary procedure of assigning values of 'real labor cost' to different
size classes of farms.

Reproduction Conditions and Exchange Activity

In order to analyze the process of exchange and the working of
the market in Indian agriculture, an alternative approach seems preferable.

That is to pose the problem within the framework of a Marxian notion of reproduction. In essence, this involves examining the roles played by the market and exchange in the various forms of economic existence of the peasantry and in the social relations of production. The neoclassical tradition does not conceive of exchange in this way; and thus a few observations are in order. Modern (neoclassical) economics treats all exchange homogeneously. Given an initial endowment of goods and/or productive resources (labor and non-labor), exchange is the process by which individuals improve their levels of well-being through access to a wider array of commodities. This is the central idea of gains from trade. When accompanied by perfect competition, gains from trade are generalized into economic efficiency for the system as a whole by the market mechanism. The price system at once unifies the whole economy and distributes the 'gains from trade' in accordance with initial endowments and the laws of supply and demand. By concentrating on the mutually beneficial aspects of exchange, this approach--as Marx argued forcefully--obscures from attention the role played by exchange in the reproduction of the capitalist mode of production. 'It does not analyze how, in the context of universal exchange, the process of production remains a capitalist process, preserving its own peculiar relations of production. Exchange as a general economic activity is rooted, of course, in the division of labor and is thus of ancient origin. To the extent that it is voluntary, there is an element of mutual gain associated with it, for otherwise it would not occur. But the underlying circumstances of the trading parties, and the economic motivations or purpose behind the exchange, are determined outside the direct activity itself.[15] Exchange takes place not only under very different economic systems--ancient, feudal, capitalist, etc.--but

also under very different states of development of the <u>market</u> itself--
from simple, localized barter systems to complex, extensive national and
international markets.

In Indian agriculture, exchange is, and has been for centuries,
widely prevalent. However, its context is not that of the capitalist
market. Much exchange occurs <u>without</u> the mediation of a market, but by
mutual agreement, as in the case of land lease. On the other hand, some
aspects of exchange--the sale of crops--are characterized by a higher
degree of mediation by the market. Thus, it is useful when discussing
Indian agriculture, to bear in mind the distinction between exchange and
the market. The former is more general and commonplace in the Indian
agrarian economy. On the other hand, the market is a specific institutional mechanism of exchange, which in the period is in a state of incomplete development. The role of the market is, of course, to socially
unify the exchange process.

What is the nature of exchange in Indian agriculture and what
constitutes the variation in the basis of exchange participation of different sections of the peasantry? These are the questions which we consider next. Differences in the basis of exchange participation among the
peasantry have their foundations in their conditions of reproduction and
the work process. A broad but fundamental analytical division of agricultural producers may be made by reference to the criterion of <u>viability</u>
referred to earlier. That is, producing households may be classified into
two broad groups: (i) those whose production conditions are <u>viable</u>, and
(ii) those whose production conditions are <u>not viable</u>. Production conditions are <u>viable</u> when the access to means of production are such that the
following potentialities are met:

The size of <u>owned</u> holdings of land (or land cultivable on a permanent, non-evictable basis), plus accumulations of other non-human means of production, are at least sufficient under the given state of technology to produce the subsistence requirements of the household. Viability imparts to the work process in the household farm an independent character. The household is <u>potentially capable</u> of reproducing itself over time without engaging in exchange or other economic relations of production. It provides the activity of production with a discretionary quality. It is the precondition of the standard or conventional conception--the Chayanov type--of the peasant farm, with production directed towards self-consumption, engaging in exchange primarily to widen the range of consumption, whose labor process is determined <u>internally</u> by the household and not by externally determined circumstances. To the extent that this type of peasant faces the market, it is essentially as a seller of his own produced <u>output</u>. Our previous discussion indicates how small a proportion of the agricultural households in India during the period meet this criterion. <u>Non-viable</u> production conditions imply circumstances which are very different; in fact, quite the opposite. While the overriding goal of economic activity is the provision of the means of subsistence, this cannot be achieved by independent self-cultivation. These cultivating households must involve themselves in economic relations as an essential part of their condition of existence. Their position is vulnerable and they must participate in exchange in order to survive. The situation here is analogous to the case of a wage laborer under capitalism who must also participate-- sell his labor power--in order to subsist. But instead of a complete specialization in the labor market, the non-viable cultivating household may participate in a combination of activities--part wage laborer, part sharecropper,

part seller of his agricultural produce. But the thrust of our argument
is that in essence, these cultivators confront exchange as sellers of
labor power. In other words, whether or not these households are involved
in leasing land or in seeking credit or selling farm output, the central
feature of economic activity is the conversion of labor power through the
exchange mechanism into means of subsistence. They cannot retain control
over their work process as they are compelled, by necessity, to seek
means of production from external sources--land and various inputs. In
return, they offer their capacity for work in whichever form is feasible
and most consistent with their overall economic reproduction. Between the
non-viable cultivating households and landless laboring households, the
difference is one of degree in this analytical sense. The former group
is merely in a superior economic position, relatively speaking. In both
cases, their condition is dictated by their (historically determined)
separation from the means of production and their involvement in exchange
is directed fundamentally towards procuring the means of subsistence.

In this connection, it is necessary, however, to bear in mind
the following caveat: the division of cultivating households into viable
and non-viable reflects an intrinsic but latent distinction with regard
to exchange participation, rather than an operational dualism. Our earlier
discussion of the distribution of land holdings by size class of holding
and of the minimum feasible holding size gives us an approximate idea of
the relative numbers of viable and non-viable peasantry. A more accurate
idea may only be obtained from detailed empirical examination which takes
account of soil quality, family size, technology and other objective conditions. This is, of course, possible to do in principle, but is not
attempted here since the main objective is to develop the idea in theoret-

ical and logical terms. Further, this scheme of differentiation does not imply that there are no useful distinctions to be made within the two broad groups. Rather than two sharply distinct categories of households, what actually exists is a spectrum within each polar category. We shall return to this point later.

Quantitative Patterns of Exchange Participation

Exchange, therefore, plays a differential role in the economic reproduction of the peasantry. So far, we have focussed on the fundamental, qualitative aspects of the distinctions. Now let us consider some of the quantitative implications. The first question which suggests itself is: Do all sections of the agricultural producers engage in exchange to the same degree? In order to deal with this question, it is necessary to be able to measure the level of exchange involvement. Let us take up the input and output 'markets' separately. Given our earlier observations regarding the heterogeneity of institutional arrangements for exchange in labor, land and credit, the difficulty of devising an aggregative measure of involvement for a household can be appreciated. One simple index which, while not perfect, seems reasonable, is the degree of monetization of inputs, as measured by the proportion of inputs purchased. Some figures for the percentage of cash expenditure to total expenditure on inputs by size class of operational holdings are presented in Table III.9. These are for the States of West Bengal and Madhya Pradesh.

As mentioned earlier, the FMS provides information classified by size of operational holding. We notice a particular pattern--the degree of monetization is high for the very small holdings; it first declines as the size of farm grows larger, and then beyond a point it rises again for still larger farm sizes. It has, therefore, a U-shaped relationship, the

Table III.9: Monetization of Inputs by Size of
Operational Holdings, (1954-57)

West Bengal

Size of Operational Holding (acres)	% of Cash Expenditure to Total Input
0.01 - 1.25	26.7
1.26 - 2.50	26.8
2.51 - 3.75	22.9
3.76 - 5.00	20.6
5.01 - 7.50	21.6
7.51 -10.00	13.2
10.01 -15.00	29.0
15 and above	33.0

Madhya Pradesh

	1955-56	1956-57
0 - 5	77.1	71.1
5 -10	67.5	64.0
10 -15	65.4	60.8
15 -20	63.1	55.6
20 -30	54.3	51.5
30 -40	52.1	51.4
40 -50	68.8	57.5
50 and above	51.3	58.6

Source: K. Bharadwaj, Production Conditions in Indian Agriculture, Table 7.1

precise turning point varying, as one might expect, from one region to another (see Figure III.1). Tacitly assuming that the size of operational holding is a good indicator of the degree of access to means of production, this observed relationship may be interpreted in the light of our discussion of viability.[16] It would seem that at the critical range of viability, where the degree of control over means of production is just sufficient to generate self-produced subsistence, the level of market participation is lowest. This is where the U-shaped curve bottoms out. On either side of the critical range of viability, the extent of market participation for inputs rises. The higher the extent of non-viability in terms of the short-

fall of means of production from the viability level, the higher the level
of market involvement. Similarly, the greater the control of means of
production above the critical range of viability, the greater is the extent of market participation. This pattern is, of course, entirely consistent with our argument thus far and indeed, it provides empirical support for the theoretical analysis. The fact that market involvement tends
to contract as the productive capacity of the household increases (the
non-viable case) suggests strongly the 'non-discretionary' character of exchange participation at this end of the spectrum. As the feasibility of
independent self-cultivation grows, the households tend to withdraw.[17]
On the other side, the rising level of market participation with size of
holdings (above viability) suggests that the basic motivation of agricultural production changes from subsistence to the raising of a marketable surplus.

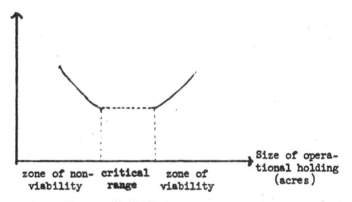

Figure III.1: Monetization of Inputs by Size of
Holding. Based on Table III.9.

The other major aspect of market involvement is with respect to
output. The common notion of the peasant household, i.e., that which does
not recognize the intrinsic differences in their economic activity, conceptualizes the sale of output in the following way. The household produces

primarily for its own subsistence and markets the surplus output to gain access to a wider variety of goods. On this basis, which immediately rules out the non-viable farms, one would expect a monotonic, positive association between the extent of market involvement (with regard to output sale) and the productive capacity of the household. But in the light of the preceding discussion, it would seem that a U-shaped pattern is plausible. That is because a high degree of monetization on the input side generates a pressure to generate cash returns in order to meet cash expenses. This is not strictly necessary (because payments-in-kind or in labor are also possible), being dependent on the level of monetization of the economic environment as a whole. However, there would be a tendency for input purchase and output sale to be positively associated. Bearing this in mind, let us consider the evidence for marketed output by size class of holdings. Dharm Narain (1961) was the first to present estimates for marketed output by size class of holdings. These pertain to all crops and their by-products (animal husbandry is excluded) and are aggregated at the All-India level. Narain's study is for the year 1950-51. Subsequent studies by Utsa Patnaik (1975) and J.W. Mellor (1976), essentially following Narain's method, provide estimates for 1960-61. The category 'output' is an aggregation of different crops and is measured in rupees. Direct data on proportion of output sold is not available. Consequently, the estimate is arrived at through a highly indirect procedure. Separate estimates are made for the value of gross output, on the one hand, and the kind-components of consumption, rent, wage bill, value of seed, and payments to artisans, on the other hand, for each size of farm. From the value of gross output, the sum of the remaining items are subtracted to yield the value of marketable output. For a number of reasons this need not correspond to the actual amounts marketed, but this can be ignored without too much damage to the general conclusions.[18] One measure of the degree of market participation is the percentage of marketable output in total production. Accordingly, the ratio of the value of marketable output to gross production for each size class of operational holdings is presented in Table III.9. For two of the three estimates--D. Narain for 1950-51 and J. W. Mellor for 1960-61--ratio of marketable to total output shows a U-shaped pattern, confirming our expectation. In the Narain estimate, the smallest size class shows a ratio of 0.336 which falls to 0.231 for the 10-15 acre size class and rises steadily thereafter to 0.551. The average for all size classes is 0.334, indicating that a third of the total agricultural crop production is marketed. Mellor's figures for 1960-61 are remarkably similar. However, U. Patnaik's estimates do not reveal the same pattern. Column 4 of Table III.10 indicates a monotonic, increasing relationship between the proportion of output marketable and the size of operational holdings, rising steadily from 0.2009 (0-2.5 acre farms) to 0.6301 at the highest size class (50 acres and over). The average proportion of output marketed for all size classes together is only slightly higher--35% compared to 33%. Patnaik's methodology and sources of data are the same as Narain's. The differences between them arise mainly with respect to the estimation of the quantitatively most important variables--output and consumption. Essentially, Patnaik argues that the Narain figures overestimate the output of the smaller farms relative to the larger farms, and that they also underestimate the value of the consumption of the small cultivators, thus tending to overestimate the marketable output of the smaller size classes. Having 'corrected' for these deficiencies, Patnaik finds a monotonic relationship.[19]

Table III.10: Marketable Output by Size of
Operational Holding

Size of operational holding (acres)	Estimate I (1)	Estimate I (2)	Estimate II (1)	Estimate II (2)	Estimate III (1)	Estimate III (2)
0 - 2.5	}33.6	26.0	20.09	5.44	}34	26
2.5 - 5.0			24.69	10.82		
5.0 - 10.0	27.4	20.5	26.65	16.98	27	20
10.0 - 15.0	23.1	7.9	30.96	11.13	23	8
15.0 - 20.0	30.1	8.0	35.55	8.44	}33	19
20.0 - 25.0	32.2	5.1	44.55	7.39		
25.0 - 30.0	39.7	5.4	49.22	6.39		
30.0 - 40.0	39.8	6.4	}54.01	16.53	}41	11
40.0 - 50.0	46.4	5.0				
50 and above	51.4	15.7	63.01	16.88	51	16
Total	33.4	100.0	35.55	100.0	35	100.0

Explanation: (1) Proportion of output marketable
(2) Percentage of total marketable output

Source: Estimate I - D. Narain, "Distribution of Marketable Surplus
of Agricultural Produce by Size Level of Hold-
ings in India, 1950-51", Occasional Paper No. 2,
Institute of Economic Growth, 1961

Estimate II- Utsa Patnaik, "Contribution to the Output and
Marketable Surplus of Agricultural Products
by Cultivating Groups in India, 1960-61",
Economic and Political Weekly, December 1975

Estimate III-J. W. Mellor, The New Economics of Growth:
A Strategy for India and the Developing World,
Cornell University Press, 1976

Granting that Patnaik's criticisms are valid and accepting her
estimates for 1960-61 to be reasonably accurate, we may, however, consider
an alternative index of market participation with respect to output. Consider the problem of market participation from the viewpoint of the utilization of land. In comparing various size classes of peasantry, we may ask

the question: Per acre of land cultivated, how much output is marketable

for each farm size? Because land is the major element of the means of

production in agriculture and the intrinsic basis of differentiation, the

extent to which it is utilized for market directed production is a useful

gauge of the level of market participation. Table III.11 provides figures

for marketable output per acre for each size class of operational holdings.

These were obtained from Patnaik's data, dividing the total marketable

output by the total operated acreage in each size group. The resultant

pattern is again U-shaped (excluding the smallest, 0-2.5 acre size class).

Marketable output per acre is lowest for farms of 10-15 acres, which is

also the size class for which the proportion of marketable to total out-

put reaches its minimum value, according to the Mellor and Narain estim-

ates.[20] A quantitative pattern thus emerges which seems to correspond well

with the notion of viability outlined earlier--a high degree of market

participation with respect to both output and input at the extremities of

the spectrum of farm size, while in the intermediate ranges, a relative

withdrawal from the market takes place. This picture is further confirmed

by an examination of cropping patterns by size class of farms. In regions

where 'cash crops', i.e., non-subsistence crops intended for sale exist--

such as jute in West Bengal, cotton in the Punjab, sugarcane in Uttar

Pradesh--it is observed that the proportion of acreage devoted to cash

crops is high for small holdings, declines for intermediate-sized holdings,

and rises again for the higher-size classes.[21]

Table III.11: Marketable Surplus per Acre
by Size of Holding, 1960-61

Size of Operational Holding (acres)	Marketable Output per Acre (10^7 Rs/acre)
0 - 2.5	6.298
2.5 - 5.0	6.909
5.0 - 10.0	6.616
10.0 - 15.0	6.248
15.0 - 20.0	6.968
20.0 - 25.0	7.976
25.0 - 30.0	8.980
30.0 - 50.0	9.896
50 and above	10.770

Source: U. Patnaik, "Contribution to the Output and
Marketable Surplus of Agricultural Products
by Cultivating Groups in India, 1960-61",
Economic and Political Weekly, December 1975

In this section we have tried to establish an analytical scheme
of differentiation appropriate to Indian agriculture. We have proposed
a fundamental though latent dualism in the conditions of their reproduction (at the micro level), which is based upon the degree of control over
means of production (land) in relation to the household's required means
of subsistence. We have argued that this latent dualism--between viable
and non-viable agricultural production--explains the character and extent
of market participation of the peasantry. The available empirical evidence on quantitative patterns of exchange participation by size of holding tends to support strongly our formulation. (See Figure III.2)

Figure III.2

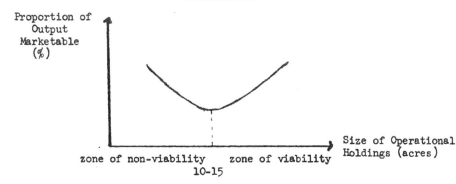

Figure III.2a: Proportion of Output Marketable by Size
of Holding, India, All-crops

Based on Table III.10, Estimates I and III

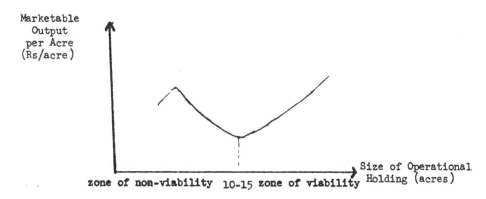

Figure III.2b: Marketable Output per Acre by Size of Holding

Based on Table III.11, All-crops, India, 1960-61.

III.6.   Economic Reproduction and Exchange in Agriculture--
         Further Theoretical Issues and Implications

We have concentrated thus far on showing that there are significant variations in the conditions of economic existence among the
Indian peasantry and that these variations find expression in quantitative aspects of their economic behavior--in resource utilization and exchange participation. We now explore some further theoretical issues
and implications which arise from our conceptualization of the agrarian
economy.

Consider first the process of exchange. We have already remarked
upon its widespread presence in the agrarian economy and the variety of its
institutional forms. Exchange is an integral element of the relations
of production and of social reproduction in agriculture. It is this aspect
which we take up now for further discussion. Exchange provides the linkage
between the modes of economic existence of the different classes of agriculturists. The latent distinctions between viable and non-viable producers
open up the possibility of economic relations of exploitation. Marx was
the first major economist to provide a thorough scientific treatment of
the concept of economic exploitation. According to Marx, the essence of
exploitation lies in production, in particular in the work process. The
form in which it is manifested in actuality is variable, depending on
specific institutional arrangements which themselves are historically
evolved. The economic relations between tenant and landlord and those
between worker and capitalist are, Marx argues, fundamentally analogous
with respect to exploitation. The qualitative essence of exploitation is
bound up with the worker's inability to control the conditions of work,
in the objective necessity to labor for another. The quantitative dimen-

sion of exploitation is connected with the distribution of the product
of labor, i.e., the alienation of the social product from the worker by
those who control the conditions of labor. Under the institutional framework of capitalism--private property, free exchange, and competition--
the relations of production (and hence exploitation) become depersonalized
and more generalized to the system as a whole, in comparison with a system
of personal bondage between serf and landlord. Exploitation takes place
through the labor market, where the level of wages reflects the conditions
of reproduction of the class of laborers as a whole. Under the specific
conditions of Indian agriculture of the mid-1950's and 1960's, is it
possible to analyze the form and content of exploitation?

Our argument here is that the distinction we have drawn between
the viable and non-viable peasantry provides an adequate basis for such
an analysis by enabling us to penetrate the welter of institutional inter-
regional varieties. The objective conditions of the non-viable peasantry,
as we have analyzed at length, do not permit the cultivators to be independent subsistence cultivators. They are therefore unable to control
their conditions of labor. In this sense, they form a group which is
potentially exploitable. The precise character of their exploitation is
determined by the economic relations in which they must engage. The
quantitative extent of their exploitability furthermore is determined by
the degree of their non-viability, i.e., by the extent to which they are
in a position to influence the terms and limits of their quantitative involvement in economic relations. As noted by Bharadwaj and Das (1975a,
1975b), the terms of tenancy, for instance, are typically more difficult
for the smaller, economically weaker classes of tenants than for tenants
of higher economic status. Rental rates gradually decline with increasing

economic position of the tenant. The principal areas of economic relations are those concerning land, labor, credit and sale of product. Their fundamental non-viability renders them vulnerable to exploitation through each of these avenues. In fact, exploitation occurs through all of these media, often simultaneously. Accordingly, 'surplus labor'[22] may be appropriated in the _form_ of money, product or labor at the same time. What is important here is the realization that exploitation is rooted not in the superficial form of the production relation, e.g., tenancy or debt, but in the underlying economic condition of non-viability. Clearly, well-to-do tenants who pay rents or who may borrow are not in an exploitable condition.

The predominant form of exploitation--of the realization of surplus labor--is determined in great measure by the conditions of reproduction (and hence economic existence) of the _exploiting_ or dominant classes. These conditions, of course, are themselves the result of an historical process. The viable peasantry, because of their resource position, are potential exploiters of the non-viable peasant with whom they engage in economic intercourse. But the intensity of exploitation, as well as the _form_ of its realization, are determined by a number of objective circumstances--relative 'bargaining power',[23] the extent of development of the market and the precise identification of the viable cultivator in it, the extent of monetization of the agrarian economy, and the degree of direct involvement of the exploiting groups in agricultural production itself.[24]

The multiplicity of forms which exist in India reflects the variety of historical experience of different agrarian regions, going back to colonial times, in addition to ecological and demographic diversities.

In spite of the fact that exploitation, in its qualitative essence, is unaltered by the form of its realization, it does make a difference from the viewpoint of historical movement. In particular, a drift towards wage labor as the predominant form is an indication of the transition of the agrarian system towards capitalism. We shall deal with this problem in detail in Chapter IV, concentrating for the present on some theoretical issues surrounding the product form of appropriation.

The simplest of these is, of course, rent in kind, whether fixed or a share of output, in exchange for leased land. But with the growth of monetization, even sharecropping may assume subtler features. When the landlord (lessor) participates increasingly in exchange with the non-agricultural sector--being involved, say, in purchasing urban consumer goods--there is a tendency towards realizing his income in money. This leads, as in Bengal, to a specification of the crops--usually more lucrative (non-food) 'cash crops' like jute--which the sharecropper must plant and which the landlord may then market for higher money returns than would be available with food crops. In this way, the small peasant whose 'natural' aim is subsistence production, is brought into closer dependence on the market. An alternative mechanism (abstracting from cash crop production) in which money plays a direct role, is analyzed in an interesting manner by Bhaduri (1974). Here, the poor peasant household, assumed to be growing foodgrains, is seen as operating under dual constraints--one of money and the other of food. Cash requirements in order to meet various impositions compel the peasant to market too high a proportion of output immediately upon harvest. Consequently, his stock of grain for subsistence consumption runs out before the next harvest, and this then compels him once more to borrow cash at high interest with which to purchase grain for consumption at 'market' prices, which are higher than the seasonally low, post-harvest prices at which he has sold his own grain output. In this manner, the merchant-cum-moneylender is able to exploit the small peasant through the difference between the buying and selling price of grain. Both these examples, while treating exploitation only partially, illustrate the manner in which the encroachment of monetized exchange affects the mode of exploitation. Bhaduri's formulation in terms of cash- and kind-accounts is useful in locating the role of money as a lever of appropriation. It also suggests a way in which monetization can be instrumental in shifting marginally viable cultivators into the non-viable category: rising cash requirements, arising from land revenue demands, increasing money rents (and even monetization of exchange for necessary artisan products), may open the marginally viable peasantry to exploitation through the above mechanism. Ultimately, through cycles of debt and attachment, this may lead in turn to gradual expropriation of land from the non-viable peasantry, which constitutes a vital aspect of historical transformation.[25]

In summary, the conditions of reproduction as analyzed through viability permit us to grasp the nature of exchange relations in agriculture. In particular, we observe the possibility of exploitative economic relations originating from non-viable reproduction conditions. Despite many fine differences in the specific terms of economic relations between regions, crops, and agriculturists within a given village, in essence exploitation is bound up with dependence in regard to the production process, rather than any specific institution, such as tenancy. The actual forms of economic relations depend on the state of historical development of the agrarian system. However, it is the forms of reproduction of the viable groups which play the critical role in the determination of the forms of economic relations. We briefly explained the working of one of these exploitative relations with an example developed by Bhaduri.

III.7.   Short-run Price Responsiveness of Agricultural Marketed Output

An aspect of market participation in agriculture which is important in the process of capitalist development in the economy as a whole is the marketing of agricultural output. This establishes a crucial link between the development of industry and of agriculture. In this section, we shall analyze the short-run responsiveness of agricultural marketed output to changes in relevant prices in the Indian case, in the light of our preceding treatment of agrarian structure.

The quantitative responsiveness of marketed output in agriculture to a change in prices has been the subject of extensive discussion in the literature of agricultural economics in India and in other underdeveloped economies, notably Latin America. It is usually observed that empirical estimates of the price elasticity of marketed 'surplus' tend to be low in these economies, and the discussions typically attempt to explain these low elasticities, when they do not focus on econometric estimation procedures. In Latin America, such discussions were at the heart of controversies between the 'structuralist' and the 'monetarist' economists, particularly in regard to their analyses of the causes and cures of inflation during the 1950's and 1960's.[26] The structuralist 'explanation' simply was that agricultural price elasticities were low because of the 'feudal' and 'semi-feudal' structure of Latin America, but despite much debate, to our knowledge no serious, thorough exposition of this idea was provided. It is perhaps fair to point out that the structuralists were not really focussing on this issue, their attention being concentrated on attempting to show the ineffectiveness of restrictive monetary policy as a counter-inflationary device. Nonetheless, the absence of a theoretical explanation for inelasticity of agricultural marketed output, remained a serious lacuna in their overall approach.

In analyzing the response of marketed output to price changes, it is useful to distinguish between short-run and long-run response. This is because the two responses operate through entirely different adjustments. The long-run response involves not merely a quantitative shift, but more often (especially in modern 'underdeveloped' agrarian systems), crucial transformations in the nature of the production system. In other words, it is an integral element of historical transformation towards capitalist agriculture, a process of structural change. The short-run response, on the other hand, reflects the adjustment to price change in the context of a given system (and the consequent limited adaptability of the conditions of production).

The Empirical Evidence

Now let us consider the empirical evidence on this issue in the case of Indian agriculture. Because of its relevance to the question of food supplies to urban areas and its obvious gravity in the Indian situation, most studies have concentrated on the case of food grains, which in this period account for slightly over half (54% in 1960-61) of 'total value of output of all crops and their by-products'.[27] The estimates generally indicate very low short-run price elasticities of marketed output of foodgrains; in fact, there appears strong evidence of 'perverse' behavior; namely, a <u>negative</u> value for price elasticity. T. N. Krishnan (1965), using data for 1959-60 to 1962-63 pertaining to foodgrains as a whole, estimated the elasticity of marketed surplus with respect to the price (index) of foodgrains to be -0.3030. Krishnan's 'model' does not allow for a response of foodgrain output itself. Other estimates--e.g., Raj Krishna (1962), which uses an indirect procedure and is based on a single crop (wheat)--point towards a positive value for elasticity. Using the indirect procedure of estimating the short-run elasticity from separate estimates of the price elasticity of cultivators' demand for foodgrains and the income elasticity of demand for foodgrains, K. Bardhan (1970) draws together plausible ranges of these values from various estimates and concludes that the short-run price elasticity of marketed surplus lies within the range -0.72 to 0.52.[28] Thus, it appears that the quantitative responsiveness of marketed foodgrains as a whole to the price of foodgrains in the short-run, is either very low or 'perverse', at least for all-India data.

In the same paper just referred to, K. Bardhan attempts a direct econometric estimate of short-run price response of proportion of foodgrain output marketed from 27 North Indian villages. It is a cross-sectional estimate with data from various years from 1954-55 to 1960-61. The observations for each variable are for the village level aggregates. The variable reflecting marketed output excludes non-market (in kind) disposals of wages and rent, and measures cash sales of output. The procedure is simply to estimate a linear regression equation with total foodgrains sold as percentage of foodgrains production as the dependent variable, and a number of explanatory variables: (i) level of foodgrain production per adult unit of population, (ii) average price of foodgrains, (iii) per capita production level of non-foodgrain, commercial crops, (iv) average income of cultivators from non-crop production, i.e., value of production of milk and by-products, which is the most significant source, (v) an index of concentration of cultivated land in the village, and (vi) non-market disposals of output (net wages and rent in kind). What is most relevant for our immediate concern is her estimate for price response, which turns out to be negative and significant for all variants of her regressions. With this sample of villages, Bardhan's estimate for the elasticity of marketed output, with respect to the price of foodgrains, works out to be approximately -0.6. This negative response is net of variation in the marketed proportion of output to changes in ratios of prices and output levels in foodgrains and other crops.[29] The other variable which has a statistically significant coefficient in all cases is per capita foodgrain output level, the sign of which is positive. We shall take up some other interesting features of Bardhan's empirical results subsequently. For the present, we note that it tends to reinforce the impression of a 'perverse' short-run response of marketed output of foodgrain to a change in its price.

Theoretical Explanations of Inelasticity

Theoretical discussions on price elasticity of marketed output have been of two major types. One explanation for the negative response of marketed output to price rise has been in terms of postulating 'fixed cash requirements' by small or subsistence farmers to meet rent, land revenue or requirements of non-agricultural necessaries. A higher price allows the same target to be reached with a smaller volume of marketed output; hence the negative supply response. This is the argument advanced by

Mathur and Ezekiel (1961) among others. It is strikingly similar to the idea of 'target-income' earning behavior of African migrant labor which arose in the context of the 'backward-bending' supply curve, and plays essentially the same role.[30]

The other major strand in the literature utilizes a Marshallian-type offer curve notion. It rejects the fixed cash requirement argument as overly restrictive and proposes a more general explanation, based on relative magnitude of income and substitution effects of a price change. A demand function for foodgrains by farmers is postulated which has as arguments the price of foodgrains and income, which includes price of food-grains times output level. In the short-run, output is assumed to be fixed. Total output is either consumed or sold. The elasticity of mar-keted output with respect to price can be expressed as a simple function of component elements--the price and income elasticities of consumption of foodgrains. Consequently, the sign of the elasticity coefficient depends on the relative magnitude of these components, and if the income elasticity is greater than price elasticity of consumption, then the price elasticity of marketed output will be negative.[31] The explanation, in terms of com-ponent elasticities, follows a standard practice of neoclassical micro-theories of consumer behavior. However, it merely provides an alternative statement of the problem, i.e., of negative elasticity of marketed output, in a more general terminology.[32] The theoretical problem which emerges from the component-elasticity formulation is, obviously, why income elas-ticity of consumption of foodgrains is higher than the price elasticity. To this question there has not yet emerged a clear and satisfactory answer.

Reproduction Conditions and Price Responsiveness of Marketed Output

A more fruitful approach to the general problem of the relationship between marketed output and price is to consider it in the perspective of motivation underlying market participation. For the agrarian
system as a whole, the principal avenue of money incomes is the sale of
output, of which foodgrains constitute a significant part. Therefore,
it would seem reasonable to think of the price responsiveness of marketed
output in terms of the reciprocal demand for money. Our analysis thus
far suggests that this varies across different categories of peasantry
and it is necessary to take this into account as it may underlie a differential quantitative response to price changes.

Very few empirical studies have attempted to estimate the market
response of foodgrains separately for different economic categories of
peasantry. Most estimates, as we have seen, are highly aggregative. An
exception to this general rule is K. Bardhan (1970), referred to earlier.
We have already discussed her estimates for village level data. These
utilized data aggregated at the level of each village as a whole. She also
repeated her regression by considering only a subset of 'richer' farmers
of each village. This was done by taking into account only those farmers
with operational holdings above 10 acres in size in each village. In a
third variant, further selectivity was exercised by considering in the regression only those observations where, in addition to the 10 acre limit,
other criteria were met, e.g., (i) an annual 'net income' of Rs 1000 and
above, and (ii) a specified amount of per capita (for large cultivators)
production of grain, sufficient to meet subsistence requirements. The idea
was to select out progressively richer subsamples of farmers who are viable,
in our terminology, and to consider their market response separately.

Table III.12 summarizes Bardhan's empirical results. We note that while the negative sign for the elasticity of marketed output with respect to price still remains valid, the level of statistical significance of the estimated coefficient drops sharply and the numerical (absolute) value of the coefficient is also substantially lower in the above subsistence subsamples, as compared with the village level general sample.[33] Thus, the non-viable peasantry must have a sharper negative response, as compared with the viable group, in the short run. But even the larger farmers in this sample do not appear to respond to higher product prices positively. A general conclusion about this for Indian agriculture as a whole cannot be drawn with great confidence without further empirical research, but the evidence does point to a differential response to price. It should be noted, however, that Bardhan's estimate is one of cross-section variations (across villages) at a given point in time, rather than one which actually takes account of short-term responses to price of a given sample of cultivators. It is in this sense a proxy indicator.

In the light of our discussion in earlier sections, it is not surprising that the short-run response of marketed proportion of output is non-positive. A positive response would be expected if the agricultural producers seek to realize their incomes solely in money, as is the case with capitalist producers under complete monetization of relations of production and exchange. This is not the case in Indian agriculture. The literature on the subject, including the studies already alluded to, implicitly takes this fact into account by attempting to analyze peasant behavior in terms of the theory of consumer behavior, rather than of producer behavior, and speaking of income and substitution effects. Thereby, profit as a criterion of economic rationality and profit maximization as

Table III.12: Bardhan's Estimates for Short-Run Price
Response of Marketed Output

	Regression Coefficient $(\partial x/\partial P)$	Level of Statistical Significance $(\%)$	Elasticity $\frac{(\partial x \cdot \bar{P})}{\partial P \; \bar{x}}$
1) General sample	-1.447	1- 5	-0.599
2) Farms above 10 acres	-0.926	10-25	-0.330
3) Farms above 10 acres plus Rs 1000 net annual income (subsample)	-1.273	10-25	-0.448
4) Farms above 10 acres plus Rs 1000 net annual income, plus per capita grain production of 100 lbs/ month	-0.840	not significant	--

Source: K. Bardhan, "Price and Output Response of Marketed
Surplus of Foodgrains: A Cross-Sectional Study
of Some North Indian Villages", American Journal
of Agricultural Economics, February 1970

the motivation of economic behavior are removed from the analysis. Even
under conditions of capitalist production, the maximization of profit by
individual producers occurs not because of some intrinsic property of
monetized exchange, but out of the necessity of economic reproduction under
conditions of competition. Capitalist producers must maximize profits in
order to survive as capitalists. The conditions of reproduction of agricultural producers vary. It is interesting to relate this to the differential basis of their response to price change. We may treat this in two
ways. First, in the abstract (theoretical) sense of the expected response
to price change; and second, in reference to the concrete process of price
formation itself.

Recall our earlier discussion of the pattern of market participation and monetization.[34] We noted the U-shaped pattern of the proportion of output marketed and monetization of inputs when graphed against
size class of holdings. These figures referred to 'all-crop' production.
Unfortunately, comparable figures for foodgrains alone are not available,
and we shall assume that the same pattern holds in the latter case as well.
We stated that market involvement for non-viable peasants is 'coercive'
or exploitative in nature. For the particular case of the market for
output, market participation is associated with the phenomenon of 'distress'
sale. The non-viable peasant under compulsion to earn cash to meet debt
and interest repayment obligations, sells his product immediately upon
harvest, sometimes to the extent that some output is bought back later at
higher off-peak prices for consumption. This can be seen from Table III.13,
where the production and disposal of an important crop, gram, is shown.

Table III.13: Production and Utilization of Gram
in Ludhiana, Punjab (1962-63)

Size of Operational Holding (acres)	Consumption	Percentage of Output Accounted for by:						Stock Carry-over
		Seed	Feed	Other Payment	Marketable Surplus	Marketed Surplus	Purchases	
0 - 5	36.67	5.33	42.67	8.00	7.33	41.33	34.00	-
5 - 10	18.08	6.03	40.15	11.20	24.54	28.85	4.31	
10 - 15	10.07	6.80	46.50	10.01	26.62	28.70	2.08	
15 - 20	9.85	7.00	41.64	13.41	28.10	25.62	-	2.48
20 - 25	8.67	7.23	37.37	12.30	34.43	31.42	-	3.01
25 and above	5.57	8.18	34.81	12.62	36.82	33.99	-	2.83
Average	10.08	7.23	39.56		31.08	30.26	1.27	2.07

Source: H. N. Dvivedi, "A Study of the Factors Governing the
Flow of Marketable Surplus of Important Crops in Lud-
hiana District," Punjab Agricultural University,
Ludhiana, Punjab

The pattern for _marketed_ output is U-shaped, but the smaller size classes actually purchase grain from the market so that the _net_ figures are quite different. The compulsive character of the activity is sharpest for the smallest holdings and gradually declines. The farmers with the smallest holdings--below 5 acres--market as much as 41% of the grain output but purchase 34% from the market, so that their net marketing is only 7% of output. Only farmers with holdings above 15 acres actually carry over a stock to the next period.

Some further supporting evidence for the notion of distress sale and differential marketing behavior is available:

> "Data. . .assembled by the Agro-Economic Research Centre at Santiniketan indicate several interesting aspects of marketing in West Bengal. The data collected in 1957-58 and 1958 -59 from six hinterland villages. . . show that the heaviest portion of arrivals is marketed in the first two quarters.... The proportion marketed in the two years in Bolpur was 67% and 74% of the annual arrivals. It was 71% and 74% in Burdwan. . . The investigation also suggests that (i) the poorer the crop, the higher the proportion marketed in the early part of the market year, and (ii) there is a distinctly different pattern of marketing between a small and a large cultivator. Small cultivators were observed to have marketed their surplus earlier in the season, pro-bably because of relatively low staying power. The data also indicated that in recent years, larger landowners have been further delaying the disposal of their surplus to the latter part of the year."[35]

It is clear that sales activity of non-viable peasants cannot be thought of as disposal of a 'surplus' of production over subsistence needs, which is then marketed in order to diversify the bill of consumption goods. Indeed, in the case of foodgrains, the purpose of production is not for profits at all. The sale of output is simply a means of not allowing debt to accumulate, so that the peasant household can reproduce itself as peasants rather than be converted into landless laborers. There is obviously a spectrum of households distinguished by their degree of non-viability, which accounts for the diminishing extent of 'distress sales' as size of holdings rises.

For the class of non-viable cultivators, what is the expected behavior of marketed output with respect to a rise in the price of output? To the extent that (i) the goal of production is obtaining the means of subsistence, (ii) the purpose of sale is to check mounting repayment obligations of debt and interest, and (iii) the magnitude of price increase is small compared with the size of debt and is not expected to erase debt permanently, and (iv) the household purchases foodgrains in the market, then the impact of a rise in the price of foodgrains is likely to be a decline in marketed output. A higher price of foodgrains lowers the rate of exploitation in the market for the product and permits a higher consumption level for the household. From this point of view, the inelastic cash demand argument has some validity because it expresses the role of debt in effecting market sales.

A Simple Analytical Model

The marketed response of the small peasant household which is being exploited through the product market may be demonstrated with a simple analytical model.[36] The household is assumed to produce only foodgrains. The model reflects the phenomenon of distress sales. The peasant household under compulsion to meet cash commitment to rentiers and creditors, sells at a price which is seasonally low and buys (with the aid of fresh loans) later to tide it over to the next period. In any given production period, let:

x = Foodgrain output at harvest (net of seed requirement for the next period) of household

c = foodgrain consumption by household

m = cash expenditures for interest or debt repayment (other than consumption loans), revenue or rent which must be made immediately following harvest

c_m = peasant consumption bought from the market, where $\propto (c_m/c) < 1$

h = Proportion of output of foodgrain sold <u>immediately</u> upon harvest by the household, $0 \leq h \leq 1$

p = selling price of foodgrain at harvest time

k = price at which the household purchases foodgrain from the market at a later point in the agricultural period

<u>Assumption (1)</u>: We assume that: k > p, i.e., the selling price by the peasant household immediately following harvest is at a price which is smaller than the price at which it buys foodgrain at a later point from the market.

<u>Assumption (2)</u>: The principal motivation of the household in selling output is to prevent debt commitments from mounting over time. Accumulation of debt beyond a point implies bankruptcy and expropriation from land. On the other hand, the lack of ownership and control over adequate quantities of means of production necessitates continuous borrowing in successive production periods.

<u>Assumption (3)</u>: Since we are considering a given production period, we assume that x, m are constant, denoted by $\bar{x}$ and $\bar{m}$, respectively. For simplicity, we assume also that the buying price of foodgrain is fixed, i.e., $k = \bar{k}$.

Following Bhaduri (1974) we analyze the household's behavior through two 'accounts' or'balances' which may be represented as follows:

<u>Kind account</u> (foodgrains): $c = (1-h)x + c_m$ (1)

<u>Cash account</u>: $m + k (c_m)_{t-1} = hpx$ (2)

Equation (1) simply says that total consumption equals the sum of the portions which are retained and purchased from the market, which gives the household's foodgrain balance over the period. Equation (2) similarly shows the balance of cash income and expenditure which it holds at harvest time. The R.H.S. shows the cash earning from sale of output. The L.H.S. shows payments. The term $k(c_m)_{t-1}$ in the L.H.S. refers to the volume of consumption loans in the **last** period which must be repaid after the harvest (the beginning of this period).

By assumption (3), $\quad x = \bar{x}, \; m = \bar{m}, \; k = \bar{k}$ $\qquad\qquad$ (3)

Consumption Gains from Market Withdrawal

Let us analyze the impact of a change in the selling price of output, p, on consumption and marketed output. In the model we are considering the behavior of a non-viable peasant household which obtains consumption goods from two sources--retentions from their own production and market purchases. By assumption (1), it is cheaper for the household to obtain consumption from the first source. However, because of the cash constraint represented by Equation (2), it is compelled to initially sell a part of its output and then seek consumption loans later in the production period. We assume that the household, given its assets, has a maximum borrowing capacity which is fixed. However, it is so poor that it seeks to increase consumption in each period by utilizing its borrowing capacity to the limit. We may formalize this assumption as follows:

Assumption (4): The volume of consumption loans is maintained by the peasant household at the maximum allowable limit, $\bar{b}$, in successive periods.

$$\text{i.e., } \bar{b} = k(c_m)_{t-1} = k\,(c_m)_t = kc_m \qquad (4)$$

This allows us to rewrite Equation (2) as:

$$m + kc_m = hpx \qquad (2')$$

This equality implies no net change in the debt position of the household. From (1), (2'), and (3) on substitution and collecting terms, we can express total consumption as a function of the price, p, and the marketed ratio of output, h:

$$c = (\bar{x} - \frac{\bar{m}}{k}) - \bar{x} (1 - \frac{p}{k}) h \tag{5}$$

If p is given, c is a negatively sloped linear function of h, as a consequence of $k > p$. The relationship is graphed in Figure III.3. For any
given value of p, consumption is a <u>monotonic declining</u> function of h.
Thus, in this model of exploitative exchange, the peasant stands to increase consumption by lowering the ratio of output marketed to the lowest
feasible point. The slope of the consumption equation with respect to h,

$$\frac{\partial c}{\partial h} = -\bar{x} (1 - \frac{p}{k}) < 0.$$ With a (parametric) rise in price p, the slope

increases, i.e., $$\frac{\partial}{\partial p} (\frac{\partial c}{\partial h}) = \frac{\bar{x}}{k} > 0.$$

The consumption line swings upward about its intercept with the vertical
axis, as shown in Figure III.3. For any given level of h, a rise in p
enables a higher consumption. If, in addition, a rise in p lowers h, a
further gain in consumption can be secured.

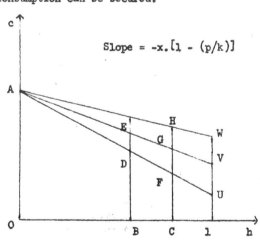

Consumption
of food-
grains

Slope = -x.[1 - (p/k)]

Proportion of
Output
Marketed

Figure III.3

Elasticity of the Marketed Proportion with Respect to Price

Now let us analyze the response of h to a change in p. Our purpose here is to examine the conditions under which this response may be negative. To do this, let us relax Assumption (4), which was effectively an assumption of a steady state. We now allow some variation to the amount of borrowing from period to period. We may now rewrite the cash constraint as follows:

$$hpx + b = m + k(c_m)_{t-1} + k \cdot c_m$$

$$\text{or, } hpx + b = z + kc_m \tag{6}$$

In the equation, b represents amount of borrowing in the <u>current</u> production period, z equals the total amount of debt (equal to $m + k(c_m)_{t-1}$) at the <u>beginning</u> of the current period, and kc_m represents the value of current market purchases.

We replace Assumption (4) by Assumption (4').

<u>Assumption (4')</u>: (a) $b \leq b'$, i.e., current borrowing is within the maximum allowable limit.

(b) Current borrowing does not necessarily equal current market purchases, i.e., $b \gtrless kc_m$

This assumption allows for a greater flexibility in the household's behavior and is more realistic.

From Equation (6), taking the differential of both sides, we have

$$d(hpx + b) = dz + d(kc_m)$$

By Assumption (3), $dx = 0$, $x = \bar{x}$, $k = \bar{k}$.

$\therefore \bar{x} \, d(hp) = \bar{k} \cdot dc_m - db$

$$\text{or, } p \cdot dh + h \cdot dp = \frac{\bar{k}}{\bar{x}} \cdot dc_m - \frac{1}{\bar{x}} \cdot db$$

Dividing both sides by dp,

$$p \cdot \frac{dh}{dp} + h = \frac{\bar{k}}{x} \cdot \frac{dc_m}{dp} - \frac{1}{x} \cdot \frac{db}{dp}$$

This may be expressed in elasticity terms after a little manipulation as:

$$E + 1 = \alpha e_1 - \beta e_2$$

i.e., $\quad E = -1 + \alpha e_1 - \beta e_2$ \hfill (7)

where $E = \dfrac{dh}{dp} \cdot \dfrac{p}{h} =$ the elasticity of the marketed ratio with respect to price p,

$e_1 = \dfrac{dc_m}{dp} \cdot \dfrac{\beta}{c_m} =$ the elasticity of purchased consumption with respect to price p,

$e_2 = \dfrac{db}{dp} \cdot \dfrac{p}{b} =$ the elasticity of current borrowing with respect to price p,

α = the ratio of the value of purchased consumption to the value of market sales,

β = the ratio of current borrowing to the value of market sales.

From Equation (7) we examine the possibility of a negative value of the price-elasticity of the marketed ratio. (Since by assumption in this short-run model total production is fixed, a negative value for E also implies a negative price elasticity of marketed output.) Clearly, the magnitude and size of E depends on α, β, e_1, e_2. We consider the following special cases:

Case 1: $e_1 = e_2 = 0$. This is the case in which the household attempts to maintain both its purchased consumption and borrowing at constant levels. In this case $E = -1$

Case 2: The household attempts to retain the level of borrowing at a constant level, i.e., $e_2 = 0$
Then $E = -1 + \alpha e_1$

In this case we would expect $e_1 < 0$, since that implies increasing current consumption. As we have seen earlier, the household withdraws from the market whenever this is feasible. Since $\alpha > 0$, in this case $E < 0$

<u>Case 3</u>: Assume that current borrowing can vary. It seems reasonable to assume that borrowing and marketed purchases would move in the same direction, i.e., e_1 and e_2 have the same sign.
Then

$$E = -1 \text{ if } \quad \frac{\alpha}{\beta} = \frac{e_2}{e_1}$$

and $\qquad E < 0$ as long as $\left| \alpha e_1 - \beta e_2 \right| < 1$

<u>Case 4</u>: Assume that the peasant household is attempting to maintain a constant consumption level. Then from Equations (1) and (3)

$$dc = -\bar{x}.dh + dc_m = 0$$

The elasticity formula (7) may be reworked, taking this into account. We now have

$$p.dh + h.dp = \bar{k}.dh - \frac{1}{\bar{x}}.db$$

$$\text{or } p\frac{dh}{dp} + h = \bar{k}.\frac{dh}{dp} - \frac{1}{\bar{x}}.\frac{db}{dp}$$

$$\text{or } \frac{dh}{dp}(p-k) + h = -\frac{1}{\bar{x}}.\frac{db}{dp}$$

After some algebraic manipulation, noting that $k > p$,

$$\frac{dh}{dp} = \frac{h}{k-p} + \left(\frac{1}{x}\right) \cdot \left(\frac{1}{k-p}\right) \cdot \frac{db}{dp} \quad .$$

Expressing this in elasticity terms, after a few steps we obtain

$$\frac{dh}{dp} \cdot \frac{p}{h} = \left(\frac{p}{k-p}\right) + \left(\frac{p}{k-p}\right)\left(\frac{b}{hp\,\bar{x}}\right).\left(\frac{db}{dp} \cdot \frac{p}{b}\right)$$

$$\text{or } E = g + g\beta e_2 = g(1 + \beta e_2) \tag{8}$$

where $\quad g = \left(\frac{p}{k-p}\right) > 1$ and E, e, β are as defined above.

In this situation we would expect $e_2 < 0$ because the only logical purpose in maintaining consumption at a constant level is to reduce the volume of borrowing.

In this case $E \gtreqless 0$ if $1 + \beta e_2 \gtreqless 0$
i.e., $\qquad E \gtreqless 0$ if $|e_2| \gtreqless \frac{1}{\beta}$

We may conclude our discussion of this model, noting the plausibility of negative price elasticity in the short run under our assumptions. The magnitude and size of E depend on the assumptions made about e_1 and e_2 and

on the values of α and β. We have examined the implications for E of a
number of simple plausible assumptions about e_1 and e_2. The model deals,
of course, only with the case of the non-viable peasant household caught
between low consumption levels and the threat of expropriation on failure
to meet debt commitments, and is based on a number of simplifying assumptions.

For the viable peasantry, the majority of which is not engaged
in profit maximization, the market response to a change in price would,
in general, be indeterminate, at least in the short run. The response
would vary according to the degree of monetization of production and the
proportion of consumption goods purchased (from the urban sector) with
money. The greater the degree of monetization, the higher the probability
of a positive response would be plausible. 'Discretionary' market involvement and the lack of competitive pressure on the other hand, where
the motive of production is subsistence rather than surplus realization,
would dull the impact of price change on marketed output.

Actual Process of Price Formation

An analysis of the relationship between price and marketed output of foodgrains at the aggregative level must take into account the concrete process of price formation itself. Two aspects are relevant:
(i) the relative quantitative significance of non-viable and viable cultivators in total marketed output and consequently, their relative significance in price formation and the total elasticity of marketed output
with respect to price change, and (ii) the question of whether both groups
of peasants face the same prices for output or whether the structure of
the foodgrain market permits a differential in prices between small and

large farmers. Let us deal with them in turn. Clearly, to the extent
that there is a difference in the magnitudes and/or sign of the elasticity
of marketed ratio of output with respect to price, then the aggregate
elasticity depends on the relative composition of marketed output between
viable and non-viable peasantry. Three different estimates of the distribution of marketed output (all-crop, all-India) by size class of operational holdings are given in Table III.1, presented earlier. The estimates
by D. Narain and J. W. Mellor are very similar. So we shall discuss only
the Narain and Patnaik estimates, which give divergent impressions of the
distribution. According to the Narain estimate, the small size groups
account for a very substantial portion of total marketed output. Farms
less than 10 acres in size contribute 46.5% of the total marketed output,
and farms below 15 acres account for 54.4%. An alternative way of looking
at it is to observe that about a third of marketed output originates from
farms above 25 acres, slightly over half from farms below 15 acres, and
approximately one-sixth coming from the intermediate 15-25 acre ('subsistence' farms) range. Patnaik's study which criticizes some aspects of
Narain's estimation procedure, provides a different quantitative impres-
sion--the contribution of smaller farms is considerably smaller. According to Patnaik, farms below 10 acres provide around 33% of the total marketed output and farms below 15 acres provide 44%. Alternatively, farms
above 30 acres provide a third of marketed output, farms in the intermediate range (10-30 acres) provide another third, and the remaining third
come from farms below 10 acres. Patnaik emphasizes the inequality of land
distribution, stating that 18% of cultivating households (accounting for
25% of population) utilize 61.2% of total operated area, produce 52% of
agricultural output and contribute 66% of total marketed output. Thus,

there remain possibilities for disagreement about the quantitative magnitude of contribution to total marketed output by viable and non-viable
peasants, especially since estimates must be arrived through indirect and
approximate procedures. However, treating 15 acres as a cut-off point,[37]
the share of non-viable farmers in total marketed output is still very
significant--between 44% and 55%. Therefore, the distress sale argument
is theoretically relevant in this context.

So far we have not directly touched upon the actual process of
price formation itself. We have tacitly supposed that all categories of
cultivators face the identical prices for identical products. Because
village markets have not been adequately studied and little data are available, most studies utilize wholesale prices. These may not, however, be
relevant for all farmers. Ignoring variations of detail with respect to
different specific crops and regions, the foodgrain market in India works
in three layers: the village markets, the primary (wholesale) markets,
and terminal (urban) markets.[38] The bulk of direct transactions between
the larger cultivators and the wholesalers takes place in the primary markets which are located in district market towns. The wholesalers, in turn,
market the foodgrains to terminal markets. Now, the prices which are
relevant for the non-viable peasantry are the village markets, and the
primary (wholesale) market prices are the ones which are relevant for the
larger cultivators who typically transport their grain to these primary
markets. There are reasons to expect that there is not a systematic relationship between village level and primary market prices.

> "It is generally believed that village-level prices
> often do not reflect the market forces of supply and
> demand and that when the produce is marketed at the
> village site, cultivators receive prices that are
> much lower than those prevailing in market places.

> Various factors are believed to be responsible for the
> phenomenon of underpricing in the village markets.
> Heavy indebtedness of the cultivator to the village
> trader-moneylender, lack of knowledge about market
> prices, a need for cash for payment taxes and debts,
> poor transport facilities linking villages with
> markets..."[39]

Village markets tend to be localized. Producers from a radius of five or
ten miles gather in these to sell small amounts. The large farmers typically
do not sell their produce in these markets. However, the proportion of
marketed output moving through village markets on to the primary wholesale
markets varies widely across different regions, but it can be as high as 90%
(Tamilnadu). Other regions with a high ratio of foodgrains marketing coming through village markets are Orissa (80%) and Uttar Pradesh (70%). It
can also be as low as 5% as in certain areas of the Punjab. The ratio
varies with the particular grain as well.[40] Detailed empirical research
is necessary to establish accurately the relationship between village
level and the primary wholesale markets. The latter are much better integrated and it appears that the wholesale trade is highly competitive.
Village markets are isolated and imperfectly linked with each other and
with wholesale markets. It would seem, however, that prices in the two
markets, especially in the short run, are not only different, but also
may not change together in a systematic fashion. This must be taken into
account when discussing differential elasticities of viable and non-viable
farmers and their relative significance. Suppose that wholesale prices
move more sharply than village market prices; then the elasticity of market response of the larger (viable) cultivators would have correspondingly
higher weight in the total elasticity relative to that of the small cultivators.

III.8.   Conclusion

In this chapter we have provided a theoretical and empirical analysis of the structure of Indian agriculture of the mid-1950's and 1960's.

1) We have established, with the aid of a variety of empirical evidence pertaining to (i) the distribution of landholdings and material conditions of living, and (ii) the patterns of variation in production conditions, productivity and resource utilization, that the Indian peasantry is not a homogeneous body of agriculturists and that there are fundamental differences between them, both in terms of objective conditions of existence, as well as in their capacity as economic agents.

2) We have analyzed the nature and implications of this differentiation from a number of perspectives. We noted the central importance of land in agrarian social hierarchy and observed that there are differences between the landed and the landless peasantry, as well as between the landed themselves. We found that there exist social categories in terms of which the peasantry define themselves, but because of historical and regional differences, these do not serve as adequate theoretical categories for a general economic analysis. Similar difficulties were noted for tenancy, whose forms and extent we analyzed; while there are economic differences between lessors and lessees, there is a large variation in the types of tenants, who range from small, insecure cultivators to large 'substantial' farmers. Consequently, the landlord-tenant distinction also does not provide a useful analytical division under current historical conditions. From the viewpoint of the analysis of economic behavior, we proposed a theoretical categorization of the peasantry, based on the concept of

viability of their conditions of production.

3) Viability was defined in terms of the degree of control over the means of agricultural production by a household in relation to its requirements of subsistence. We noted the significant quantitative extent of non-viability in Indian agriculture. We used the concept to provide a categorization of agriculturists into viable and non-viable households which takes account of the intrinsic difference in their conditions of economic reproduction. We then applied the concepts of viability, non-viability and reproduction to the analysis of peasant economic behavior. We focussed in particular on agrarian exchange and market participation. We observed first that the agrarian market was only partially monetized. A significant portion of exchange took place outside the scope of monetized exchange, but that exchange in general was a significant, widespread and vital aspect of the agrarian economy. Our analysis led to the conclusion that there is a fundamental qualitative difference in the character of exchange-and-market-participation between the viable and non-viable peasantry. This consists of the essentially non-discretionary or coercive character of exchange involvement by the non-viable peasantry, and the opposite being true of the former group. The non-viable peasantry engages in exchange in essence as sellers of labor-power to procure means of subsistence in a manner analogous to the wage worker. Our hypothesis of viability as a fundamental analytical tool of differentiation is supported by two sets of quantitative evidence--the U-shaped patterns of market participation for both output and agricultural inputs when graphed against the size of operation holding--the curves bottoming out at the holding size corresponding to viability.

4) We next examined the character of exchange <u>between</u> viable and non-viable peasantry from the viewpoint of exploitation in the Marxian sense. We find that the non-viable peasants are potentially exploitable for much the same reason as wage laborers under capitalism are -- their inability to control their conditions of production and reproduction. But the <u>form</u> of exploitation--whether through the product market, through credit and interest, through tenancy or through the exchange of labor, or indeed, through a combination of all these--depends on the historical state of development of the agrarian system as a whole. More specifically, it is determined by the form of economic existence of the viable farmers, which dominates the form of reproduction of the agrarian system.

5) Finally, we applied our theoretical formulation to an analysis of the observed 'perverse' response of marketed output of foodgrains to price change. We developed a simple analytical model for the case of the non-viable peasants as an alternative to the usual analysis in terms of income and substitution effects. We noted the reasons for expecting a <u>differential</u> response between viable and non-viable cultivators and concluded with some observations on the relative magnitudes of the contribution of these groups to total marketed output and on the actual process of (differential) price formation in the foodgrains markets in India.

6) This chapter lays the theoretical groundwork for the analysis of agrarian change in the modern period, which is the subject of Chapter IV. There we shall argue that the difference in conditions of reproduction lies at the root of differential development of the peasantry.

FOOTNOTES - CHAPTER III

1 See Bharadwaj (1974), p. 32, and Khusro (1973), Ch. 5.

2 See Vaidyanathan (1972), pp. 13-21.

3 A. K. Sen (1962), initiated a large literature on the question.

4 For assessments of the literature on this subject, see A. K. Sen (1975), Appendix C, and Bharadwaj (1974), Ch. 2.

5 There is no contradiction involved between this observation and Table III.5. In the latter, the measures of yield are in value terms, as opposed to physical yields. The inverse relation between value yield per acre and size of operational holdings is attributable therefore to selection of crops, and higher intensity of land and labor utilization through choice of labor intensive crops and multiple cropping, as the following observations indicate.

6 The discussion on agrarian social hierarchy has drawn upon Beteille (1974).

7 See Bharadwaj (1974), p. 52, Table 6.1.

8 For a brief summary of the statistical evidence on interstate variations on types of tenancy, see Laxminarayan and Tyagi (1977).

9 The positive association between the level of tenancy and rural unemployment suggests that the majority of tenants are the underemployed petty tenants or the landless, seeking land. The picture is further strengthened by the finding that tenancy is positively related to labor intensive crops, since we know that small farms are more intensively cultivated. Together, they seem to imply, though not conclusively, that tenancy is an unequal relationship.

10 See, for example, Beteille (1974), especially Ch. 5 , "Agrarian Relations in Tanjore District", and studies by Bharadwaj and Das (1975a), (1975b).

11 In other words, negative profits show up entirely due to imputation of market prices to household resources. If we were only to consider cash transactions on purchased inputs, we should find households for the most part staying within the constraints imposed by their cash incomes. The alternative would be steady accumulation of debt which seems unlikely. Detailed data on the cash transactions of agricultural households are, unfortunately, not available.

12   Because of a history of high levels of agrarian political tension in
     this state particularly, it is difficult to obtain an accurate
     picture of the actual extent of tenancy, owing to concealment
     in the face of land reform legislation. However, we notice that
     it has one of the highest preponderance of non-cultivating land-
     lords--almost 70% of tenanted area is accounted for by non-cul-
     tivating landlords; also, it has the highest figure for the
     percentage of cash loans from landlords and agricultural money-
     lenders among all the states. (See Bardhan (1976), Tables 1 and 2).
     This may account for the discrepancy if the conditions of tenancy
     are highly exploitative.

13   Chayanov (1966) analyzed the economic behavior of the peasant house-
     hold in terms of the 'labor-consumer' balance and incorporated
     the idea of diminishing marginal utility of work into the analysis.
     See especially the section on "Peasant Farm Organization",
     Chs. 1 and 6.

14   See, for example, A. K. Sen (1966), (1966a) and (1975). See Chap-
     ter II of this study where this is discussed in more detail.

15   The underlying conditions of exchange are determined (in the Marxian
     conception) by historical development in the course of which the
     means of production are distributed. The concentration of means
     of production affects conditions of economic reproduction which
     decides, in turn, the qualitative content of exchange.

16   We defined viability as an analytical concept in terms of owned means
     of production. But FMS data are available classified only by
     operational holdings which includes land leased-in. We noted
     earlier (see Footnote 7) that the ratio of owned to operational
     area shows no systematic variation and appears to be clustered
     around a constant value. Ignoring the large landlords (who
     might be net lessors and are in the upper end of the spectrum),
     if we assume that the ratio of owned to operated area is a con-
     stant ratio by size class, this implies a stronger U-shaped
     relationship. Let
     x = size of owned land, y = size of operational holding,
     p = proportion of inputs purchased.
     We have given a U-shaped relationship $p = f(y)$, $\frac{df}{dy} \gtrless 0$, for
     $(y-y^*) \gtrless 0$.
     Assume $y = (1 + r)x$ where r is a constant--the proportion of
     owned area which is leased in; $r > 0$. Then
     $p = f[(1 + r)x]$. Therefore,

     $\frac{dp}{dx} = \frac{df}{dy} \cdot \frac{dy}{dx} = \frac{df}{dy}(1 + r)$ Therefore,

     $\frac{dp}{dx} \gtrless 0$ if and only if $\frac{df}{dy} \gtrless 0$

     Hence, the U-shape remains valid and is in fact sharpened because
     $r > 0$.

17   This was first observed by Bharadwaj (1974), p. 62.

18   See Patnaik (1975), p. A-91, where she distinguishes between 'market-able' and output marketed to the market centres. She notes possible retentions by the agricultural sector as a whole because of internal exchanges within the village economy.

19   Patnaik uses a 3 year average, 1954-57, for variation in yields per acre by size class of holding, whereas Narain had access to the first year, 1954-55, only. Narain thus has higher estimates for the output of small farmers. See Table III.5.

20   Interestingly, this size class with the lowest ratio of market participation in terms of output corresponds closely with Khusro's (1973) estimates of the 'minimum feasible holding' in Indian agriculture.

21   For detailed empirical information with respect to specific crops in various regions and discussion of this type of cropping pattern, see Bharadwaj (1974), Ch. 7, especially pp. 62-84.

22   Because exploitation in this sense inevitably involves the labor process, a natural abstract or theoretical measure of the degree of exploitation is 'surplus labor' which is what Marx utilized. Under capitalist conditions, 'surplus labor' appears as surplus value and the labor theory of value bridged the gap between the two concepts in Marx's analysis. In our specific context, 'surplus labor' appropriated not only as labor directly but also through product and interest. But we are not directly concerned here with measuring exploitation. We merely locate its objective origin in non-viability. See also footnote 41.

23   This would depend on such factors as population size, open unemployment or underemployment.

24   Thus, in regions where monetization is at a low level and the viable agriculturists are non-cultivating landlords, the mode of exploitation is predominantly in the form of product or labor surrendered as rent; where monetization of the rural economy is highly developed, usury and trade in the product are more prominent as modes of exploitation; and where the viable agriculturists have taken to direct production for the market, the chief form of exploitation is likely to be through the labor market--hiring of wage workers

on the large farms. Actual configurations can be best explained by concrete empirical studies at the local level.

25   See the analysis of expropriation in the case of colonial Bengal in Chapter II.

26   See Baer (1967) and Baer and Kerstenetzky (1964) for accounts of this controversy.

27   See K. Bardhan (1970), p. 52, Footnote 6.

28   See K. Bardhan (1970), p. 52.

29   See K. Bardhan (1970), p. 55, Table 1 and p. 57.

30   See E. Berg (1961)

31   For analyses along these lines, see K. Bardhan (1970), Krishnan
     (1965), Dandekar (1964), and also the discussion by Bhagwati and
     Chakravarty (1970). Viewed in this way, a negative price elas-
     ticity is not 'perverse', but explainable as income effect
     dominating the substitution effect.

32   It is useful, however, for empirical estimation purposes.

33   Fortunately, Bardhan's variants correspond well to our general dis-
     tinction between viable and non-viable cultivators. Operational
     holdings of 10 acre size in this region appear to represent the
     critical size for viability. When farms below this size are in-
     cluded in the regression, the price elasticity of marketed output
     is negative and highly significant. When they are excluded, the
     picture changes remarkably. 10-25% level of significance implies
     that a probability of Type I error (i.e., concluding that the
     regression coefficient is different from zero when it is actually
     zero) can be as large as 25%.

34   See pp. 144-149 above.

35   Lele (1971), p. 129. See also Krishnan (1965).

36   The following model adapts and extends the one set out in Bhaduri
     (1974).

37   Using Khusro (1973), criterion 1. See pp. 132-133 above.

38   The distinction is made in Lele (1971).

39   See Lele (1971), p. 21.

40   See Lele (1971), pp. 48-52.

41   Patnaik (1976) suggests a differentiation scheme based on the ratio
     of hired-in to hired-out labor on farms ("labor-exploitation"
     index). Focussing on labor-relations to locate class categories,
     it ignores markets for credit, output, etc. Our approach is
     preferable for studying agrarian change, since viability characterizes
     the entire reproduction process. It determines the potential
     response to market and non-market mechanisms of change. See Ch. IV.

Chapter IV

AGRARIAN TRANSFORMATION IN INDIA, 1948-EARLY 1970's:
A PROCESS OF DIFFERENTIAL DEVELOPMENT OF THE PEASANTRY

IV.1.   Introduction

In this chapter we analyze the structural transformation of the
agrarian system in India in the period following independence. Since
1947, several important developments have contributed towards the transformation of India's agrarian economy. There are unmistakable signs that
the agrarian system--in terms of its form of productive organization and
relations, as well as the material conditions of production--has been responding to these influences. The central feature of this systemic
change is a process of differentiation within the agrarian society and
economy. The groundwork for this analysis was laid in the preceding
chapter where the agrarian structure of the 1950's was expressed as a
dichotomy between viable and non-viable households. The dichotomy was
based upon essential differences in conditions of economic reproduction.
In this chapter, we analyze how this differentiation evolved over time.
This transformation of the agrarian system was integrally connected with
the processes and mechanisms by which capital enters that sector. We
shall try to show how the infusion of capital propels and intensifies
the existing differentiation and imparts to it an increasingly capitalist character.

The forms and intensity of the transforming mechanisms emerged from the nature of the capitalist accumulation process taking place in the industrial sector. In other words, they were related to the specific orientation of industrial accumulation (for a domestic market rather than export) which implied a particular type of intersectoral economic linkage. The most important link in this case being the increased demand for agricultural products by industry. In the Indian case, this formed the principal structural factor underlying the penetration of capital. While these mechanisms of penetration are closely interrelated, they may be classified broadly as: (a) Political and legal mechanisms; (b) Economic mechanisms operating through monetary incentives; and (c) Promotion of technological change in agricultural production. We should note in this context the organic connection between the government's economic and social policies and the process of capitalist accumulation. Consequently, the state has played a key role in all of the above-mentioned forms of intervention in the agricultural system. This role is so central here that in this chapter, we do not treat the policies of the government as a distinct and separate influence on the agrarian system. Rather, we analyze it as an aspect of the general process of development of capital in the agrarian system.

If the penetration of capital provides the impetus for agrarian transformation, the nature of the response, i.e., content of change, depends upon the manner in which these stimuli of change are integrated into the agrarian structure and become part of the on-going process of differentiation. The heart of the matter in this whole process of capitalist differentiation is that the penetration of capital into the agrarian system affects different sections differently--it accentuates the process of polarization of the peasantry. In the following pages we analyze the differential manner in which the economic units in the agrarian system have developed in connection with various mechanisms of capitalist penetration. For example, we show how land reform legislation and the promotion of the 'Green Revolution' technology have intensified the polarization within the agricultural producers--the viable and the non-viable cultivators have evolved along different lines in response to the same general impetus. Thus, the existing agrarian structure determines the nature and direction of development. However, with the penetration of capital, the broad tendency of the evolution of the differentiation (or more precisely, the relations of production and conditions of economic existence) is towards the capitalist type. Thus, we find a tendency towards the development of wage labor on the one hand, and of profit-motivated production on the other.

This chapter is organized as follows: In Section IV.2, we present our theoretical conceptualization of agrarian transformation in India. The ideas expressed there are substantiated with the help of empirical and historical evidence in the succeeding sections. In Section IV.3, we describe the principal components of state policy towards agriculture and the main features of output trends. Section IV. 4 presents and analyzes the evidence on structural transformation (and its determinants). We examine in turn the trends towards 'capitalist' cultivation, towards the formation of an agricultural proletariat, and the patterns of change in terms and conditions of tenancy. The connection between technological change and that of economic structure is probed in the Indian context. Section IV.5 concludes the chapter with a summary.

IV.2. A Theoretical Conceptualization of Agrarian Change in India Since Independence

In Chapter I we explained our methodology and contrasted it with the leading theoretical approaches to agricultural development. In India, several attempts have been made (especially by Indian economists writing in the Marxian tradition) to achieve a theoretical understanding of the process of agrarian transformation.

The discussion has generated a literature which is generally known as the debate on the mode of production in Indian agriculture.[1] We shall not deal with it in any detail here as it has been ably surveyed and commented on in Alavi (1975) and Cleaver (1976). We note simply its central feature, which is to identify whether or not Indian agriculture had made a transition to capitalism, using as a criterion the attainment of key attributes of capitalist production--viz., wage labor, accumulation. The main weakness of this discussion is that it reduces to a mechanical labelling exercise, to the relative exclusion of theoretically confronting the concrete process of change.

To restate briefly what we elaborated more fully in Chapter I, agrarian change is viewed in this study as a process which has multiple dimensions. It consists of a set of changes in the form of reproduction of production units and correspondingly, in the means of economic existence of units of agrarian society, i.e., households. There are changes in the objective conditions of relations of production--form of exchange, terms of work--and in the motivation or aim to which production is directed, i.e., subsistence or profit. Alongside changes occur in the role and importance of specific material elements in the scheme of production and re-

production in the agrarian system, such as land, money and non-human inputs. Finally, the social and economic structure is refashioned with
changes in the distribution of means of production and wealth, political
realignments and class formations on new bases of political-economic
polarization. Essentially, these are the qualitative dimensions of change
which obviously have their counterparts and reflections in the quantitative aspects of change as, for example, in productivity, labor- and
capital-intensity, monetization, elasticity of response to price changes,
and so on.

We characterize agrarian change in India in the present historical context in the following way: The central process is one of evolving
differentiation of the peasantry in response to the penetration of capital.
The entry of capital into the agrarian system provides the dominant, underlying dynamic factor which sets in motion, activates and propels the process of transformation during this period. This formulation allows us to
view the transformation process in terms of two component aspects:
(i) the mechanisms of change, i.e., the set of stimuli which provide the
impetus for structural change, and (ii) the existing agrarian structure
with its patterns of differentiation (which we have analyzed in terms of
conditions of reproduction). The actual process of change takes place as
an interaction between these two elements.

The precise mechanisms are historically specific. They flow from
the broad process of capitalist development in the Indian economy as a
whole. In this case, as in most others, the nucleus of capitalist accumulation is in the industrial sector. From there the development of capital
spreads towards agriculture. For this reason, the former element (i.e.,
the mechanisms of penetration of capital) is determined outside of agri-

culture proper. At the same time, its precise forms and intensity are not accidental occurrences but rather, they have a systemic logic, originating in the process of capitalist expansion in the industrial sector. Further-more, the extent to which national capital is interlinked with and dependent on the international capitalist system has an important determining influ-ence on the logic of the process.[2] To be a little more specific, we may make the empirical observation here that the basic orientation of the industrial accumulation process in India following independence has been its domestically directed, import substituting emphasis,[3] in contrast to the export-based pattern observed in other less developed countries in East Asia. This pattern of accumulation, accompanied by imports of machinery and heavy equipment, led quickly to a state of chronic shortage of foreign exchange. Meanwile, growing money incomes and employment in-creased the demand for items of consumption. Most important from the view-point of smooth accumulation were wage goods, chiefly foodgrains. Soon excess demand emerged, which for the reason just mentioned above, could not be met by imports without straining foreign exchange resources. Infla-tionary pressures came to be generated through rising agricultural prices. The resolution of this problem of secular imbalance between food demand and supplies thus became in India the primary determinant of the mechanisms of penetration of capital into the agrarian system during the last two decades.

What has been the precise content of the penetration of capital? It has the following distinct forms:

(a) Political/legal, effected through the passage and implementation of land reform legislation by the state;

(b) <u>Price movements and monetization</u>--the improvement of terms of trade between agriculture and industry which increases the monetary incentive to
transfer agricultural output to urban markets.[4] This is accompanied by
the expansion of rural credit from institutional sources; both these
facilitate increasing monetization both of asset holding and of exchange
activity in the rural economy;

(c) <u>Direct public investment</u> in agricultural productive base and infrastructure. The most important feature is the expansion of irrigation
through government investments, which has been a vital factor in facilitating
yield and acreage expansion;

(d) <u>Provision of a finance-intensive, productivity-increasing new technology,</u> together with credit, which simultaneously expands the possibilities for private profitability in agricultural production.

Each of the above forms of penetration of capital has been directed
towards increasing supplies of agricultural commodities to the industrial
sector of the economy. Over time, the relative emphasis on a particular
form has varied, depending upon the intensity of the economic crisis encountered in the accumulation process. For example, in the early phase,
when food supplies in the urban areas were relatively plentiful and it
was widely believed that land reforms, plus irrigation expansion would
increase production and sales sufficiently, (a) and (c) were relatively
more important. In the course of time, (b) became more significant through
the automatic mechanisms of the market process. Finally, most recently,
as the crisis deepened, (d) grew dominant. (This last shift was catalyzed
by two years of severe drought, deepening foreign debt and the correspondingly stronger bargaining position of foreign capital, which was responsible
for the development of the new technology.[5])

The actual process of change, i.e., the 'response' of the agrarian sector, depends on the interaction between these mechanisms and the structure of the economic system into which these mechanisms are articulated. Our analysis of Chapter III introduced the most essential aspect of the pre-existent differentiation in the agrarian system from the theoretical point of view. This is the identification and empirical location of a basic differentiation between agriculturalists relative to our notion of 'viability'. Viability of the production unit as defined there is related in a direct (though not mechanical) way to the degree of control over the means of production, and on the subsistence requirements of the operating household. At any **given** point in time and geographical location, when technology and reproduction demands are known, it is in principle possible to give an operational meaning to the criterion of viability. It can be used to classify the production units in the agrarian system in two ways: First, to decide whether a **particular farm** is viable or non-viable; and second, to locate it within a spectrum on the basis of 'distance' from the margin of viability. As we showed in the previous chapter, the importance of this classification lies in the correspondence between viability of the production unit and the qualitative nature of the mode of economic reproduction of the social unit (the household) to which it is attached and its relations to other units. This determines the situation of the household in the relations of production and its vulnerability to exploitation. The viable peasant household which can control the conditions of its reproduction is thereby in a relatively independent position in its economic relations. By contrast, the non-viable peasant household (in direct relation with its degree of non-viability) is unable to control its conditions of reproduction, is dependent on economic rela-

tions in order to obtain its means of livelihood, i.e., not an independent
producer, but essentially a supplier of labor power--a quasi-proletarian.
This fundamental division between a small minority of viable farmers and
a large majority of non-viable farmers, gives us the analytical starting
point from which to study the changes in the agrarian system which occur
in response to the penetration of capital between the 1950's and 1960's.
The theoretical analysis consists of the logical reconstruction of the
connection between the processes of penetration of capital during this
phase and that of on-going differentiation.

The reasons for conceptualizing the central event of the process
of agrarian change as one of evolving differentiation are the following:
(1) There are two distinct but interrelated aspects of agrarian change
which must be understood simultaneously for a correct and complete com-
prehension of the process. These are, first, the transformation at the
micro level, namely the conditions of production and reproduction of the
units of economy and society; and second, the change at the macro level
of patterns of distribution of productive resources and income, the impact
on social and economic structure and social relations of production, i.e.,
the perception of the agrarian system in terms of classes or groups which
are identifiable on the basis of certain critical common attributes and
unified by common experience in the process of change. Our conceptualization permits us to think simultaneously of these twin dimensions in a connected manner. (2) Given the pattern of differentiation in the agrarian
system already existent as a result of prior historical evolution,[6] the
entry of capital cannot but affect the agrarian system in a differential
fashion and indeed, we notice on empirical grounds that economic polarization is increasing and new alignments in social structure and economic

relations based on this are taking place, which our approach permits us to analyze.

The capitalist mode of production has, of course, its own patterns of economic differentiation and conditions of reproduction, viz., the polarity between wage labor and capital. A question which is relevant in connection with agrarian change in response to mechanisms of penetration of capital is whether or not the differentiation in the agrarian system which existed in the 1950's is gradually being transformed and reconstituted along capitalist lines.

There are, however, two sides to this question. One is the development of capitalist relations of production at the farm level, and the other is the development of social classes, approximating that of capitalists and workers in terms of their forms of economic reproduction and economic motivations. Our formulation is in terms of a pre-existent differentiation in which a non-viable peasantry who, directly or indirectly, engage in exchanging labor for means of subsistence, and a surplus-realizing group are identified. This provides us with a way of analyzing this question in a flexible, yet analytically sound and empirically grounded manner, their subsequent (differential) development as capital enters.

Our approach to this problem contrasts with the categorization of production units into 'capitalist' and 'non-capitalist' types which has been quite common in the literature. While an identification of the pre-existent pre-capitalist attributes of the social formation are interesting and informative, from the viewpoint of analysis in the current historical context, the fundamental features of the pre-existent system may be grasped with greater generality by using the notion of 'viability'. Moreover, the entire period is one of transition of forms of reproduction.

"Pure" categories do not exist, e.g., the "capitalist" farm. Nor are these organizational forms static. To grasp the essentials of change, we have taken the direct analytical route--namely, to examine the relationship between the existing unevenness of agrarian structure and its dynamic historical response to capitalist pressure.

Phases of Change

Because of important differences in emphasis and because also of actual chronological phases in the penetration of capital, it is useful to divide our theoretical reconstruction into two parts: (1) the pre-'Green revolution" phase, and (2) the post-'Green Revolution' phase.

The Pre-'Green Revolution' Phase. As noted earlier, the principal forms of penetration of capital in phase were political and legal, and direct public investment in irrigation and rural infrastructure. The response to this from the agrarian system took the form of some key changes in social and economic structure which we shall explain and elaborate. What is significant here is to note the manner in which these forms of penetration are absorbed and integrated into existing differentiation and in turn mould it. Consider the land reform legislation. Its impact is different on viable and non-viable peasantry. For the viable peasantry, the land reforms implied a significant political restructuring. The abolition of intermediary tenures implied the relative decline of absentee landlordism and the breakup of large estates through ceiling laws. Even though these reforms are only imperfectly enforced, they signal the end of the colonial forms of rural reproduction by the creation of an adverse political climate for it. On the other hand, the reforms facilitate the ascendence and consolidation of a new class of rich and middle farmers, who are the prime beneficiaries of the land reforms. These rich and middle farmers were primarily the 'large' tenants whose control over the land was strengthened by the reforms, since they possessed the political and economic ability to benefit from them. Their position was improved further by the panchayat and cooperative movements which enhanced their political and economic power within rural society. Thus, a new form of economic reproduction came to grow in importance among the viable farmers who were directly involved in agricultural production, unlike the traditional landlord. It should, however, be noted that while landlordism by no means disappeared under the impact of the reforms, and petty tenancy often went underground, some erstwhile landlords also resumed land and undertook directly supervised cultivation, joining the ranks of the middle and rich farmers. Meanwhile, the rising prices of foodgrains in the urban sector turned the terms of trade increasingly in favor of agriculture and greatly facilitated the growing monetary accumulation[7] in the hands of farmers who raise a surplus over their subsistence and market agricultural products. These funds are put, in part, into moneylending. These viable farmers derive income simultaneously from a number of sources--part from supervised cultivation, part from interest from moneylending (loans made within the rural economy chiefly to poor farmers), part from rent on tenanted land, and part from trade.[8]

The effect of this phase of penetration of capital on the non-viable peasant households presents a sharply contrasting picture. Specifically, they are unable to obtain a more firm control over land through land reforms. Many petty tenants are evicted and thereby dispossessed of land. For the majority of the petty tenants, the level of security of tenure is not improved. In fact, quite the contrary may be observed due

to the phenomenon of 'tenant switching' by landlords anxious to evade the
impact of tenancy legislation by which tenants may gain occupancy rights
on the basis of prolonged cultivation of particular plots. One important
reason, among others, why the non-viable tenant-cultivators are not able
to gain control over land is the fact that they do not possess the accumulation of money funds with which they may legally purchase the plots from
former landlords. Control over the means of production not having improved
for the non-viable peasant households, they respond to their condition by
increasing their labor intensity of cultivation to the extent possible,
and by engaging in off-farm occupations (of which agricultural wage labor
forms an important part) to supplement earnings and meet subsistence re-
quirements--in direct relationship to the degree of their non-viability.
They are, furthermore, unable to gain access to significant amounts of
institutional credit or to benefit from the marketing cooperatives. They
are not able to realize actual gains from the trends in agricultural
prices at the wholesale level because of the structure of village level
exchange, where petty cultivators part with output to local merchant-land-
lord-moneylenders on terms that bear little relation to the prices of
agricultural commodities ruling in wholesale or urban markets.[9] Therefore,
they are unable to accumulate money funds, even though the rural economy
is gradually being monetized and their own participation in money exchange
is increasing. To summarize the discussion thus far concerning the pre-
'Green Revolution' phase:

1) The viable and non-viable agricultural households evolve in distinct
ways; differentiation is accentuated. The productive base of the bulk of
viable households is strengthened, the opposite being true for non-viable
households. The latter is an effect of the former development.

2) Within the category of viable households, an economic and political re-structuring takes place. There is a relative decline of landlordism and a rise of rich and modern farmers. Direct supervision of cultivation grows correspondingly more prevalent, but a multiplicity of sources of income exists for the viable households.

3) The very mechanism through which rich and medium supervisory farmers consolidate themselves in the course of penetration of capital, viz., consolidation of landholdings, favorable movements in terms of trade, credit and marketing cooperatives, accumulation of money holdings, are precisely the ones from which the non-viable households are excluded because of the conditions of their reproduction. This results in a further weakening of their control over means of production (land) and a growing reliance on wage or quasi-wage incomes.

The reasons for the exclusion of the non-viable peasantry arise from a combination of factors. These are: (a) The incomplete development of the market mechanism itself leads to the "interlocking" of the market for output, labor, land and credit.[10] The non-viable peasant household finds its range of feasible choice possibilities limited by the fact that its sources of borrowing, of leasing land, marketing outlets, are often controlled by the same individual because of the combination of functions by a viable cultivator. (b) Not only are its options limited in this way, but also the terms of exchange it receives are worse because of poor "bargaining" power. Their basic economic vulnerability also makes them higher credit risks, for example, which is likely to be a factor inhibiting access to institutional sources. (c) Relative lack of political organization and political power makes it impossible for these groups to gain access to the various governmental distributional agencies, which is in sharp contrast to the richer peasants.

Before turning to the 'Green Revolution' phase, we note two
other related developments which are relevant--the increase in rural
population which is taking place, and the increasing displacement of
the rural non-agricultural households from their traditional lines of
employment. The latter event is related to the fact that many of the
artisans had stable supply relationships in the past with the zamindars
and traditional landlords. The changes in the agrarian system have led to
a displacement of the zamindari style of life and demand patterns. The
consumption patterns of the rural rich, particularly the newly emergent
middle and rich farmers, are oriented more towards urban consumption goods.
Meanwhile, the shrinking economic base of the non-viable cultivators has
not allowed a substitution to the mass market sufficient to sustain the
artisans in traditional activity.

Finally, public investments in irrigation also play an important
role. Irrigation, by improving the productivity of land and thereby
raising the returns to cultivation, is positively associated with corresponding evictions of the tenants. It therefore catalyzes and quickens
the process just outlined. On the other hand, those small farmers whose
holdings are mostly owned, benefit relatively more from irrigation because
it improves productivity and the employment capacity of a piece of land
by permitting multiple cropping and affording a wider selection of crops.
However, here also, the tiny absolute size of small peasant plots and the
limited availability of complementary inputs, acts as a deterrent to the
increase in the degree of viability.

The 'Green Revolution' Phase. This phase of penetration has two
principal aspects: First, it involves technological innovation which is
capable of substantially raising physical productivity of agriculture.

Second, because of the fact that the new technology is <u>finance intensive</u>
by requiring the utilization of <u>purchased inputs</u> from outside the sphere
of household production, the adoption of 'Green Revolution' technology
simultaneously introduces the <u>direct involvement of capital in the process of production</u>. Specifically, this takes the form of the increased
activation of the M-C-M' circuit of capitalist production[11] which steadily
becomes the dominant rationale of production among the viable 'Green
Revolution' responsive farmers. In other words, the utilization of money
for the purchase of production as 'circulating capital' in the purchase
of inputs--fertilizer, pesticides, HYV varieties, and also wage-labor--
grows, and the motivation of production shifts increasingly to profit,
which is realized in money. The involvement of capital in production takes
not only the form of increased money as circulating capital and the establishment of the profit motive, but also of fixed investments in land
improvement, tubewell irrigation and farm mechanization. It signifies
also a restructuring of the relative importance of the various sources of
income in favor of agricultural production for those who adopt the new
technology, i.e., farming becomes more important than before in relation
to, say, moneylending and trading.

The implication of this switch in forms of income-earning activity
by the viable groups and their relative concentration on agricultural
production, are very important for changing production relations in agriculture. Typically, the tendency is towards the growth of production
based on wage relations and away from the traditional types of tenancy
contracts. Several writers, including Marx, Lenin and Kautsky, have discussed the role of usury in the transition to capitalism in European agriculture. These writers held the position that usury was an important

historical forerunner and catalyst in the development of capitalist farming, the reasons for this being that these activities led to both accumulations of money capital with these groups which could be transferred to
production, and also they served to expand the monetized market. Moreover,
the logic of these is profit-motivated. In the Indian context, however,
several authors[12] have expressed a contrary opinion, which is that the
relative profitability of usury has proved a deterrent to investments by
the richer agrarian groups in agricultural production directly. In other
words, usury has had a retarding influence on the development of agricultural capitalism. It is not our purpose here to engage in a deep discussion of the relation between moneylending and production investments. However, it would seem clear that this issue cannot be settled at the level
of an abstract proposition. We should note that in the present context
of India, the importance of cheap credit from institutional sources
(especially government) in the 'Green Revolution' areas, lessens the role
of profits from usury and trade as sources of investible funds. We
should note also that when the objective conditions for profitable investments emerge, (e.g., when the possibility of technological change raises
the profitability of agricultural production sharply and when irrigation
and credit is available), the shift to agricultural production investment
does occur. As we shall see later, even in regions where petty tenancy
remains prevalent, the nature of moneylending alters under these conditions.
Credit to sharecroppers becomes tied to the adoption of 'Green Revolution'
technology in the form of cost-sharing credit in place of pure consumption
loans.

What is the nature of evolution of differentiation during this
phase and what are the reasons underlying it? Once more, the entry of

capital is integrated into the existing differentiation in agrarian structure and further accentuates and modifies it. The fact that the transition to the new technology requires considerably higher[13] levels of monetization of production, implies at once that those with higher levels of monetary accumulation and/or access to finance, are able to adopt the high cost-high profit technology. As noted during our discussion of the pre-'Green Revolution' phase, the viable and non-viable peasants are placed on opposite positions in this regard. As a general rule, the availability of finance varies in direct relation to size of land owned and security of tenure on rented land. Even where finance may be available, the risk-bearing capacity of the non-viable households is low and is a deterrent factor. Therefore, the frequency of adoption of 'Green Revolution' technology is much higher among the rich and medium (viable) farmers than among the non-viable farming households.

The immediate and most obvious impact of the adoption of 'green technology' is two-fold: (a) a sharp increase in the level of monetization of production and exchange in the agrarian economy, and more important, (b) increasing economic distance between viable and non-viable cultivators. In the pre-'Green Revolution' phase, the inequality of land ownership and operational holdings between households, was partially counterbalanced by the more intensive cultivation and harder work (higher labor intensity in cropping pattern) of the non-viable peasantry. But in the 'Green Revolution' phase, the productivity of land and labor is altered drastically by the introduction of capital in the production process in the shape of new inputs. Productivity and incomes on 'Green Revolution' technology- using farms increase sharply, reversing the formerly observed inverse relation between (value) yield per acre and size of operational holdings.[14] There is evidence from a major 'Green Revolution' area that 'big farms' were more efficient than 'small farms' in terms of output per acre and net farm business income per acre, thus clearly indicating the effect on productivity of capital-intensive cultivation.[15] The effect on distribution of income is obvious. This is confirmed by other empirical and statistical studies.[16] To sum up the discussion thus far, the direct entry of capital in agricultural production occurs through adoption of 'Green Revolution' technology. It accentuates existing differentiation because of finance-intensity and therefore non-uniform accessibility of the new technology. Capital coagulates in large and medium farms to the exclusion of small farms. Within the ranks of the viable households, an innovative, profit-motivated, capital investing, capitalist type of farmer begins to emerge. However, this is a minority of agricultural households. The level of monetization of the agrarian economy increases sharply. Meanwhile, inequality of incomes among agricultural households is intensified.

The 'Green Revolution' phase, along with increased involvement of capital in production, also affects the relations of production in agriculture. The terms and conditions of tenancy in 'Green Revolution' areas change rapidly. Cash and fixed rents grow more prevalent. Cost sharing arrangements, where landlords invest funds in production, transform the nature of sharecropping. Cultivation under personal supervision by landholders, with the help of a wage paid work force, grows more important in 'Green Revolution' areas. A class of permanent agricultural laborers, hired on an annual or longer term contracts, grows quantitatively more significant in widely dispersed areas, such as Haryana and Birbhum, West Bengal. The numbers of agricultural laborers increase very

rapidly in rural areas. A wage labor force, in other words, seems to be
developing as possibilities of wage employment in agriculture expand,
relative to alternative sources of income for non-agricultural and non-
viable peasant households. Cash wages become more frequent. However,
the demand for labor in 'Green Revolution' areas increases more sharply
in the harvesting season, i.e., there is a seasonal peak associated with
the high yields rather than in year-round labor services. This tempers
the pace of formation of a regular wage force because of the use of casual
wage labor. As far as the development of relations of production is concerned, we conclude by noting that trends towards capitalist wage relations are indeed noticeable, and that a class of capitalist producers and
a class of wage laborers is visible, if still in embryonic form, more
markedly in the 'Green Revolution' regions.

Capitalist Production Relations and Proletarianization in Agriculture

We shall conclude this theoretical section with some observations regarding the logic of emergence of capitalist production relations
in Indian agriculture. The development of capitalist production relations
is essentially a process of reconstitution of existing agrarian differentiation along capitalist lines--i.e., in the form of wage laborers and
capitalist employers. The degree to which this takes place in Indian
agriculture depends fundamentally on the intensity and nature of the
mechanisms of penetration.

It is possible to trace the evolution of the viable peasant households in the direction of becoming capitalist producers. Two factors determine the pace of this movement: (a) the quality and efficiency of the land
reform implementation, and (b) the relative feasibility of profitable

investment of private capital funds in production. These two factors
influence the development from opposite directions. Because of (a),
the former basis of economic existence of the large landlords is threatened.
Land reforms tend to impose ceiling limits and more important, to reward
the landowners who reserve land for self-cultivation. And (b) works
through the incentives of higher incomes. The availability of the new
technology thus accelerates the process of transformation by making
feasible a highly profitable alternative avenue of investment. The availability of irrigation is an important prerequisite for the adoption of new
technology and in general, for the productivity of land. For this reason,
we may expect a positive association between irrigation levels and the
incidence of profit-motivated farming. The higher the orientation of production towards realizing profits through the use of capital advanced by
the landholder, the more complete the switch to cultivation through the
use of wage labor.

The process of proletarianization, however, depends not only on
the creation of a demand for wage labor by the viable agricultural households, but also involves a transformation of the conditions of reproduction of the non-viable peasantry. But proletarianization of the non-viable
peasantry is not a once-for-all change, but involves a gradual transition in which wage labor as a means of economic existence grows progressively more important. Further, it does not necessarily involve the disappearance of the small peasant farm, at least in the first instance. In
other words, the development of a wage labor force does not automatically
present a barrier to the continued existence of petty cultivation, and
vice versa. Their mutual co-existence is possible, to the extent that
the means of subsistence of the small peasantry can be met without relin-

quishing control over the land. In this sense, we must distinguish between the process of proletarianization and of expropriation. The condition of non-viability guarantees the supply of wage labor, and the higher the degree of non-viability, the more complete the degree of proletarianization.

IV.3. The Evolution of State Policies towards Agriculture

State policies towards agriculture have played a significant role in the evolution of agriculture and we shall review them here briefly, along with trends in the growth of output. These policies were integrally connected with the pattern and momentum of industrial accumulation taking place in the towns. The overall nature of state policies towards agriculture has been influenced by the specific role played by Indian agriculture in capitalist industrial accumulation, and policy shifts moderated by crises encountered in this process of accumulation.[17]

IV.3(a) Policies During the Pre-'Green Revolution' Phase (1948-1965)

Land Legislation: After the transfer of power, steps were taken by the new government towards reform of the agrarian structure through land legislation. The stated purpose of the land reform legislation was to relieve the exploitative system that had grown under the British and to increase thereby the productive performance of agriculture. It was acknowledged that the system of landlordism and insecure petty tenancy created motivational obstacles in the path of increased agricultural productivity.[18] The chief elements of land legislation were:

(a) the abolition of intermediary tenures (the zamindari system),

(b) the reform of tenancy to guarantee security of tenure and to limit the amount of rent that could be legally collected,

(c) the imposition of ceilings on land holdings and redistribution of land aimed at reducing inequalities in landholding,

(d) the consolidation of fragmented agricultural holdings in order to increase efficiency in agricultural production.

The impact of land reform legislation was uneven across different regions in the country. It is generally accepted that in terms of its stated objectives, these land reform measures were unsuccessful. However, they did have a significant impact on the agrarian structure. Essentially these reforms helped to consolidate the economic position of the viable peasantry and correspondingly, to weaken the economic base of non-viable peasant households. The reforms effectively abolished the colonial system of landlordism and intermediary tenures in most areas. In place of these groups, a broad group of middle and rich farmers (the viable cultivators) emerged as an economically secure and politically powerful social group in the countryside. Many of the old landlords resumed lands for self-cultivation rather than surrender them under the law to the "actual cultivator". Where the implementation of reforms was relatively weak, this was more nominal than real and as we shall see, there is evidence of concealed tenancy and tenant-switching to prevent any one tenant from claiming permanent occupancy rights. The major gainers from the legislation were the larger and economically more secure tenants who did successfully claim ownership on the basis of permanent occupancy. On the other hand, the non-viable tenants were adversely affected. This took the form of their eviction by landlords resuming land, whether genuinely or, more frequently, as a result of tenant-switching. In any case their position with respect to the legal definition of "tenant" was specifically made so as to exclude the petty sharecroppers from the reform legislation.

Due to loopholes in the legislation and political problems in its implementation, de facto both inequality in land distribution and insecurity of tenure have remained widespread.[19] According to the Planning Commission's Task Force on Agrarian Reform (1973):

> "A broad assessment of the programmes of land reform
> adopted since Independence is that the law for the
> abolition of intermediary tenures has been imple-
> mented fairly efficiently, while in the fields of
> tenancy reform and ceiling on holdings, legislation
> has fallen short of proclaimed policy and implemen-
> tation of the enacted laws has been tardy and
> inefficient... . The programmes which could have
> led to a radical change in the agrarian structure
> and the elimination of some of the elements of ex-
> ploitation in the agrarian system...were those of tenancy
> reform, ceiling on agricultural holdings and distri-
> bution of land to the landless and small holders. As
> already pointed out, these programmes cannot be said
> to have succeeded. Highly exploitative tenancy in the
> form of crop-sharing still prevails in large parts of
> the country. Such tenancy arrangements...have also
> become insurmountable hurdles in the path of modern
> technology and improved agricultural practices."[20]

The manner in which the land reforms failed reflected the grow-ing political and economic strength of the middle and upper peasantry. Intermediary tenures could be abolished because they had been closely identified with the colonial system and opposition to the zamindari system was an important part of the anti-imperialist political movement which brought independence. Abolition of insecure tenancy and of social and economic inequalities proved another matter. Actual conditions of pro-duction, particularly in relation to tenancy, varied greatly across states. However, in most regions at the end of the colonial period there existed a spectrum of tenants, ranging from the very insecure share-

cropper to more secure, 'substantial' tenants who also owned some land.
The legislation affected these groups differently, not only in its implementation but also in its conception.[21] Several features of the laws
also made evasion by large landowners possible. Of these, the principal
one was the provision allowing resumption of tenanted lands for 'personal
cultivation' by landowners (subject to a loosely specified limit). But
because of a very liberal definition of the term 'personal cultivation'--
which included the possibility of "cultivation through servants or laborers
provided they are remunerated in cash or kind, but not in crop share",
with or without personal supervision--effective implementation was made
very difficult. Ceiling limits on land holdings could be evaded by the
well-known practice of nominal redistribution of land among family members. Other legal loopholes were afforded by the definition of the term
'tenant' and the status of land records. In several states the laws
specifically excluded the sharecropper from the tenant status, which included only those paying cash or kind fixed. This is true for West
Bengal and Uttar Pradesh, where sharecroppers constitute the bulk of
poor peasantry. This meant that landowners could resume such lands in
full. And since most of the insecure leases are oral, with no written
records in many states, the implementation of protective legislation where
such existed was an impossibility. The prevailing conditions of political
and economic power obstructed implementation. There is evidence of
numerous cases of 'voluntary surrender' of tenancy rights by tenants, of
tenants not appearing before tribunals at the time of hearing, or declaring an unwillingness to purchase land, all of which reflect the coercion
of the weak by the strong. Similarly, despite stipulated limits on the
magnitude of rent, actual rents prevailing (under highly insecure condi-

tions) remain high--50:50 shares being common where the law calls for 20% or 25%. Fair rent laws are effective only for the larger and more secure tenants in actual practice.

In spite of the above-mentioned failings of land reforms in India since independence, it is incorrect to suppose that the legislation left the agrarian structure unaffected. One important impact was that it cleared the way for the ascendance of the group of middle and rich peasants who were also large tenants. These groups were the principal beneficiaries who were able to increase their owned holdings. Interestingly, the legal provisions which called for the abolition of intermediarie and transfer of ownership to tenants, did not recommend an outright expropriation and transfer from the landlord, but merely that tenants be given the right of purchase. The larger tenants were in an economic position to take advantage of such rights and did so. Meanwhile the mode of existen of the old absentee landlords was rendered politically more risky than previously, creating a climate slightly favorable to their direct involvement in agricultural operation. On the other hand, the insecure tenants-at-will and sharecroppers experienced no improvement in their conditions, both with respect to security of tenure and magnitude of rents. Rather than reversing the historical trends towards immiserization and proletarianization and converting them to viable peasants, the land reforms at best preserved the status quo as far as this group was concerned. It is likely that with evictions and uncertainties created by the reforms, the conditions of some actually worsened.

Community Development Programs and Cooperative Movements: The community development programs were small-scale state investments in the rural sector. Begun during the early 1950's, they were considerably ex-

panded in the course of the decade. The projects were administered through
a bureaucratic machinery and involved small irrigation works, village
roads, schools, and hospitals. Rural communities were expected to colla-
borate and cooperate, but public response was insignificant. The impact
of these programs was insignificant and the chief beneficiaries were the
economically and politically dominant sections.

The principle underlying the community development programs was
that these would catalyze rural self-development through the joint participation of all sections of rural inhabitants. They were expected to contribute resources and effort towards these social investments. The community development programs failed because of the implicit assumption
that the village could be treated as a harmonious community. As we have
seen, this was unrealistic in the Indian context. The social and economic
relations between different sections--the viable and the non-viable house-
holds--are those of conflict. What might be beneficial to one group is
harmful to the other. Besides, the relative political power of the viable
households enabled them to have freer access and influence over the low-
level government officials administering the projects. For a detailed
discussion of the conception and implementation of the community development projects in India and the reasons for their failure, see Gunnar Myrdal (1968).[22]

Efforts at promoting cooperative societies were also made during
the 1950's. Most of these (80%) were credit societies and the rest were
marketing cooperatives. The underlying strategy apparently was to dis-
place the agricultural moneylenders and trading intermediaries who imposed
difficult terms on the peasantry and thus to promote greater economic
equality. However, the cooperatives themselves were marked by the domin-

ance of the rich peasantry. The share of total rural credit from cooperative and government sources has been gradually increasing, but even in 1970-71, only 40% originated from these sources.[23] Cooperative marketing societies were similarly controlled by the larger landholders. Thus, both these sets of policies served to strengthen the larger cultivators and did not include the non-viable cultivators. The usual (pre-independence) channels of credit and marketing on exploitative terms continued to exist as the only alternative to the non-viable peasantry.

The "cooperative movement" failed for essentially the same reason as the community development program. As Myrdal puts it:

> "Unfortunately the notion that cooperation will have an equalizing effect is bound to turn out to be an illusion... Indeed, it aims at improving conditions without disturbing that [unequal] structure and represents, in fact an evasion of the equality issue. If as is ordinarily the case, only the higher strata can avail themselves of the advantages offered by cooperative institutions--and profit from the government subsidies for their development--the net effect is to create more, not less, inequality. This will hold true even when the announced purpose is to aid the disadvantaged strata."[24]

In other words, the basic viable - non-viable dichotomy in the conditions of reproduction of the agrarian households lies at the root of the actual response to a mechanism, i.e., the structure determines the response. A classic example of this is found in the case of cooperative credit societies. The nominal membership by poor cultivators in these societies is no guarantee in practice of their getting loans from these sources, because they do not have the ability to offer any acceptable collateral, nor the political influence to claim these resources.[25] Cooperative credit societies moreover do not possess the ability to employ coercive methods to exact repayment of debts, which is demonstrated by the rural moneylenders. Thus, what occurs is a dualism in the credit market, with the viable household borrowing at cheap rates from cooperative credit institutions at (subsidized) rates and the non-viable peasants borrowing at much higher rates from the rural moneylender and local landlord.[26]

Irrigation: The state also invested directly in the production base of the agricultural sector in the form of irrigation projects. This helped to increase the productivity of agriculture, to extend acreage and to lay the foundations for the technological innovations of the 'Green Revolution' phase. These investments thus had a positive impact on production levels and marketed surplus to the industrial sector. During the decade of the 1950's and early 1960's, substantial expansion in irrigation occurred. Gross irrigated area increased 38.1% (from 22.6 to 31.2 million hectares) between 1950-51 and 1964-65. There is little doubt that this contributed significantly to the increase in agricultural production. One study[27] estimates that irrigation accounts for nearly 54% of the variation in interregional output growth during this period. However, excluding two states (Rajasthan and Gujarat), irrigation explains nearly 70% of the growth of crop output. Other material inputs which registered notable increases were unirrigated land and the use of chemical fertilizers. Increase of unirrigated land in net acreage terms kept pace with that of irrigated land.[28]

It is clear that state investments in irrigation works were largely responsible for the expansion in irrigated acreage. Major and medium canal irrigation were directly funded by the government. The large part of minor irrigation was also increased through direct public investment in tanks. Well irrigation has been an area where private investment by farmers has taken place, but this, too, has been facilitated greatly by government loans and subsidies. Thus, direct public investment financed over two-thirds of irrigation expansion and through indirect methods made possible part of the remainder. This was one aspect of state policy which underwent a sharp reversal relative to the colonial era. As might be expected, the growth in irrigated acreage between 1951 and 1966 showed considerable variation between states. (See Table IV.1.) Increase in gross irrigated area over the 15-year period as a percentage of the level of gross sown area at the beginning of the period grew sharpest in the states of Madras, Punjab and Kerala--the difference between the fastest and slowest growing states in this respect was nearly tenfold.

The impact of irrigation expansion has been to make possible impressive gains in agricultural production over the period 1951-66.[29] However, it is likely that it has been partly instrumental in deepening regional disparities and economic polarization between wealthy and poor peasantry within regions. What is rather interesting to note is that public investment in agriculture has tended to favor those regions of the country which have a relative preponderance of rich farmers in the cultivating population.[30] It is also extremely likely that private investments in well irrigation have been made mostly by the richer farmers who have had easier access to government loans and subsidies within any given region. It should also be noted that in some major irrigation schemes, the actual utilization of irrigated capacity has been poor. A study[31] has claimed that for the Kosi project, which involved a large public investment in Bihar state, the estimated use of capacity has been 40% of potential in autumn, 15% in spring and 10% in the summer. The study suggests that this is due to disincentives inherent in the land relations in the area, which dissuade the sharecroppers working the area

Table IV.1: Growth of Crop-Output and Irrigated Area
              by State, 1951-1966

State	Percent Increase in Crop Output, 1952-53 to 1964-65	Percent Increase in Gross Irrigated Area, 1951-52 to 1964-65	Percent Increase in Gross Un-irrigated Area, 1951-52 to 1965-66
Punjab	78.5	20.1	10.4
Gujarat	78.3	12.6	-4.6
Madras	70.0	21.8	-2.9
Mysore	57.2	8.1	4.0
Bihar	46.3	6.8	3.6
Maharashtra	45.6	6.7	0.1
Rajasthan	42.2	9.1	33.7
A.P.	41.6	14.8	-9.0
Orissa	37.5	15.2	-1.9
M.P.	37.6	2.6	15.4
Kerala	33.9	18.2	2.4
West Bengal	28.3	15.1	-4.8
U.P.	23.9	8.2	2.6
Assam	16.3	6.5	11.1

Source: S. K. Rao, "Inter-Regional Variations in Agricultural
         Growth, 1952-53 to 1964-65: A Tentative Analysis in
         Relation to Irrigation," Economic and Political
         Weekly, July 3, 1971, Table 3. Rao's sources are
         publications of the Ministry of Food and Agriculture
         and the Agro-Economic Research Centre, Delhi.

from realizing its potential.[32] Thus, even in the case of expanding irrigation through public investments, in which the role of the market is
minimal, the actual impact has been conditioned significantly by the
existing agrarian structure, both with respect to allocation and utilization.

IV.3(b) Structural Reasons for the Shift Towards the 'Green Revolution'
          Policies

         Components of Agricultural Growth (1951-65: While irrigation
has been the major factor underlying growth of agricultural production
since independence, it is useful to have an idea of the relative importance
of specific component elements--acreage expansion, yield effects and changes

in crop-patterns--in the growth of output. Index numbers of agricultural production have been growing at an average compound rate of between 2.5% to 3.0% per year, but year-to-year output magnitudes have fluctuated sharply. Figures for rates of change of output, area and value yield per acre between 1952-53 and 1964-65 in India by states are shown in Table IV.2. Considerable regional variations may be noted.

Table IV.2: Relative Contributions of Different Elements to the Growth of Crop Output - All-India and States, 1951-54 to 1958-61

	Area	Yield	Crop Pattern	Interaction	Total	Overall Rate of Growth
			Percent Increase Attributed to			
Punjab	69.93	7.98	22.38	-0.29	100.00	5.14
	(3.59)	(0.41)	(1.15)	(-0.01)		
Madras	19.70	52.70	25.00	2.60	100.00	5.12
	(1.01)	(2.70)	(1.28)	(0.13)		
Gujarat*	22.16	21.29	68.21	-11.66	100.00	4.53
	(1.00)	(0.97)	(3.09)	(-0.53)		
Mysore	37.29	48.71	11.32	2.68	100.00	4.36
	(1.63)	(2.12)	(0.49)	(0.12)		
Rajasthan*	102.00	-18.37	6.90	9.47	100.00	4.20
	4.28	(-.77)	(0.29)	(0.40)		
Kerala*	21.42	74.57	6.41	-2.40	100.00	4.08
	(0.87)	(3.04)	(0.27)	(-0.10)		
Madhya Pradesh	40.44	53.32	6.45	-0.21	100.00	4.07
	(1.65)	(2.17)	(0.26)	(-0.01)		
Maharshtra	31.92	42.60	46.43	-0.95	100.00	3.07
	(0.98)	(1.31)	(0.81)	(-0.03)		
Andhra Pradesh	9.74	48.75	36.61	4.90	100.00	3.05
	(0.30)	(1.48)	(1.12)	(0.15)		
Bihar	17.73	76.51	16.72	-10.96	100.00	2.42
	(0.43)	(1.85)	(0.40)	(-0.26)		
Uttar Pradesh	45.98	34.12	19.39	0.51	100.00	2.20
	(1.01)	(0.75)	(0.43)	(0.01)		
Assam	99.27	15.89	-14.23	-0.93	100.00	1.24
	(1.23)	(0.20)	(-0.18)	(-0.01)		
Orissa	32.34	61.87	7.33	-1.54	100.00	1.05
	(0.34)	(0.65)	(0.08)	(-0.02)		
West Bengal	83.96	-54.02	74.92	-4.86	100.00	0.21
	(0.18)	(-0.11)	(0.15)	(-0.01)		
All-India	45.38	45.83	8.16	0.63	100.00	3.57
	(1.62)	(1.64)	(0.29)	(0.02)		

*Base is two-year (1952-54) average.

Source: B.S. Minhas and A. Vaidyanathan: "Growth of Crop-Output in India, 1951-54 to 1958-61: An Anlysis of Component Elements," Journal of the Indian Society of Agricultural Statistics , December, 1965, Table II.

A careful study for the period 1951-61 by Minhas and Vaidyanathan (1965) attempted to break down the effect of component elements,
using an additive decomposition scheme. Percentage of increase in output
attributable to area, yield, crop-pattern and 'interaction' between physical yield and crop-pattern changes were estimated.[33] They noted the
absence of a common national pattern. For India as a whole, contributions
of area and yield increases were roughly equal (around 45%) and shifting
crop-patterns accounted for only about 8% of the net change. Yet for
individual states, there were large variations. Some states. such as fast-
growing Punjab and stagnating Bengal, showed a high relative dependence
on area. Some, such as Kerala, Madras, Mysore, registered significant
increases in physical yields per acre. Change in crop-patterns were insignificant in relative contribution to output growth at the national
level, but in Gujarat it was the major factor (accounting for 68% of growth),
where a large switch from millet to cash crops (oil-seeds and cotton)
took place.

On the question of which systemic influences underlie the switch
to the new agricultural strategy by the Indian Government, a few key elements may be noted. The decades following independence have witnessed
sharp increases in urban incomes. These have been the by-product of the
effort at achieving rapid industrialization through both public and private capital accumulation during successive five-year plans. Consequently,
urban demand for foodgrains has been rising, and even though the growth
rate of agricultural production markedly rose compared to the last few
decades of the colonial era, agricultural production did not keep pace with
the demand.[34] Moreover, the orientation of industrial production was not
towards exports, but the domestic market and thus foreign exchange reserves

were low. Repeated droughts of 1965-66 and 1966-67 contributed to concern over the 'food crisis' and the readiness to adopt a technological solution to the problem of food supply. It was, in other words, prompted by the need to contain a crisis in food supplies which, by raising wage-goods prices, was emerging as a contradiction in the process of domestic capital accumulation. In addition, however, was the influence of international capital. As noted by Cleaver (1972), the 'Green Revolution' was a world-wide phenomenon and an integral aspect of official and private American foreign policy. As India's dependence on foreign official borrowing ('aid') grew and as the food shortages of the mid-60's were met through direct, subsidized foodgrain imports under P.L.480, the Government of India became more receptive to the imported seed-fertilizer package that was to be the building block of the 'Green Revolution'. Table IV.3 shows the figures for foodgrain output, imports and the ratio of foodgrain prices to the wholesale price index for the 1950's and 60's. Also shown are the trade deficit in the balance of payments and the column of gross aid from non-socialist sources. Note the trend in foodgrain imports and the sharp increase in the drought years of the mid-60's. Despite the upward trend in output, sharp year-to-year fluctuations due to the vagaries of the monsoon and the parallel upward trends in demand (associated with rising population, employment and earnings) led to rising foodgrain imports. The figures clearly illustrate the mounting food crisis and foreign-aid dependence which contributed to the switch in agricultural strategy.

TABLE IV.3: Production, Imports and Index Number of Prices of Foodgrains to Wholesale Price Index and Net Foreign Resource Transfer, India 1950-70.

Year	Net Production (Millions of Metric tons)	Net Imports (Millions of Metric tons)	Year	Foodgrains Price Index (Base Year 1960-61)	Wholesale Price Index 1950-51	Foodgrains Price Index / Wholesale Price Index	Net Foreign Resource Transfer (Millions of U.S.$)
1951	48.2	4.8	1950-51	100.0	100.0	100.0	335
1952	48.7	3.9	1951-52	108.0	105.5	102.4	193
1953	54.1	2.0	1952-53	106.3	89.4	118.9	87
1954	63.3	0.8	1953-54	102.5	93.6	109.5	132
1955	61.9	0.7	1954-55	80.5	87.2	92.3	123
1956	60.7	1.4	1955-56	77.6	82.6	93.9	123
1957	63.5	3.7	1956-57	99.3	94.2	105.4	590
1958	58.3	3.2	1957-58	103.6	97.0	106.8	841
1959	69.0	3.9	1958-59	112.8	100.9	111.8	692
1960	67.3	5.1	1959-60	108.5	104.7	103.6	675
1961	72.0	3.5	(Base year: 1960-61)				
1962	72.6	3.6	1960-61	100.0	100.0	100.0	1007
1963	70.3	4.6	1961-62	106.5	104.1	102.3	903
1964	70.6	6.8	1962-63	110.2	107.9	102.1	937
1965	78.2	7.5	1963-64	137.6	119.1	115.5	903
1966	63.3	10.4	1964-65	152.9	128.9	118.6	1119
1967	65.0	8.7	1965-66	171.0	144.3	118.5	1267
1968	83.2	5.7	1966-67	225.0	166.0	135.5	1229
1969	82.3	3.9	1967-68	208.2	165.3	125.9	1079
1970	87.1	3.6	1968-69	202.8	168.8	120.1	735
			1969-70	209.7	179.2	117.0	225

Net Production = 87.5 of gross production, 12.5% being the provision for feed, seed and wastage.

Net Foreign Resource Transfer = Imports less Exports.

SOURCE: Government of India, Ministry of Finance, Economic Survey (1974-75), J. W. Mellor (1976), Tables IX.1, Appendix Table 3.

IV.3(c) New Agricultural Strategy and the 'Green Revolution' Phase

The set of policies comprising the 'new agricultural strategy'[35] began in 1960-61 on an experimental basis and was extended in 1964-65 under the so-called Intensive Agricultural Districts Program (IADP) and the High Yielding Varieties Program (HYVP). The basic strategy here was to raise agricultural production sharply within a relatively short period by means of a technological breakthrough in production. Essentially, this involved the concentration of a 'technical package'--high yielding seeds, fertilizers and pesticides, along with agricultural credit, in a number of selected districts all over India which were specifically selected because of abundant and controllable irrigation. Foodgrain production did, in fact, increase from 89 million tons in 1964-65 to 99 million tons in 1969-70, though it fell drastically during the drought years 1965-66 and 1966-67, indicating the continued dependence on the monsoons. The new agricultural strategy marked an explicit break in emphasis from agrarian reforms and a shift towards technological advances in agriculture. But the new strategy had a significant impact on Indian agrarian structure and its own results were modified by it. By its very nature, the strategy increased regional and intra-regional disparities in agricultural production and incomes, and reinforced and exacerbated the inequalities in agrarian structure--mainly because small cultivators were excluded from access to improved inputs and credit. In contrast to small farms, the application of fertilizer and water in large farms has been high. In fact, one study suggests that this has proceeded to the point where, by a more equal spreading of these inputs over the cultivated land, higher total output would be obtainable.[36] Not all states have participated

to the same extent in the so-called 'Green Revolution' introduced through
the new agricultural strategy, partly because wheat has been the major
crop in which high-yielding varieties have been most successful. Punjab
state, a major wheat-growing area, is the acknowledged heart of the
'Green Revolution'.

The impact of the 'Green Revolution' on agricultural production
has been very favorable. Output has increased substantially, if good
harvest years prior to and following the new agricultural strategy--
1964-65 and 1970-71--are compared when wheat production rose 90%.[37] However, many writers have argued that high rates of output growth are unlikely to be sustained. A number of very different reasons have been
cited. One view is that the 'Green Revolution' technology relies crucially
on controlled irrigation (which is indeed correct) and points out that
such areas are limited. In fact, in 1969-70 the proportion of acreage
under HYV seeds was 36.8% for wheat, but this represented as much as 80%
of the irrigated area under wheat.[38] Consequently, expansion of irrigation was vital to the continued spread of the new technology. Another
'input constraint' argument has been that nitrogenous fertilizers (another
indispensable ingredient) are mostly imported and dependent on India's
foreign exchange position, which has been poor throughout the post-inde-
pendence era and is further weakened by rising prices of other critical
imports, such as oil. The fact has also been pointed out that the HYV
seeds (dwarf strain) suitable to Indian soil conditions have been developed
successfully in a single major foodgrain--wheat (and some lesser crops as
well), but they have not yet emerged for rice. This latter crop, which is
the predominant foodgrain in all-India output, but particularly so in the
Eastern and Southern states, apparently is the 'orphan of the Green Revolu-

tion'. Area under HYV seeds for rice in 1969-70 was only 11.6% of acreage under the crop. Part of the problem in developing high-yielding strains has been the non-contiguous, widespread regional pattern of rice cultivation which implies a great diversity in temperature, soil and water conditions. For all these various technological reasons, there has been skepticism about the continued progress of the 'Green Revolution', unless these impediments and obstacles are overcome.

A very different set of arguments, however, locate the problems not in overall technical constraints, but in rural structure and conditions of production. In areas where the new technology has been taking hold, it has been noted that it is only the richer cultivators who have adopted it. By and large, the small peasantry have not.[39] This has been seen as a limiting factor. A variety of reasons are cited, including imperfections in the credit and distribution system, in which the larger farmers have exercised a dominating influence, the financial risks associated with the new technology, involving sharply increased cash outlays on purchased inputs, especially where there is variability of yields.

An alternative explanation drawn from the experience of areas where the 'Green Revolution' has been slow in making inroads, is advanced by some writers working in the Marxian tradition. A rather different level of argument is advanced. It was suggested by Bhaduri (1973) that the explanation lay in the contradiction between forces and relations in non-capitalist agriculture. The argument was that, given a system of sharecropping by a semi-proletarian class of tenants who are bound by consumption loans to the landlord, the decision to introduce the new technology rests with the latter. The landlord does not introduce changes which would improve productivity on the grounds that this would lead to the eventual independence of the tenant from debt-bondage and thus to the breakdown of the exploitative production relations. Others have argued that it is the relative profitability of usurious moneylending under these production conditions that retards a shift to the new technology. There has been considerable debate in the literature on these issues.[40] This set of arguments is rather interesting for it indicates the fact that the existing economic structure plays an important role in determining the systemic response to the 'Green Revolution' mechanisms. Thus, it is in conformity with our basic position. On the other hand, we should note that when the mechanisms are sufficiently strong and objective technical conditions favorable, there is nothing absolute about the pre-existent structure which would permanently withstand the opportunities made available by the new technology. Indeed, even in Bengal where Bhaduri draws his evidence, there is increasing evidence of technological innovation taking place within the framework of debt-bondage.[41]

To summarize, there has been a growing consensus in the literature that the 'Green Revolution' is being retarded, either because of technological or institutional constraints, but the explanations vary greatly. However, its effect on agricultural productivity has been dramatic, especially for wheat during the late 1960's, and should not be minimized.

IV.4. Structural Transformation of Agricultural Production-- Evidence and Analysis

During the pre-'Green Revolution' phase, the economic polarization between the non-viable and the viable household was intensified, as we have already seen. From the point of view of transformation of production structure, however, the 'Green Revolution' phase was relatively more dramatic. Income inequalities were sharply intensified and production relations altered more markedly. On the question of the impact of the 'Green Revolution'on agrarian structure, there has been a great deal written from various theoretical perspectives. Assessments have accordingly varied. However, there is consensus on a number of points, viz., (a) inequality in Indian agriculture has increased, both between regions and, more important, within the village economy, because the larger, dominant sections of the peasantry have benefited from the profitable new technology, while the smaller cultivators are excluded. Specific studies for the Punjab region (a major 'Green Revolution' state) have shown that relative inequality in (real terms) in terms of consumption in rural Punjab has distinctly worsened. The same is generally true of other 'Green Revolution' areas and in terms of other measures, such as 'farm business incomes';[42] (b) despite increased agricultural production and per capita consumption, the **absolute** levels of living of the bottom three deciles of the rural population (per capita monthly consumption at constant prices) declined between 1960 and 1970. Bardhan (1970) found that real wages of agricultural laborers fell in the Punjab, Haryana wheat belt during 1960-68. Contrary, therefore, to a diffusion of agrarian prosperity, there seems to be evidence of worsening absolute conditions of living among the poorer segments of the population. The proportion of population below the 'poverty' line has been increasing in 'Green Revolution', as well as non-'Green Revolution' areas.[43]

Disparate assessments have been made on the question of the extent to which the 'Green Revolution' has contributed to the transformation of the mode of production in Indian agriculture. Specifically, dis-

cussion has focussed on whether, and to what extent, there has been a
transition to agrarian capitalism. Assessment is difficult because of a
lack of comprehensive data, because of the bewildering variety of existing production relations and distributional arrangements in different
regions, and because different areas have had different historical experience before and during the 'Green Revolution' period. One view holds
that capitalism has made significant inroads into Indian agriculture,
in the sense of a distinct switch to capitalist production relations, a
change catalyzed by the 'Green Revolution' technology. There seems to be
some evidence of this.   A contrary position has been that the capitalist
farmer is very difficult to locate as a 'pure' type because of the continued existence of 'pre-capitalist' attributes. Others have argued that
pre-capitalist relations--sharecropping and petty tenancy--continue to
exist in large sections of the country and while there may be some changes,
they seem to be achieved __within__ the overall framework of pre-capitalist
relations, rather than a transition towards wage labor. Again, there is
evidence of this too.[44] A third view holds that there is no meaningful
sense in which it can be said that Indian agriculture in the modern period
is 'pre-capitalist' in the first place. It is dominated by and is an integral part of the world capitalist system, without explicit reference
to which it cannot be analyzed, and that pre-capitalist forms are superficial aspects.[45]

The basic problem with this literature, it would seem, is that
it poses the theoretical issue within a narrow framework of whether or
not the agrarian structure at any point in time meets a set of criteria
which would justify the label "capitalist". In what is clearly a transitional period, this leads inevitably to a debate over definitions and cate-

gories. The discussion tends also to be a static exercise of comparing existing structures with abstractly conceived norms--(a problem which is further bedeviled by the vagueness of the term "pre-capitalist"). But the underlying economic phenomenon here is really a dynamic one, namely structural transformation. In this dynamic historic process there are certain dominant tendencies. Our approach has been to focus on the process of change directly and to isolate, identify and relate these tendencies to the mechanisms of penetration of capital.

Another area in which there is disagreement deals with the issue of rural proletarianization. Some writers see this as proceeding apace as an integral part of the transition to capitalist agriculture. They cite the rise in the numbers of agricultural laborers. Others urge caution, saying that some of the census figures may be illusory because of data collection procedures and because of widespread concealment of tenancy by landlords evading land reform laws. One aspect of the controversy relates to whether or not the small family farm is disappearing as peasant households are proletarianized. There is some village level evidence, even in 'Green Revolution' regions, which suggests that small farms persist and often even partly utilize hired labor. Thus, it is argued, in the absence of a marked polarization in the course of which the peasant family farm disappears, how meaningful is it to claim that agricultural production is being transformed to capitalism? At one level, the extent and pace of proletarianization is an empirical question for which we need to examine the evidence. At another level, viz., that of the structural determinant of wage labor, proletarianization raises theoretical questions. We shall deal with both sets of issues below. Once again, we shall view this problem within the general context of agrarian change (or more pre-

cisely, the differential development of the peasantry). What we might
note here is that it is not necessarily inconsistent to observe the development of proletarianization and the simultaneous persistence of the small
peasantry. Expropriation of the small peasant and proletarianization are
related but not identical phenomena. Specificities of structure and
history can make their mutual coexistence possible, at least within brief
periods of time. We shall return to this point later.

The above discussion has provided us with a general idea of
major events and trends relating to the agrarian economy. This enables
us to properly situate the more detailed examination of specific issues
concerning agrarian change which follows, in terms of their historical roots
and overall significance.

Evidence on Structural Transformation of Agricultural Production

What evidence do we have that the social basis of production in
agriculture has been undergoing transformation? Are production relations
changing, and in particular, are they changing towards capitalist ones?
In the present section, let us gather together the available information
on these questions. Evidence has been accumulating slowly from two types
of studies--aggregate level analyses based on decennial census reports
and National Sample Survey reports, and second, a number of local village
or district level studies of various scattered parts of India based on
field surveys by individual authors. Given the vastness of rural India,
the information cannot be said to be comprehensive, but it is sufficient,
we believe, to permit a grasping of the essential patterns of change.

The sense in which we use the term 'structural transformation'
in agriculture should be further clarified at this point. Essentially,

it refers to changing <u>conditions of reproduction</u> in the agrarian system.
This has three major aspects: first, <u>relations</u> of production; second,
the principal <u>motivation</u> of production; and third, the role of specific
<u>material elements</u> in the distribution and accumulation process. These
define the basic character of the social and economic process underlying
production activity. Relations of production specify the social organization of production at the level of the production unit and derive
ultimately from the control of means of production. The principal motivation of production defines the logic of the economic activity--the form
of realization of the labor of production which drives the allocation
process. Finally, in any system of production there are certain key
material elements, in terms of which the distribution and accumulation
mechanisms are defined. Examples in the agrarian context are money,
fertilizer and land. Within a social formation and its institutions,
these material elements play a specific role. Land may be the principal
accumulated asset--the dominant source of income and wealth in a system
based on landlord-petty tenancy, for instance. Under capitalist farming
on the other hand, the role of money is likely to be dominant--in
accumulation, in controlling the production process (through purchased
inputs), and in the mechanism of social distribution. When structural
transformation occurs, these conditions of reproduction are altered and
it is by grasping these mutations that we hope to understand agrarian
change. There are two interrelated dimensions of conditions of reproduction which must be grasped simultaneously for an integrated conceptualization of the economic process. The first refers to the 'micro' dimension,
namely, the production-distribution-accumulation process at the level of
the unit of production, the farm. And second, there is the 'macro' dimen-

sion, referring to the systemic unit into which the individual production units are articulated. These micro-units of production obviously do not function in economic isolation, but are bound by specific economic ties to other units of society in a pattern of alignment and interlinkage. There are relations of exchange (with characteristics of dominance and subservience) and cross flows of commodities, money and labor under specific institutional arrangements. Clearly, the economic reproduction of the individual unit is bound up with that of others with which it is linked. When systemic change occurs, both the 'micro' and the 'macro' aspects are changed simultaneously. Our theoretical task in this chapter is to identify and locate these twin dimensions of transformed conditions of reproduction. Let us first consider the evidence.

IV.4(a) Tendency toward 'Capitalist' Cultivation

Whether or not the term 'capitalist' may be applied to characterize an individual farm in current Indian conditions has been a matter of controversy in the literature.[46] As noted earlier, such an approach leads inevitably to the necessity of deciding (rather arbitrarily) on the necessary and sufficient set of attributes of a capitalist farm. This may have its usefulness in compelling a sharp appraisal of concrete conditions of production from an empirical standpoint. However, it obscures attention from the actual process of change in which certain capitalist tendencies begin to manifest themselves at the level of production. These tendencies, which also mark a break with pre-existent behavior, are: (1) farming carried out with the motivation of profit, (2) investment of capital in agricultural production, and (3) employment of wage labor. There is reason to believe that such trends have been emerging in Indian agriculture, but just how pervasive these are, is not entirely clear.

In a field survey conducted in 1969, U. Patnaik examined 66 farms from ten districts over five states--Tamilnadu, Mysore, Andhra Pradesh, Orissa and Gujarat. Note that this excludes the 'Green Revolution' heartland, Punjab. The farms were deliberately chosen in order to take account of the 'most progressive' cultivators in each of these areas. The majority of these farmers turned out to be capitalists of an 'impure' form, i.e., the capitalist tendencies noted above would be accompanied by such 'pre-capitalist' attributes as moneylending, lease of part of land-holding to petty tenants, and forms of labor exploitation through debt-bondage (i.e., consumption loans). However, most of them had invested substantial sums of money on land improvement through irrigation- boring wells, using electric or oil pumpsets; they had switched to new HYV seeds and other high valued crops, utilizing purchased inputs such as pesticides and fertilizer. They all made very substantial annual returns on cash investment; rates as high as 200%-300% per year were observed. There were many cases of farm mechanization through purchase of tractors. Clearly, the potential for profitable capitalist cultivation exists in Indian agriculture, in the sense of realizable returns on capital investment. Thus, there are some clear signs (though rare) from scattered regions of the country of the coming into existence of a mode of agricultural operation characterized by a profit-oriented, highly-diversified crop-pattern, intensive cultivation which has been supplemented by substantial private investment in irrigation, land improvement, and even farm mechanization, together with the adoption of new technology.

Patnaik attempted to identify the 'class origins' of the incipient capitalist farmers. She classified them under four major headings: landlord-turned-capitalist, the dominant landholder, the rich peasant, and urban entrant. Significantly, only a small proportion of the sample (6 out of 66) were from the landlord class whose major source of income used to be rent. By far the bulk of the sample was made up of dominant landholders(17) and rich peasants (35). The remaining 8 were the new urban entrants--professionals, retired military officers, or bureaucrats and even industrialists. She characterized the last group as 'capitalists pure and simple'. Thus, the focal point of incipient capitalism would appear to be located in a rich peasant class. This would form the bulk of what in the last chapter we called the 'viable' farmers.

The distinction between the dominant landholder and the rich peasant is not sharp--the former plays only a supervisory role in actual cultivation, while the latter participates to a minimal degree in manual work on the farm. The big landowners of the colonial period have, by and large, not responded to the changed situation by turning into Junker-type capitalists operating large estates. Instead, the estates mostly have either been disintegrating--the larger tenants gaining occupancy rights under land reforms--or have been nominally subdivided to evade the ceilings, but essentially continuing as before. Yet there are isolated instances of clear transition to capitalist farming, where large farms (ceilings evaded by nominal partitioning) are intensively cultivated on a capitalist basis and where profits have become the major source of income (crop-sharing and lease of land still continuing however). This pattern is more visible only in a few states--Tamilnadu, Gujarat and Mysore--which have shown higher-than-average agricultural production increases. By comparison, dominant landholders prefer not to lease out owned holdings and have traditionally cultivated them through farm servants. They have considerable accumulated liquid funds which have traditionaly been invested in moneylending and trade and, in rare cases, industry as well. The enhanced profitability of agricultural production in recent times has prompted some reallocation of investment towards farming. But here, there is an interesting dichotomy. In 'wet' areas (with canal irrigation), agricultural productive investment by dominant landowners is very insignificant. They have simply reaped the benefits of rising agricultural prices, shifting some acreage to cash crops, but disposed of their enhanced cash earnings in luxury consumption (automobiles), housing construction or real estate in neighboring towns and even shares in local factories, or in acquiring more land. In other words, technological innovation in agricultural production is rare; old wooden ploughs and simple implements continue to be utilized (though some investment in processing machinery has been observed). The pattern is strikingly different in the 'dry' (rain-fed) tracts. Here, the dominant landholders have made substantial sums towards land improvement, mostly in the form of irrigation (well irrigation, bunding), but also in farm machinery. There is evidence of technological change-- scientific utilization of fertilizer, high-yielding seed variety, diversified crop-pattern, multiple cropping, and so on. However, old forms of investment such as moneylending still persist in these areas. This sharp dichotomy in the behavior of similarly placed agriculturists in relation to innovation and its connection with irrigation is noteworthy and deserves further analysis. Without going into a deep examination of this problem, we might suggest some reasons for this dichotomy. It seems likely that several contributory factors are at work. Areas which have

had irrigation for a long time are likely to have (prior to innovations
in technology) a higher land productivity, and a higher level of population density. A labor intensive mode of farming based on petty tenancy
is likely to have evolved over time in these regions.[47] The rents per
acre received by the landlord in the 'wet' region are likely to be relatively high. For this reason, the relative <u>differential</u> in economic returns available from a switch to the new technology would be <u>lower</u> in the
'wet' regions than in the 'dry' regions, where the initial productivity
of land is low.

The 'rich peasant' category differs from the dominant landholder
in performing a portion of work in the field, as mentioned earlier. It
differs also in having much less accumulated funds, as compared to both
dominant landholders and the landlords. There is a great deal of variation in the production characteristics of this group of farmers. Here,
access to credit from state-controlled finance and commercial banks is
closely associated with tendencies towards innovation and incipient
capitalist production. There are cases where rich peasants have made investments, have acquired and reclaimed scrub land with government help,
have switched to HYV and displayed other characteristics similar to the
dominant landholders. But cases of 'peasant capitalism' are more frequent in the fast-growing regions of the country, which is to be expected
given the concentration of public funds in these regions.

Finally, the urban entrants are a very new group and negligible
in numbers relative to the agricultural population. They are more noticeable in highly commercialized states such as Gujarat and Punjab. Funds
accumulated in industry or urban commerce are invested purely for profit.
Investments (sometimes financed by large urban private commercial banks)

and profits are relatively very large. Sometimes they are run by salaried managers who jointly manage the holdings of several individuals as a joint estate. But these are rare and it is unlikely that 'industrial capital' will extend itself into agriculture in this manner in a pervasive way. These farms in Patnaik's sample seem to specialize in products with high returns in urban markets, such as fruits, cane and cotton, and hardly at all in foodgrains.

All these farms surveyed by Patnaik are capitalist in the sense of reflecting a tendency toward production for profit realized in money, rather than in the sense of productive organization. The conditions of employment in these farms vary somewhat, but the pattern by and large is cultivation through a combination of hired annual or permanent farmworkers and of casual laborers hired on a daily basis. The permanent laborers are paid partly in cash and partly in kind in the local staples. Debt is a factor in tying permanent laborers to the farm. Often the cash-part is advanced at the beginning of the year and 'deducted' monthly. Casual labor is increasingly paid in cash, which reflects both growing monetization and the fact that employers are able to keep real wages down since agricultural prices are rising. It is frequently pointed out that pre-capitalist labor relations persist in these farms because of the persistence of tying permanent farm servants through consumption loans (and leasing out tiny parcels of land to them in some cases). In this sense, it is argued, these are not capitalist farms. Clearly, this reflects the incomplete development of the labor market. However, this should not obscure recognition of the penetration of capital in the production process and the setting up of profit-motivated production.

Are these tendencies towards capitalist production rare and isolated occurrences? To what degree do these represent a trend in Indian agriculture? At the present state of knowledge, this question cannot be answered except as cautious hypotheses. A recent study by Raj provides information about trends in the 'activity status' of the rural male working force between 1952 and 1972 for India as a whole. Raj's calculations show that the number of rural male 'employers' has risen quite significantly from 1.6 million in the 1950's to well over 24 million in the 1960's.[48] But, as Raj points out, this dramatic rise reflects in large part an illusory change linked to landlords falsely declaring themselves as 'employers'. Raj's findings, however, support the idea of a possible shift towards capitalist cultivation in the sense of employing wage labor. It is not possible to gauge the magnitude of this shift. This doubt is further reinforced by Visaria (1977), who argues that the NSS estimate (19th round, 1964-65) on which Raj bases his calculation may have contained (unspecified) non-sampling errors. Raj himself seems to suggest, on the basis of trends in numbers of households by size class of operational holding, that shift towards wage-based agriculture is likely to have taken place in around 5 million households during 1954-72.[49] This seems a more plausible upper limit.

Thus, the evidence seems to support the view that there is a notable trend towards the conversion of the viable cultivators into profit-motivated, capital-investing farmers. This transformation is more marked in regions where the 'Green Revolution' technology is taking hold. In fact, there is a logical connection between technological change and this trend because the new technology involves substantial private investments. The commitment of private capital to the production process by the viable households integrates their economic activity more closely with production and

tends to convert them to employers of wage-labor. In the present state
of knowledge, it is not possible to settle definitively the question of
why the pace of this transformation (of viable peasantry into capitalist
producers) is not faster than it has been. One retarding factor to the
adoption of innovations, and thus to this process of conversion, is the
fact that the viable peasantry are not under competitive pressure to
innovate. Agricultural price trends have been favorable, as we have
seen. There is no compulsion to cut costs, as was the case in Europe
and Russia, through international competition.

IV.4(b) Trend Towards the Emergence of Capitalist Production Relations and a Wage-Labor Force

To what extent can it be said that the non-viable peasant households are being transformed to a class of wage-workers? Our discussion
thus far could lead us to anticipate that this is occurring. We have noted
the economic polarization taking place in connection with the mechanisms
of penetration of capital, particularly state policies. Our analysis in
Chapter III noted the essential similarity in conditions of reproduction
between this category and the wage-worker. Given the switch of the viable
producers to profit-motivated employers, we might expect the evidence to
indicate a rise in 'capitalism'. This, indeed, turns out to be the case.
It is well-known that due to frequent changes in data collection procedures,
coverage, and in definitions and terminology, assessment of aggregative
economic statistics in India over time requires caution. Judgment and
interpretations are seldom uncontroversial. However, there is consensus
that over the 1950's, 60's and early 70's, a trend is observable in rural
India towards the growth of a class of workers who depend for their sub-

sistence for the most part on being suppliers of agricultural labor.
Moreover, this takes place in a situation of relatively slow expansion
of employment opportunities in the economy as a whole, with the consequent
exacerbation of relative inequality and absolute poverty in the rural
economy. To some analysts of the agrarian scene, this is significant because the emergence of a working class is a precondition of the development of capitalist relations of production in agriculture. But how rapid
this trend has been, what its significance is for the evolution of agrarian
India, and what its determinants are constitute issues yet to be settled.

K. N. Raj (1976) presents an interesting analysis of empirical
trends. His findings indicate a sharp and significant trend towards proletarianization. Estimates are presented for three years--1954-55, 1961-
62, and 1971-72. There has been a rapid increase in the number of landless rural households, especially during the first period, but continuing
on in the second interval as well. Over the entire 17-year period, out
of a total increase in rural population of 19 million households, the
increase in landless households has been 15.3 million households. The
bulk of this occurs in 1954-62--12 million--and this is attributed by
Raj to the eviction of tenants immediately following land reforms,
estimated at 6 million. At the same time, the numbers of small cultivators (with holdings of 0.01-2.49 acres) registered a decline of about the
same magnitude, confirming the hypothesis of a conversion of petty tenants
into landless laborers. At the same time, an increase occurred in the
average size of holdings of the small farmers, indicating that the ones
with the smallest holdings had been proletarianized. Of course, the landless households are not the only households that provide wage labor--the
small holders are also included. This group first declines sharply but

grows over the next decade--a net decline of 1.6 million households. So, together with the landless, the net increase is 14 million over the whole period--a compound growth rate of about 2% per annum. Raj cites supporting evidence from decennial census figures which show a large increase of 'agricultural labor households' between 1961 and 1971. Further, from NSS figures on rural male population by 'activity status', he notes the increase of the proportion of 'employees'. Raj's analysis is criticized by Visaria (1977) who disputes the plausibility of the 19th round NSS figures. But his analysis also indicates that the proportion of employees in rural male population and in male 'workers' has been steadily increasing, but at a slower rate than implied by Raj. According to Visaria's estimates, the trends in rural economy were as follows:

(a) the rural male population grew at an average annual (compound) growth rate of 2.27%;

(b) the number of employees grew much faster at 3.28%;

(c) however, the participation rate of rural males in the labor force fell. (The labor force is defined as the sum of workers and the unemployed. 'Workers', however, include self-employed family workers and working employers in addition to employees).

Thus, we find fairly conclusive all-India evidence of a steady trend towards the emergence of a laboring class who either have no land to operate on their own, or have holdings so small that they must earn a significant, and even major part, of their income from the sale of labor-power. To get an idea of the relative importance of the agricultural proletariat, we may note that according to the 1971 census reports, 25.2% of all rural males actively engaged in gainful work were 'agricultural laborers'--defined as their 'main activity'.

Patterns and Determinants of Proletarianization

The overall national trend established, the question comes up about the process of proletarianization itself. Let us note some possibilities which have been suggested in the literature. One view is that it is to a great degree a process by which small cultivators are being converted into agricultural laboring households. There are two aspects of this: one is eviction of small tenants, following first, the 'resumption for personal cultivation' by landlords upon land reform, and more recently associated with the 'Green Revolution'. The other is a more gradual economic process, by which small cultivators attempt to overcome the non-viability of their agricultural operations by selling or leasing out land and becoming wage-laborers. In this latter scenario, long-term demographic and economic pressures create the conditions for proletarianization of the peasantry, whereas in the former, it is an abrupt political mechanism. But both these scenarios are unified by the common notion that it is the small peasantry which is being proletarianized. An alternative opinion, based on certain specific regional studies, is that the addition in the number of agricultural labor households has little to do with the small peasantry. Instead, it is accounted for by the displacement and loss of means of livelihood of rural artisanry and other similar non-agricultural households because of competition from industry and the breakdown of landlordism and lifestyles associated with it. Clearly, this is an empirical issue. But with the limited information available, this cannot be settled decisively. Regional specificity is very important here; both mechanisms are operative and in some areas, one mechanism is quantitatively more significant than the other, and vice versa for other areas. But it is equally apparent that the conditions of reproduction of the small peasantry have been undergoing significant transformation towards proletarianization, and an increasing proportion of their income comes from labor sale. It is incorrect to state that the small peasantry has been unaffected by pressures towards proletarianization.

The logic of transition to capitalist wage relations may be viewed in the light of our theoretical formulation outlined earlier in this chapter. The initial impetus emerges from the impact on the viable peasantry, resulting in a tendency towards resumption of 'self-cultivation', which is the first step towards capitalist production relations. The intensity of the transformation varies with the quality and efficiency of the implementation of the land reform. The major impetus comes with the 'Green Revolution'. Consistent with our discussion thus far, we may advance a set of hypotheses concerning the patterns and determinants of proletarianization:

(1) The development of wage labor increases with the rate of adoption of 'Green Revolution' technology by viable farmers.

(2) Proletarianization of the non-viable peasantry is inversely related to the existence of a pool of unemployed non-agricultural households who are displaced via different mechanisms from traditional means of livelihood. Households traditionally engaged in cultivation are not the only source of wage labor. The artisanry whose supply outlets are drying up because of shifting consumption patterns, are likely to seek wage employment in agriculture, especially since there is high urban industrial unemployment. Meanwhile, the non-viable peasants seek to retain their landed status for reasons of security of income and social status in the village.

(3) 'Green Revolution' technology is associated with a sharp differentiation <u>between</u> the <u>non-viable</u> peasants. Those with <u>owned</u> holdings and
some access to credit are able to improve their condition by limited
adoption of the new technology. Those who are petty tenants face
eviction and become landless laborers. Among the non-viable peasant
households, the degree of non-viability is positively associated with
the degree of proletarianization.

(4) Exclusion from 'Green Revolution' technology and expanding agricultural
wage employment opportunities, however, make incomes from agricultural
labor progressively more important. The fact of non-viability implies
that underemployed members of the household seek employment as agricultural laborers. Over the long term, however, with the increase in
population (and the slowdown of expanding acreage), this tends to grow
in importance. This breaks down the cohesive structure of the household and corresponding fragmentation of the extended family, leading
to subdivision of owned holdings. The faster the growth of employment
opportunities, the faster also this process of subdivision. However,
there is a limit to the size of the farm and in the absence of new and
more productive technology, this would lead to conversion to wage
laborers.

(5) Expropriation is associated with the growth of demand for land by the
economically powerful groups. But with capital intensive farming,
expansion of land in acreage terms is no longer the only source of
increased income. Investments in land improvement and the use of
purchased inputs on the one hand, and the existence of ceiling laws
on landholding on the other, act as countervailing influences on the
demand for land. This tends to retard the pace of proletarianization.

This accounts for the difference between the current period and the case of colonial Bengal. (Chapter II)

(6) The fact that the increase in demand for labor during 'Green Revolution' introduction on viable farms rises more sharply for casual (i.e., temporary) employment, retards the pace of proletarianization. The non-viable peasants with owned holdings are able to earn supplementary cash incomes without having to sell or mortgage land.

(7) The role of the state in recent years has tended to provide support to small farmers through special credit programs. Ceiling laws are maintained. This reflects a concern over worsening rural open unemployment, leading to a deepening political crisis. This tends to preserve the small farm.

These are not alternative hypotheses but rather, different combinations of these mechanisms operate in different regions of India. With these hypotheses in view, let us examine the evidence which is available from local-level empirical studies.

Evidence from Local Level Studies

A clearer picture of the process by which an agricultural proletariat is emerging may be obtained from the more detailed evidence of local and region-specific studies. At the same time, of course, one must be cautious about sweeping generalizations. In this part of the discussion, we shall draw upon a number of recent studies obtained from scattered parts of India, in which soil and water characteristics, the extent of the impact of new technology, pre-existent production relations, are all different. Our aim will be to identify in each case the emergence of an agricultural wage labor force. The examination of the proletarianization process under diverse circumstances is also likely to aid us in locating a unifying pattern and thus enhance our understanding of the general process.

Haryana: Consider first the state of Haryana,[50] adjacent to Punjab and formerly part of it, which has been a fast-growing region in agricultural production due to the adoption of 'Green Revolution' technology. In this state, there has been a marked tendency towards proletarianization. According to population census figures, the absolute number of agricultural laborers rose two and a half times over the decade 1961-71. There was no marked shift of population out of the rural areas--rural population as a percentage of total, remained at around 80% since 1951. The proportion of male agricultural laborers in total active rural population increased about two and a half times between 1961-71--a remarkable increase from 7.38% to 15.78%. There are other striking signs of change: the growth of a new category of permanent farm workers, called 'naukars', who are paid in cash with some in-kind benefits such as meals, tea, tobacco. This category is increasing, replacing the traditional farm laborers, 'sanjhis', who are paid a share of the crop. But even where 'sanjhis' are employed, because of the increasing complexity of the 'Green Revolution' technology and (working) capital-intensity of production, the share received by the sanjhi is calculated after deductions are made for various inputs paid for by the owner. Thus, there is an increasing emphasis on monetary accounting practices, rather than a simple share of the crop and the actual payment varies from farm to farm. Permanent labor contracts have also grown very formal and the contracts are now two, three and four years long instead of the customary one-year contract. The form of payment being practised is rather interesting in that it reveals how the enhanced demand for labor leads to attempts by employers to guarantee supplies of labor for their farms. Wages are paid in two in-

stallments to permanent workers. The first payment, made immediately
after the contract is agreed upon (in the presence of witnesses), is
an advance for about four months. The second installment is made after
about six months (with workers having to borrow to cover their needs in
the interim), also contains an element of advance payments (basically a
consumption loan) beyond the end of the harvesting year so that the worker
ends the working year with a debt to his employer. In the event of his
working for different employer the following year, the debt is cleared
by the new employer with the previous employer. Also, workers sometimes
obtain loans from local shopkeepers under a guarantee of collateral from
the employer--a case of intermediated debt. Thus, the mechanism of indebtedness for consumption loans is used in this situation not so much to earn
interest income through usury, but in order to ensure a permanent and
'attached' labor force in agricultural operations. In this sense, the
agricultural laborers are not 'free', but this is effected by their financial stringency and not by any quasi-feudal bonds. Therefore, there
is no question that in Haryana, a process of proletarianization and a
switch to a production system based on wage labor is under way.

A more revealing picture of the determinants of the process is
brought out by a comparison between different regions of the state. These
regions, designated A, B, and C, are distinguished by the extent to which
the 'Green Revolution' has made inroads and this, in turn, is closely related to the availability and controllability of irrigation water. Region A
is the most receptive to the 'Green Revolution', being the best irrigated
and having the highest proportion of area under HYV seeds. Region B is
less affected by the 'Green Revolution', partly because it is irrigated
by a canal system which cannot supply water in the optimum amounts needed.

Less area is under HYV seeds, about half the percentage in A. Region C
is arid, semi-desert, and has very little irrigation and also has a very
small acreage under the new seeds, growing mostly low-value sturdy crops.
In terms of average incomes generated, the level of technology in agriculture and the growth of capitalist wage relations, Regions A, B, and C
are ranked in descending order. As noted earlier in the chapter, agricultural laborers in India are of two types--permanent or attached, and
casual. The first kind is engaged on an annual or longer-term contract,
while the second type is engaged on a daily basis for specific tasks,
such as peak time harvesting. From the proletarianization perspective,
obviously the first kind is more important.[51] The number of permanent
agricultural laborers is highest in A, followed by B and C--the magnitudes are 57%, 30% and 9%, respectively, for males. Most of the permanent
agricultural laborers in A originate from landless agricultural labor
households, and also most landless agricultural male laborers are permanent laborers. In B, the proportion of permanent agricultural laborers
who come from landless labor households is fairly high, but less than in A;
however, the majority of landless laborers are casual workers. There are
hardly any permanent agricultural laborers in C by comparison, and they
all come from landless agricultural households. Thus, it is clear that
the importance of permanent laborers diminishes as we move from the regions
affected most by the 'Green Revolution' to those least affected. This
finding is therefore in line with our hypothesis (1).

Also interesting is the fact that in all regions, agriculturists
whose main source of income is self-cultivation, participate in agricultural
labor to a significant extent--comprising around 21-25% of total (permanent
plus casual) labor in each region. Most of this is casual labor, but in A

and B, some permanent laborers originate from this category as well.
The point we had made earlier about proletarianization and expropriation
being non-identical processes is very pertinent here. The possibility
of a partial proletarianization, i.e., the incomplete specialization of
incomes in wage forms, actually may retard the expropriation of the small
peasantry from land in the short-run (hypothesis [6]). The relative importance of agricultural labor households with land, i.e., those who own
or operate some land but devote the major part of their time to agricultural labor, is lowest in A (11%) and rises to about 20% in B and C.
It is evident that in the 'Green Revolution' regions, opportunities for
farm employment are more plentiful and there are even some permanent
laborers in A who come from households operating 10-15 acre farms and
in B from 5-10 acre farms, whereas in C, the demand is for casual labor
from all landed operational size groups.

In support of hypothesis (2), it is noteworthy that a sizable
proportion (19.3%) of male agricultural laborers in C are classified as
originating from households whose main income source is non-agricultural
activity--artisans and household industry, petty self-employment operating
tea shops and the like, and other unskilled laborers. Apparently, the
class of landless agricultural laborers in A and B also have the above-
mentioned activities as subsidiary sources of income, but earn the major
part from agricultural labor. The significance of this is that it gives
an indication of non-agricultural workers being an important source of the
landless agricultural proletariat, a factor which must be borne in mind
when analyzing the effect of the 'Green Revolution' on proletarianization
of the peasantry.

In support of hypothesis (3), we may note the sharper pattern
of differentiation associated with the 'Green Revolution': (1) the
number of landless households per 1000 households with 5 acres or more in
A, B and C is 599, 340 and 246, respectively; (2) among landed households,
the percentage of households whose main income source is agricultural
labor is zero for acreage class above 2.5 in A, and zero for above 5
acres in B, but in C there are households in this set in the 5-10 acre
class. (See Table IV.4.)

Table IV.4: Proletarianization Patterns in Haryana
by Regions

	Number of Landless Households per 1000 Households with 5 Acres or More	Percent of Households with Land Whose Main Source of Income is Agricultural Labor, by Operated Acreage Class			
		0-1.25	1.25-2.50	2.50-5.00	5-10
Region A	599	21.6	9.3	0	0
Region B	340	38.4	16.2	3.3	0
Region C	246	13.2	10.0	4.6	1.8

Source: Sheila Bhalla, "New Relations of Production in
Haryana Agriculture", Economic and Political Weekly,
Review of Agriculture, March 27, 1976. Tables 2 and 3.

(Note: Regions A, B and C are in descending order with respect
to adoption of 'Green Revolution' technology).

As might be expected, in each region the percentage of landed households
with principal income from agricultural labor, falls sharply as we move
upwards in operated acreage class. However, it is quite remarkable that
the total relative magnitude of this set is much higher in the intermediate region B--57.9%, compared with 30.9% in A and 29.6% in C. This
seems to suggest that in C, opportunities for agricultural employment
and incomes are meager. But in A, most of the enhanced demand for agricultural labor is met from the landless category, whereas in B, a mix-
ture of agricultural labor and household cultivation is far more prevalent--
employment opportunities exist, but the tendency is to retain self-cultivation.

To sum up, the évidence presented thus far indicates:

(1) the relative importance of permanent agricultural laborers is posi-
    tively associated with the extent of adoption of 'Green Revolution'
    technology;

(2) the relative importance of landless laborers is also associated posi-
    tively with the 'Green Revolution';

(3) the demand for farm labor and remuneration in farm employment is higher
    in the 'Green Revolution' regions;

(4) relations of production have been changing most in the 'Green Revolu-
    tion' areas, with a shift away from payment in shares of crop to long-
    term annual contracts, with a system of payment geared to ensuring a
    more stable work force;

(5) landed agriculturists take up agricultural employment, but the rela-
    tive importance of this form of income in different size classes of
    operated acreage varies according to region and so does the numerical
    composition of agricultural laborers originating from different house-

hold types classified by main source of income;

(6) previously non-agricultural households are likely to be significant

contributors to the pool of landless agricultural laborers.

The above conclusions, based on a regional comparison at a given point in

time (1972-73) are suggestive of the impact of the 'Green Revolution' on

proletarianization, but leaves open many questions on the process of

proletarianization itself, for which purpose some intertemporal evidence

is required.

In a follow-up study[52] added light is shed on acreage structure changes

in Haryana between 1962-1972. From this we may infer the extent and the

manner in which the small peasantry has been brought in the proletarian-

ization process, a point we have already touched on above. The issue

here is to what source can we attribute the 150% decadal growth of agri-

cultural laborers in the state and, in particular, whether it is caused

by a process of expropriation of the small peasantry from their landhold-

ings. The evidence here seems to be that while substantial numbers--

some 10,500 households concentrated in the 'Green Revolution' intensive

region particularly--were pure tenants who were evicted and thus rendered

landless by the 'resumption' of tenanted land, the total growth in agri-

cultural labor households cannot be attributed to the expropriation of

the small peasantry, either by eviction or through an economic process

of indebtedness, mortgage and sale, as was the case in colonial Bengal

(studied in Chapter II). In fact, not a single household in the sample

lost any land through the latter mechanism. Only 5.3% of landless labor

households in 1972 cultivated land as tenants in 1962. In other words,

while a significant proportion of cultivating households with land per-

form agricultural labor (as we saw earlier), a very small component has been rendered landless. However, some rather interesting changes have taken place. Most striking is the sharp fall in the average size of operational holding among farms below 15 acres in size. Especially in the 'Green Revolution' areas and particularly below 5 acres, the majority of households 'lost' land in the decade--95.18% in A and 65.22% in B (of households cultivating below 5 acres) experienced diminution of holdings. As a result, the percentage of households cultivating 0-2.5 acre farms, and of households cultivating 2.5-5 acre farms, in total cultivating households, rose dramatically from 6.22% to 26.70%, and 9.92% to 18.88% between 1961-71.

How did this happen? It appears that two factors contributed--subdivision of owned holdings and resumption of tenanted land, of which the first is quantitatively more significant, both by frequency and in terms of acreage changes especially in 'Green Revolution' areas. For some reason, apparently unconnected with financial strain, many small holdings subdivided--typically three ways--associated with the simultaneous breakdown of the joint or extended family. The author of the study suggests that the rising productivity of land following adoption of the new technology, "any prior economic bonds holding joint families together, were loosened". Resumption was also important in lowering the acreage under small farms. This, too, was more prevalent in the 'Green Revolution' areas, where landowners responded to the profitable opportunities opened up by the new technology. In the lesser irrigated, non-'Green Revolution' regions, resumption of land was directed more towards 'tenant-switching', motivated by the fear of tenants demanding occupancy rights, than to genuine self-cultivation. Tenants in 'Green Revolution' areas affected by resumption often responded by improving their remaining

land by sinking tubewells. All this seems to suggest that as far as the
small farmers in Haryana are concerned, the initial impact of the 'Green
Revolution' has not been to dispossess them completely of landholdings,
and to the extent that they have had access to 'Green Revolution' technology and supplementary incomes through agricultural labor, they have
been able to counterbalance the impact of loss of land through resumption
and subdivision. Whether or not this will be maintained in the long
run remains an open question.

We thus find that the evidence from Haryana is in close conformity
with what we might expect from our theoretical analysis. The association
between 'Green Revolution' technological change and the growth of wage
labor is very close. On the other hand, the development of wage labor
in this case does not automatically coincide with the disappearance of
the non-viable production unit. This is due to a number of factors--the
existence of alternative sources of labor supply, and also because of
the nature of technological change. The seed-fertilizer innovation allows
the possibility of capital accumulation by the viable farmers without
necessarily examining the physical size of the farm, i.e., there is slower
expansion of the demand for land.

Gujarat: For information on this state, we rely mostly upon a study by
V. S. Vyas (1976) which deals specifically with the problem of proletarianization. In this state too, according to census figures, the absolute
numbers of agricultural laborers have grown—almost doubling between 1961-71.
As a proportion of active agricultural population, the figure has increased
from 14.9% to 22.77%. Gujarat is one of the states in which the land reforms have been more effectively enforced and it is also commercially
very well developed. It was one of the fastest growing states in terms

of agricultural output in the 1952-64 period, but in the following decade
its agricultural growth rate has been more modest. Trends indicate that
the number and proportion of small farmers has been increasing and so
has been the area under small farms (0-5 acres), with average farm size
remaining approximately the same. Incidentally, the largest size category (25 acres or more) has been distinctly declining in importance.
The growth in the agricultural proletariat may be explained in part by
each of the following four sources: (a) the natural increase of population in agricultural labor households, coupled with lack of alternative
opportunities, (b) the influx of dispossessed small farmers, (c) the
additional (underemployed) workers in small farm households seeking off-
farm employment, and (d) the breakdown of artisan households who are
unable to find a means of living in their traditional occupations. Vyas
puts emphasis on the third and fourth sources. There is evidence of a
growing trend in the supply of labor by small farmers and some indication
in the rise in the size of the average family (of all groups combined).
Both macro and micro level evidence points also to the dwindling of artisan and other similar categories of workers. On the other hand, there
is virtually no evidence of any quantitatively significant sales of land
by small farmers. In fact, there have been very few market transactions
in land since the mid-1950's, most changes in landholdings having occurred
with land reform. Thus, in Gujarat, small farmers have been able so far
to retain their landholdings but seem to be increasingly supplementing
household incomes by allowing members of the family to earn wage incomes
as agricultural laborers and also through dairy farming. Data on production characteristics indicate furthermore that small farms have not been
able to improve land productivity, investment in irrigation and other forms

of land improvement have been meager and they have not adopted the new
technology. They are characterized by Vyas as relatively inefficient and
undergoing a process of immiserization. Part of the reason why small
farmers have not become landless lies in the fact that ceiling laws on
landholdings have prompted the progressive middle and larger farmers to
invest in land improvement--private wells--and to adopt the new capital-
intensive technology instead of seeking to expand their landholdings.

The evidence from Gujarat state lends further support to our
interpretation of the Indian experience with respect to the growth of
wage labor. Basically, the data support the view that wage labor is
gradually increasing in its incidence. It originates basically from non-
viable agricultural householders and from the marginalized artisanry.
The development is consistent with the persistence of the small farm.
However, indications are that the essential non-viable character of the
small farms remained generally unchanged since they continue to remain
outside the rubric of the new technology.

Uttar Pradesh: A study of a west U.P. village[53] provides detailed information on the process of agrarian change in an irrigated, wheat growing
village which has experienced the 'Green Revolution' in the form of tubewells, HYV seeds, chemical fertilizers, tractors, and so on. A large
section of the village households--108 out of 185--are designated 'poor
households'; 40 of these are peasant cultivators and the remaining 68 are
primarily non-agricultural workers. All of these households engage in a
phenomenal variety of occupations, various types of petty trade, artisan-
ship, transport and agricultural labor, typically combining activities
to make ends meet. In terms of land distribution and other fixed assets,
all the usual characteristics of extreme inequality prevail. Among the

small cultivators, the size of operated holdings is extremely small
(average size below 2 acres), which is definitely insufficient to support the subsistence needs of the household by self-cultivation alone.
A total of 36 households in the village performed agricultural labor as
their main occupation and 44 additional households have agricultural
labor as a subsidiary occupation. Thus, wage labor in agriculture is
once more numerically important.

According to the authors of the survey, the poor households
have been affected differently by the 'Green Revolution' according to
their major occupation. Most hard hit have been the artisanry and other
non-agricultural occupations, first by the collapse of the pre-existent
supply arrangement with the old landlords, and also because of competition
from industrial products from urban areas--for example, the replacement
of leather buckets for irrigation by modern equipment. Many craftsmen
have been forced to shift to petty trading and agricultural labor. Among
cultivators, the small minority of owner-cultivators may have benefited
from the 'Green Revolution', but given the tiny size of owned plots, it
is doubtful how much absolute gains may have been realized. For tenant
cultivators (sharecropping being the most prevalent type), the gains have
been even less--partly because they are often compelled by landlords to
use farmyard manure as a condition of lease,[54] and partly because insecurity
of tenure and financial requirements of the new technology. Thus owner
and tenant-cultivator households of the poor category remain a potential
source of agricultural wage labor.[55]

There is some evidence of increasing concentration of landownership since the 1950's and sale of land by the poor peasants, but in absolute
acreage this turns out not to be very important and the land sold by the

poor households is only a small fraction of the land purchased by the rich households. However, leasing land to small tenants for a share is still quite prevalent--a factor which counterbalances the pressures making for their conversion to a landless agricultural proletariat. The impact of 'Green Revolution' on labor demands seems to have been concentrated mostly in increasing sharply the seasonal harvesting requirements which are met by the existing pool of potential suppliers--agricultural and non-agricultural poor households, and with temporary employment of workers from other villages.

The evidence from this U.P. village with regard to the formation of a wage labor force may be summed up as follows: A large wage labor force in relation to working population in agricultural production does exist. This is drawn from a wide range of agricultural, as well as non-agricultural occupational groups, some of whom are gradually tending to take up agricultural labor as a main occupation. The non-agricultural landless group is quantitatively quite large and in recent times has been gradually deprived of their traditional means of livelihood. The small peasants also participate in wage labor, but have for the most part retained their landed status, even though they have derived marginal benefits from 'Green Revolution' technology as far as their own cultivation is concerned. The continued existence of small tenancy, plus the fact that the existing pool of labor supply is able to meet the growth in demand for wage labor without a rapid rise in wages, contributes to the possibility of the continued existence of small farms.

Other States: Scattered evidence from village level studies in other states also tend to support the idea that the growth of an agricultural wage labor force is taking place. A study of two West Bengal villages[56] in Birbhum district indicates that the 'kishan' system of annual crop-sharing contract between cultivator and laborer is being replaced almost completely by a system of annual farm servants and casual (daily wage) laborers. Part of the change is simply a shift in the form of payment from share to fixed wages, but it indicates the emergence of more usual capitalist relations of production and the capitalist rationale in maximizing profit from a combination of permanent and casual labor. There is a sharp increase in the number of landless 'mahindar' (permanent farm servant) families and an even sharper increase in landless day laborers. In contrast to the findings of the other studies reported on above, the growth of the landless labor force in these villages can be accounted for mainly by expropriation of former landed peasants through sale by auction, direct negotiation and unrecovered mortgages. In Orissa too,[57] there are cases of small tenants being evicted and of owners of small plots leasing out under financial strain.

We may conclude our discussion of the empirical basis on pro-letarianization, noting that there is widespread and very convincing macro and micro level evidence that agricultural wage labor exists and is growing fairly rapidly as a major occupation in rural India. This phenomenon is closely associated with the land reforms of the 1950's and the adoption of 'Green Revolution' technology of the 1960's, and consequently there are regional variations. The origin of this wage labor force is a combination of both agricultural and non-agricultural occupational groups. The extent of conversion of landed cultivators into landless wage laborers, however, has been limited. The evidence is in conformity with our theoretical formulation of agrarian change in India in terms of differential development of the peasantry. The local and regional level data bear out quite reasonably our expectations regarding the patterns and determinants underlying proletarianization, which were set out earlier in the subsection.

IV.4(c) Evidence on Changes in Extent and Structure of Tenancy

Because tenancy has been the most important basis of agrarian production relations in the past, no discussion of agrarian change is complete without a treatment of the changes in tenancy. Moreover, any major transformation of the agrarian system is bound to be reflected in some way in changes in tenancy. Consistent with our preceding discussion, we should expect the evidence to indicate the following broad tendencies:

(a) The institution of tenancy should be declining in favor of owner-cultivator (with hired labor), especially in the 'Green Revolution' areas. '

(b) The economic distinction and distance between the large tenants (viable cultivators) and the petty insecure tenant or sharecropper (non-viable cultivators) should be increasing with the spread of the 'Green Revolution'.

(c) The petty tenants should be expected to be increasingly proletarianized.

Based on a scrutiny of NSS Landholdings Survey data for 1953-54, 1960-61 and 1970-71, Bardhan (1976) provides a broad picture of national trends. Roughly speaking, tenancy (as measured by percentage of operated area leased-in) has decreased during the period 1953-71 in most states, with the exception of Bihar, Orissa and U.P. where it has increased. In the period 1960-61 to 1970-71, i.e., well after the land reform legislation, the extent of tenancy at the all-India level, has declined very slightly. In a number of states, including fast-growing Punjab, Haryana, Karnataka and in Kerala, Tamilnadu, Gujarat and Maharashtra, it has significantly declined. But it has increased in U.P., Bihar, Orissa and Assam, which includes some of the regions where agricultural output has expanded most slowly. Tenancy appears to have declined the most in those states where there has been a rise in the index of land improvement, which in turn is positively associated with the 'Green Revolution'. Thus a shift is occurring in these regions towards owner cultivation in place of landlordism, which is a significant trend consistent with our expectations.

Another important trend pertains to the structure of tenancy itself. This underscores the significance of the 'viable-non-viable' distinction in relation to differential evolution of the tenant. There is a widespread growth in the percentage of landed tenants; a distinct shift is occurring, especially in the 'Green Revolution' areas, away from landless or petty tenant cultivation towards a more affluent capitalist type tenant. The concentration index of net leased-in area by size class of farms has distinctly increased in Ferozepur district, Punjab between 1956 and 1970 and the average tenant there has a bigger and better irrigated farm. This is accompanied by the demise of the small tenant--whereas 25% of primarily tenant farms were in the less than 10 acre size category in 1956-57, not a single farm belonged to this category in 1969-70. This general pattern is supported by state level data in Punjab and Haryana, and by micro studies by Vyas (1970) for Gujarat, Bandopadhyay (1975) for West Bengal, Nadkarni (1976) for Maharashtra, and to a limited extent by Bharadwaj and Das (1975) for Orissa. This change is particularly marked in irrigated areas and where HYV seeds are being introduced. The process

in this regard may be one where farmers with medium-sized holdings and with
financial access to the 'Green Revolution' inputs have been able to obtain
increased operational holdings by offering high cash rents in advance, as
in parts of Orissa. While insecurity of tenure, caused by frequent
'tenant switching', higher than average rents per acre, inadequate or no
access to the new technology remain the prevailing condition of production
of small tenants, a new type of capitalist farmer is also acquiring land
on lease.

National trends in the relative growth of the form of tenancy
contract--share tenancy vis-a-vis fixed rental arrangements--are mixed.
Fixed rent tenancy seems to be rising in the more progressive, and newly
irrigated areas, but this is not universal by any means. From the NSS
data, it appears that the area under sharecropping as percentage of total
tenanted area at the all-India level has been rising over time and that
it remains the prevalent mode of tenancy except in South India. But
against this, we may note that the content of the sharecropping contract
has been undergoing significant changes in many regions, especially in
'Green Revolution' regions, in the increasing practice of cost sharing
(coupled with higher share) by the landlord in order to avail of the new
technology, a trend which might lead to the landlord getting directly involved in supervision of actual production.

Regional level studies underscore the relation between the nature
and content of changes in tenancy and irrigation. In Haryana, widespread
resumption of tenanted land for owner cultivation took place primarily in
better irrigated areas by landowners responding to opportunities provided
by the 'Green Revolution'.[58] In the poorer irrigated areas of the state,
repeated evictions of tenants took place without genuine resumption, in

apprehension of tenancy legislation. In irrigated villages of Orissa, where HYV are being adopted, there is a shift occurring toward fixed rents from sharecropping and conspicuously shortened leases and towards the payment of cash rents in advance. Rents are also being revised upwards. The net effect is the gradual displacement of petty tenants by more substantial peasants who can grow HYV.

To sum up, the most important features of changes in tenancy from the perspective of our analysis are:

(1) Tenancy appears to be declining in favor of owner cultivation in the areas most affected by the 'Green Revolution';

(2) Among tenants, there is a shift (once again associated with the 'Green Revolution') in the importance of landed and larger tenants as opposed to landless or petty tenant farmers; a class of technologically progressive, capitalistically motivated farmers with medium-sized farms seems to be emerging;

(3) Petty tenants are increasingly marginalized and face partial proletarianization;

(4) The terms and conditions of sharecropping are being substantially modified to incorporate growing 'finance-intensity' of production with the new technology;

(5) Irrigation appears to be a significant factor underlying regional variations.

The first three trends lend direct support to our contentions. The fourth trend indicates the resilience of the institution of tenancy to the profitable opportunities presented by the technological innovation, but at the same time, opens up the possibility of further change. It tends to contradict those writers who, as we noted above, have suggested that tenancy might block innovation. The fifth pattern, which we do not pursue in detail here, confirms the observations we made in Section IV.4(a) regarding the relationship between irrigation and the economic behavior of viable cultivators.

Section IV.5. Conclusion

In this chapter we have analyzed the process of development of the agrarian economy in India since independence. We have interpreted the essential features of this process as ongoing differentiation and structural transformation, which are catalyzed and influenced by the operation of certain economic mechanisms. The mechanisms, in turn, emanate from the nature of capitalist development in the Indian industrial sector (e.g., the determination of state policies towards agriculture).

The theoretical basis of our analysis, both of agrarian structure and its transformation, has been the concept of reproduction. We have viewed the essence of differentiation within a structure in terms of differences in the conditions of reproduction (the viability-non-viability distinction introduced in Chapter III). Our analysis in this chapter has dealt with the consequences of these differences in the dynamic process of change--i.e., the differential response to the infusion of capital. Our basic formulation appears to be well supported by the available empirical evidence. A number of significant changes have been occurring in the agrarian economy--there is increased economic polarization, increased development of wage labor relations and of profit motivated production, and some changes in the terms and conditions of tenancy, which we have analyzed. In general, we find that the extent and speed of change is closely associated with the degree to which the

new technology is adopted by the viable groups. Because of their
dominant position in economic relations, this affects the conditions
of economic existence of the non-viable groups. Proletarianization is
positively associated with 'Green Revolution' technology. However,
this can proceed without necessarily leading to expropriation of the
petty farmers from their non-viable holdings.

FOOTNOTES - CHAPTER IV

1. The main discussants in this debate are S. C. Gupta (1962), Rudra, Majid and Talib (1969), (1969a), (1970), Patnaik (1971), (1972), (1972a), and Chattopadhyay (1972), (1972a), among others. For a discussion of this literature see H. Cleaver (1976) and H. Alavi (1975).

2. See Cleaver (1972) for an analysis of the close connection between the adoption of the 'Green Revolution' strategy and U. S. foreign aid policies. The U.S. Government directly and indirectly had supported the 'Green Revolution' in Third World countries. The strategy was adopted in India at a time when the Indian economy was feeling the strain of two successive drought years and was reliant on emergency food aid from the U.S.

3. Since the state played an important role in industrial accumulation, its five-year plans and economic policies set the basic pattern of industrial growth. The domestically directed, import substituting emphasis evolved as a consequence of the so-called "Mahalanobis" strategy underlying the Second Five Year Plan which emphasized the building of a capital goods sector and an autarkic growth strategy.

4. The price index for food articles and industrial raw materials rose at an increasing rate between 1950-1966. Food article prices increased at a compound rate of 2.8% per year between 1950-1966 and at 6.9% during 1955-1966. For the same intervals industrial raw material prices increased at 2.5% and 6.7% per year. Both were consistently higher than the price increases for industrial manufactures. (A. B. Ghosh (1974), p. 36, Table 4.2). The pattern remains valid also for 1966-71.

5. Mellor (1976), p. 46.

6. The essential features of this pattern were analyzed in Chapter III. The agrarian structure of the 1950's was the result of a long period of evolution on which the policies of the colonial state had an important influence. The specific historical experience of different regions in India were different, which is a reason why there were differences in rural structure between them (e.g., in the patterns of tenancy). Nonetheless, the basic polarity between the viable and non-viable seems to be a common feature in all regions of agrarian India.

7. For statistics on price trends, see Ghosh (1974), op. cit. There is both micro- and macro-level evidence suggesting that monetary accumulations in the hands of the viable farmers occurred. See Patnaik's account of her field observations on 66 rich farmers. (Patnaik (1972b). Also, an aggregative study of agriculture-industry economic linkages by R. Tamarajakshi (1969) indicates a "surplus" in agriculture's trade balance with industry during 1951-1966, i.e., the value of sales by agriculture to industry exceeds its purchases of industrial products.

8. Bharadwaj (1974), Patnaik (1972b) among others.

9. U. Lele (1971), p. 21, P. 129.

10. Bharadwaj (1974), Chapter I.

11. The M-C-M' circuit is Marx's representation of the circulation process
    of capital. The idea simply is that the logic of production is
    governed in this case by making profits realized in money.
    Money is invested as capital in production (M), the process of
    production yields commodities (C) and these are sold for money
    (M'). M' exceeds M and hence profit. This contrasts with the
    circuit C-M-C', where producers directly produce commodities
    (c) which are ultimately exchanged for other commodities (C'),
    the purpose of exchange being the diversification of consumption.

12. P. Prasad (1974), N. K. Chandra (1974).

13. Mellor (1976), p. 59, P. 80, Table IV-1.

14. This pattern was discussed in Chapter III.

15. P. Bhattacharya and A. Majid (1976), P. A-147, P. A-149.

16. For example, G. R. Saini (1976) comes to the same conclusion.

17. Cleaver (1972), Mellor (1976).

18. P. S. Appu (1974). Insecurity of tenure and high rents imply that
    the actual tenant producers have little incentive to invest in
    land.

19. The structure of land holdings in 1960-61 was discussed in Chapter III.
    The continuation of insecure conditions for petty tenants,
    especially sharecroppers, is found by all studies on land rela-
    tions. See Chapter III, Section 4, and the works referred
    to there.

20. Quoted in P. S. Appu (1974), op. cit., P. A-72.

21. A good discussion of tenancy reform legislation and its implementa-
    tion in various states is available in P. S. Appu (1975). See
    particularly Section II, pp. 1347-1355, and Appendix II,
    "Definition of Personal Cultivation in the Various State Laws".

22. Myrdal (1968), Chs. 18 and 26, pp. 1334-1356.

23. Mellor (1976), op. cit., p. 35.

24. Myrdal (1968), op. cit., p. 1335.

25. D. Thorner(1962) on the basis of a field survey of agricultural co-
    operatives noted: "In general, I found that the heads of co-
    operatives were the big people of the village". (p. 257) and,

"The little people, desperate to get land, cannot sit as equals with important people who have significant amounts of land to give out" (p, 252). Also, "In case after case among the best cooperatives, the leadership turns out to be the trader-moneylender" (p. 259) who often acquire funds from them. Quoted in Myrdal (1968).

26. Myrdal (1968), op. cit., p. 1337.

27. S. K. Rao (1971), p. 1337-1339.

28. Acreage is measured in both gross and net terms. Gross acreage counts a plot of land twice if it is sown twice in the year. Net acreage concerns only the physical land area regardless of intensity of cropping.

29. Rao (1971), op. cit., p. 1342. Figures on agricultural production are given in Table IV.3.

30. Rao (1971), ibid., p. 1343.

31. Appu (1974), op. cit.

32. The argument given by Appu is that rents are very high, all inputs have to be provided by sharecroppers. The main crop is paddy. A second crop (of wheat) can be planted in January. But because growing wheat is more expensive, the farmers need financing which is available at very high interest rates. The crop is consequently foregone.

33. The additive decomposition scheme is, of course, only one of many possible schemes. In addition, output changes may be decomposed into component elements using a multiplicative scheme.

34. See Table IV.3 for figures on domestic production and imports. Also Mellor, Cleaver, Lele and Simon (1968), pp. 21-28.

35. The literature on the 'Green Revolution' is enormous. For a compact discussion, see Mellor (1976), Ch. III.

36. C. H. H. Rao (1974).

37. Mellor (1976), op. cit., p. 50.

38. Ibid., Appendix Table 5.

39. Ibid., Chapter IV, Patnaik(1972b), G. Saini (1976), Bhattacharya and Majid (1976), among others.

40. The main proponents of this view are Bhaduri (1973), P. Prasad (1974), and N. K. Chandra (1974). A critical comment was made by Rudra (1974).

41. Rudra (1974) argues that there is evidence of landlords advancing a portion of the cost of improved seed and fertilizer to small tenants in return for increased rent.

42. Bhattacharya and Majid (1976), op. cit.

43. See I. Rajaraman (1975), especially Table 3.

44. See the "mode of production debate" cited above. The second strand is the contribution of authors such as Bhaduri and Prasad, op. cit., who have used the term "semifeudal" to describe Indian agriculture.

45. This view was introduced in the Indian context by A. G. Frank (1973).

46. A complete bibliography is given by Cleaver (1976).

47. This type of a dichotomy between regions with old and new irrigation is noted by Beteille (1974) for Tanjore district. The 'wet' regions on the irrigated deltaic regions showed a more complex, highly stratified tenurial and social structures as compared with the newly irrigated regions of the district.

48. Raj (1976), p. 1288. The figures given there are 2 million and 30 million, respectively. But Raj had indicated the presence of computational errors. (See Visaria (1977), footnote 1). We have therefore given corrected figures.

49. Ibid., p. 1287.

50. Sheila Bhalla (1976).

51. This is the case because a stable workforce with long-term employment contracts would allow a sharper development of wage relations and wage earning in the agricultural production system, as compared to a casual workforce which subsists on a multitude of activities.

52. Sheila Bhalla (1977).

53. A. Saith and A. Tankha (1972).

54. Ibid., p. 718. The landlords believe that the use of organic manure is necessary for the soil to recover its natural fertility. So they insist that when petty tenants cultivate the land organic fertilizer be used. However, when they themselves cultivate, they use inorganic fertilizer, preferring to alternate the type of fertilizer used on a given plot of land.

55. Rudra and Newaj (1975).

56. Bharadwaj and Das (1975a), (1975b).

57. A very recent, fairly comprehensive survey of research on the labor market is K. Bardhan (1977).

58. Bhalla (1977), op. cit.

REFERENCES

H. Alavi (1975), "India and the Colonial Mode of Production", Economic and Political Weekly, August 1975, special number

L. Althusser and E. Balibar (1970), Reading Capital, NLB, London, 1970

P. S. Appu (1974), "Agrarian Structure and Rural Development", Economic and Political Weekly, September 28, 1974

_____ (1975), "Tenancy Reform in India", Economic and Political Weekly, August 1975, special number

G. Arrighi (1970), "Labor Supplies in Historical Perspective: A Study of the Proletarianization of the African Peasantry in Rhodesia", Journal of Development Studies, April 1970

W. Baer (1967), "The Inflation Controversy in Latin America", Latin American Research Review, Spring number, 1967

W. Baer and I. Kerstenetsky (1964), Inflation and Growth in Latin America

A. Bagchi (1976), "De-Industrialization in India in the Nineteenth Century: Some Theoretical Contributions", Journal of Development Studies, January 1976

J. Banaji (1976), "Summary of Selected Parts of Kautsky's The Agrarian Question", Economy and Society, February 1976

N. Bandopadhyay (1975), "Changing Forms of Agricultural Enterprise in West Bengal", Economic and Political Weekly, April 26, 1975

K. Bardhan (1970), "Price and Output Response of Marketed Surplus of Food-grains: A Cross-Sectional Study of Some North Indian Villages", American Journal of Agricultural Economics, February 1970

_____ (1977), "Rural Employment, Wages and Labour Markets in India-- A Survey of Research", Economic and Political Weekly, June 25, July 2 and July 9, 1977

P. Bardhan (1970), "Green Revolution and Agricultural Labourers", Economic and Political Weekly, July 1970

P. K. Bardhan (1972), "The Pattern of Income Distribution in India-- A Review", mimeo

_____ (1976), "Variations in the Extent and Forms of Agricultural Tenancy: An Analysis of Indian Data Across Regions and Over Time", Economic and Political Weekly, September 11 and 18, 1976

E. Berg (1961), "Backward-Sloping Labor Supply Functions in Dual Economies--
The Africa Case", Quarterly Journal of Economics, August 1961

A. Beteille (1974), Studies in Agrarian Social Structure, Oxford University
Press

A. Bhaduri (1973), "Agricultural Backwardness Under Semi-Feudalism",
Economic Journal, March 1973

_____ (1974), "Towards a Theory of Precapitalist Exchange", in
A. Mitra (ed.), Economic Theory and Planning, Ch. 10

J. Bhagwati and S. Chakravarty (1970), "Contributions to Indian Economic
Analysis: A Survey", American Economic Review, Supplement

Sheila Bhalla (1976), "New Relations of Production in Haryana Agriculture",
Economic and Political Weekly, March 27, 1976, Review of
Agriculture

_____ (1977), "Changes in Acreage and Tenure Structure of Land
Holdings in Haryana, 1962-72", Economic and Political Weekly,
March 26, 1977

K. Bharadwaj (1974), Production Conditions in Indian Agriculture, Cam-
bridge University Press

K. Bharadwaj and P. K. Das (1975a), "Tenurial Conditions and Mode of
Exploitation: A Study of Some Villages in Orissa", Economic
and Political Weekly, Annual Number, February 1975

_____ (1975b), "Tenurial Conditions and Mode of
Exploitation in Agriculture: A Study of Some Villages in Orissa--
Further Notes", Economic and Political Weekly, June 1975

P. Bhattacharya and A. Majid (1976), "Impact of Green Revolution on
Output, Cost and Income of Small and Big Farmers", Economic and
Political Weekly, December 1976, Review of Agriculture

G. Blyn, Agricultural Trends in India, 1891-1947: Output, Availability
and Productivity, University of Pennsylvania Press, Philadel-
phia, 1966

E. Boserup, (1965), The Conditions of Agricultural Growth, Aldine Publishing Co., Chicago, 1965

Bipan Chandra (1968), "Reinterpretation of Nineteenth Century Indian
Economic History", Indian Economic and Social History Review,
March 1968

N. K. Chandra (1974), "Farm Efficiency Under Semi-Feudalism: A Critique of Marginalist Theories and Some Marxist Formulations", Economic and Political Weekly, August 1974, Special Number

P. Chattopadhyay (1972), "On the Mode of Production in India Agriculture: A Preliminary Note", Economic and Political Weekly, March 25, 1972

_____ (1972a), "Mode of Production in Indian Agriculture: An 'Anti-Kritik'", Economic and Political Weekly, December 1972, Review of Agriculture

A. V. Chayanov (1966), The Theory of Peasant Economy, D. Thorner, B. Kerblay and R. Smith (eds.), American Economic Association Translation Series, R. D. Irwin, Homewood, Illinois, 1966

H. M. Cleaver (1972), "The Contradictions of the Green Revolution", Monthly Review, June 1972

_____ (1976), "Internationalization of Capital and Mode of Production in Agriculture", Economic and Political Weekly, March 27, 1976, Review of Agriculture

V. Dandekar (1964), "Prices, Production and Marketed Supply of Foodgrains", Indian Journal of Agricultural Economics, July-December 1964

K. Davis (1951), The Population of India and Pakistan, Princeton University Press, Princeton, 1951

R. C. Dutt (1950), The Economic History of India, (Volumes I and II), Routledge and Kegan Paul, London, 1950

R. P. Dutt (1949), India Today, People's Publishing House, Bombay, 1949

H. N. Dvivedi (unpublished), "A Study of the Factors Governing the Flow of Marketable Surplus of Important Crops in Ludhiana District", Punjab Agricultural University, Ludhiana, mimeo

R. S. Eckaus (1955), "Factor Proportions in Underdeveloped Countries", American Economic Review, September 1955

Famine Enquiry Commission (1945), The Report on Bengal, Government Publication, Calcutta, 1945

D. K. Foley (1975), "Problems versus Conflicts; Economic Theory and Ideology", American Economic Review, Papers and Proceedings, May 1975

A. G. Frank (1973), "On 'Feudal' Modes, Models and Methods of Escaping Capitalist Reality", Economic and Political Weekly, January 6, 1973

R. E. Frykenberg (1969) ed., Land Control and Social Structure in Indian History, University of Wisconsin Press, Madison, 1969

A. Geddes (1937), "The Population of Bengal, Its Distribution and Changes: A Contribution to Geographical Method", Geographical Journal, 1937

_____ (1946), "Half a Century of Population Trends in India: A Regional Study of Net Change and Variability, 1881-1931", Geographical Journal, 1946

N. Georgescu-Roegen (1960), "Economic Theory and Agrarian Reforms", Oxford Economic Papers, February 1960

A. B. Ghosh (1974), Price Trends and Policies in India, Vikas Publishing House, Delhi, 1974

Government of India, Ministry of Finance, Economic Surveys

_____ , Ministry of Food and Agriculture, Studies in the Economics of Farm Management

S. C. Gupta (1962), "New Trend of Growth", Seminar No. 38

S. Nurul Hasan (1969), "Zamindars Under the Mughals" in Frykenberg (1969)

D. W. Jorgenson (1961), "The Development of a Dual Economy, Economic Journal, Volume 71

_____ (1967), "Surplus Agricultural Labor and the Development of a Dual Economy", Oxford Economic Papers, November 1967

C. Kao, K. R. Anschel and C. K. Eicher (1964), "Disguised Unemployment in Agriculture", in C. K. Eicher and L. Witt (eds.), Agriculture in Economic Development, New York, McGraw-Hill

K. Kautsky (1970), Le Question Agraire, Maspero, Paris, 1970

A. M. Khusro (1973), Economics of Land Reform and Farm Size in India, Institute of Economic Growth, Delhi, 1973

Raj Krishna (1962), "A Note on the Elasticity of the Marketable Surplus of a Subsistence Crop", Indian Journal of Agricultural Economics, July-September 1962

T. N. Krishnan (1965), "The Marketable Surplus of Foodgrains: Is It Inversely Related to Price?", The Economic Weekly, February 1965

W. Ladejinsky (1970), "The Ironies of India's Green Revolution", Foreign Affairs, July 1970

H. Laxminarayan and S. Tyagi (1977), "Inter-State Variations in Types of Tenancy", Economic and Political Weekly, September 1977, Review of Agriculture

Land Revenue Commission of Bengal (1940), The Report, Bengal Government Press. Calcutta, 1940

Uma J. Lele (1971), Foodgrain Marketing in India: Private Performance and Public Policy, Cornell University Press, 1971

V. I. Lenin (1974), The Development of Capitalism in Russia, Progress Publishers, Moscow, 1974

W. A. Lewis, "Economic Development with Unlimited Supplies of Labor", Manchester School of Economic and Social Studies, May 1954. Reprinted in A. N. Agarwala and S. P. Singh (eds.), The Economics of Underdevelopment, Oxford University Press, New York, 1958

K. Marx (1967), Capital, Volume I, International Publishers, New York, 1967

P. N. Mathur and H. Ezekiel (1961), "Marketable Surplus of Food and Price Fluctuations in a Developing Economy", Kyklos

R. McKinnon (1973), Money and Capital in Economic Development, The Brookings Institution, Washington. D.C., 1973

Shakuntala Mehra (1966), "Surplus Labour in Indian Agriculture", Indian Economic Review, April 1966

J. W. Mellor (1966), The Economics of Agricultural Development, Cornell University Press, Ithaca, 1966

_____ (1967), "Toward a Theory of Agricultural Development" in H. Southworth and B. Johnston (eds.), Agricultural Development and Economic Growth, Cornell University Press, Ithaca, 1967

_____ (1976), The New Economics of Growth: A Strategy for India and the Developing World, Cornell University Press, Ithaca, 1976

J. W. Mellor, T. Weaver, U. Lele and S. Simon (1968), Developing Rural India, Cornell University Press, Ithaca, 1968

B. S. Minhas (1970), "Rural Poverty, Land Distribution and Development Strategy: Facts and Policy", Economic Development Institute, IBRD, mimeo

B. Minhas and A. Vaidyanathan (1965), "Growth of Crop Output in India, 1951-54 to 1958-61: An Analysis by Component Elements", Journal of the Indian Society of Agricultural Statistics, December 1965

Radhakumud Mukherjee (1933), Land Problems of India, Longmans, 1933

Ramkrishna Mukherjee (1957), The Dynamics of a Rural Society, Akademe-Verlag, Berlin, 1957

Ramkrishna Mukherjee (1974), The Rise and Fall of the East India Company, Monthly Review Press, New York, 1974

G. Myrdal (1968), Asian Drama: An Inquiry into the Poverty of Nations, Pantheon, New York, 1968, Volume II

M. V. Nadkarni (1976), "Tenants from the Dominant Class: A Developing Contradiction in Land Reforms", Economic and Political Weekly, December 1976, Review of Agriculture

Dharm Narain (1961), "Distribution of Marketable Surplus of Agricultural Produce by Size Level of Holding in India, 1950-51", Occasional Paper No. 2, Institute of Economic Growth, Delhi

W. Neale (1957), "Reciprocity and Redistribution in the Indian Village: Sequel to Some Notable Discussions" in K. Polanyi, C. Arensberg and H. Pearson (eds.), Trade and Market in the Early Empires, Gateway, Chicago, 1957

U. Patnaik (1971), "Capitalist Development in Agriculture: A Note", Economic and Political Weekly, September 25, 1971

_____ (1972), "On the Mode of Production in Indian Agriculture: A Reply", Economic and Political Weekly, September 30, 1972

_____ (1972a), "Economics of Farm Size and Farm Scale", Special No., 1972

_____ (1972b), "Development of Capitalism in Agriculture", Social Scientist, Sept.-October, 1972

_____ (1975), "Contribution to the Output and Marketable Surplus of Agricultural Products by Cultivating Groups in India, 1960-61", Economic and Political Weekly, December 27, 1975

_____ (1976) "Class Differentiation within the Peasantry", Economic and Political Weekly, Review of Agriculture, September, 1976

K. N. Raj (1976), "Trends in Rural Unemployment in India: An Analysis with Reference to Conceptual and Measurement Problems", Economic and Political Weekly, August 1976, Special Number

I. Rajaraman (1975), "Poverty, Inequality and Economic Growth: Rural Punjab, 1960/61-1970/71", Journal of Development Studies, July, 1975

C. H. H. Rao (1974), "Socio-Political Factors and Agricultural Policies", Economic and Political Weekly, August 1974, Special Number

S. K. Rao (1971), "Inter-Regional Variations in Agricultural Growth: A Tentative Analysis in Relation to Irrigation", Economic and Political Weekly, July 3, 1971

G. Ranis and C. H. Fei, Development of the Labor Surplus Economy: Theory and Policy, R. D. Irwin Inc., Homewood, Illinois, 1964

T. Raychaudhuri, "A Reinterpretation of Nineteenth Century Indian Economic History?", Indian Economic and Social History Review, March 1968

_____ (1969), "Permanent Settlement in Operation: Bakarganj District, East Bengal", in Frykenberg (1969)

A. Rudra (1974), "Semi-Feudalism, Usury Capital, Et Cetera", Economic and Political Weekly, November 1974

A. Rudra, A. Majid and B. D. Talib (1969), (1969a), "Big Farmers of the Punjab", Economic and Political Weekly, September 27, 1969, Review of Agriculture, and December 29, 1969, Review of Agriculture

_____ (1970), "In Search of the Capitalist Farmer", Economic and Political Weekly, June 27, 1970, Review of Agriculture

A. Rudra and K. Newaj (1975), "Agrarian Transformation in a District of West Bengal", Economic and Political Weekly, March 29, 1975

A. K. Sen (1966), "Peasants and Dualism with or without Surplus Labor", Journal of Political Economy, October 1966

_____ (1968), Choice of Techniques, Blackwell, Oxford, 1968

_____ (1973), "Behavior and the Concept of Preference", Economica, August 1973

_____ (1975), Employment, Technology and Development, Oxford University Press, Oxford, 1975

G. R. Saini (1976), "Green Revolution and the Distribution of Farm Incomes", Economic and Political Weekly, March 27, 1976

A. Saith and A. Tankha, (1972), "Agrarian Transition and the Differentiation of the Peasantry: A Study of a West U.P. Village", Economic and Political Weekly, April 1, 1972

R. K. Sau (1976), "Can Capitalism Develop in Indian Agriculture?", Economic and Political Weekly, December 1976

E. S. Shaw (1973), Financial Deepening in Economic Development, Oxford University Press, London, 1973

R. Tamarajakshi (1969), "Intersectoral Terms of Trade and Markets, Surplus of Agricultural Produce, 1951-52 to 1965-66", Economic and Political Weekly, June 28, 1969

D. Thorner (1962), "Context for Co-operation in Rural India", Economic and Political Weekly, February 1962, Annual Number

D. Thorner and A. Thorner (1962), Land and Labor in India , Asia Publishing House, Bombay, 1962

A. Vaidyanathan (1972), "Some Aspects of Inequalities in Living Standards in Rural India", New Delhi, mimeo

P. Visaria (1977), "Trends in Rural Unemployment in India--Comment", Economic and Political Weekly, January 29, 1977

V. S. Vyas (1970), "Tenancy in a Dynamic Setting", Economic and Political Weekly, June 27, 1970

_____ (1976), "Structural Change in Agriculture and the Small Farm Sector), Economic and Political Weekly, January 10, 1976

For Product Safety Concerns and Information please contact our EU representative GPSR@taylorandfrancis.com Taylor & Francis Verlag GmbH, Kaufingerstraße 24, 80331 München, Germany

Printed and bound by CPI Group (UK) Ltd, Croydon, CR0 4YY

01/05/2025

01858439-0001